"CHARLES GABY has opened a gateway to understanding how consciousness awareness, meditation, and somatic practices can merge together. *Choosing to Evolve* is necessary reading especially for all yoga teachers who wish to help their students inform their practice with these powerful insights and thoughtful practical teachings."

— Nicole Shaw, Co-Founder SunstoneFit, Yoga Teacher Trainer E-RYT 500, Yoga Alliance Continuing Education Provider YACEP, and Meditation Teacher 300 RMT

"WHEN TALENTED MUSICIANS turn to a career in psychotherapy, they bring with them a unique ear to the emotions of others. *Choosing to Evolve* exposes an additional side of Charles Gaby — the ability to put into words his insights into the motivational motifs from which human personalities are woven. This book is informative of complex theory but eminently readable because of Gaby's unique style of teaching by sharing his personal experiences. As a result, he is able to provide the reader interested in changing unpleasant patterns in the self with practical advice and exercises that he himself and those who have worked with him have found beneficial."

— Vernon C. Kelly, Jr., MD, Psychiatrist and author of *The Art of Intimacy and the Hidden Challenge of Shame* and co-author of *The Upside of Shame*.

CHOOSING TO EVOLVE
A User's Guide to Waking Up

Charles Gaby

Choosing to Evolve: A User's Guide to Waking Up
Copyright © 2018 My Leap Year, LLC

ISBN: 978-1-947758-04-9

Lyrics to the song "Holy Now" from the album *Million Year Mind* is used with permission of the artist, Peter Mayer. His website is blueboat.net.

Production by:
Indie Author Books
12 High Street, Thomaston, Maine 04861
www.indieauthorbooks.com

This Edition Published by:
The Folse Group LLC
Fort Worth, TX
www.folsegroup.com

Printed in the United States of America

Table of Contents

Life Is But a Dream
We all have the capacity to retain images from our past experiences like little scenes from our inner theater, and then project them onto new experiences. We can't change the way consciousness works but we can change the way we participate in it!

The Images That Row Your Boat
Images from our past help define our present and anticipate our future — and the more experiences we have, the more automated this process becomes. By gaining awareness of this process, we can begin to understand the true source of habitual suffering — our own and in the world.

The Secret of Going Gently
When we learn how to slow down and question the habituated images we carry, we can become more curious, open, and ready to learn. "Meekness" in this context is neither shy nor retiring; it is to participate in our own consciousness without defensiveness. Freedom anyone?

The Art of Waking Up
When you get stuck in a repetitive cycle, think of your consciousness like a team that includes both players and coaches. Sometimes we have to trade a player, draft a new one, or fire a coach — it's easier than you might think!

Shift Happens!
Understanding the scripted nature of our emotions has been the missing key to understanding our motivations. It is our scripted emotion – attached to our stored imagery – that often defines our lives. This awareness offers a clear path for addressing suffering at its source in our lives and in our world.

Meet the Affects, Part 1: Distress-Anguish
Affects are the biological basis of emotions that are visible on the faces of babies even before they can talk. You don't have to teach a baby how to cry when this Affect is triggered, but how does our response to it change as we grow older?

Meet the Affects, Part 2: Shame-Humiliation
Did anyone teach you how to blush? Of course not! The Shame – Humiliation Affect is a part of your biological experience from birth. Here's how and why the scripts we develop to manage Shame define much of our life and relationships.

Meet the Affects, Part 3: Two Ways to Feel Good
Of the nine Affects we inherit as humans, only two of them feel good. If we were shaped by our life experiences to limit, deny, or repress these happy Affects, it's high time to break free of that prison — and make the most of feeling good!

Meet the Affects, Part 4: Anger-Rage

In every culture humans are trained to channel Anger in some form or other. By learning more about your own scripts for honoring this energy, you can make a big difference in your relationships, from setting boundaries to transforming conflict.

Meet the Affects, Part 5: Surprise-Startle

The experience of being surprised is universal, but depending on your body's sensitivity, this Affect can be more or less intense. Exploring the differences in how we Startle can offer life-changing insight into how our scripts work — and how to work with them!

Meet the Affects, Part 6: Dissmell and Disgust

From the moment of birth these two Affects help keep us safe, but they can also become associated with anything or anyone, including certain types of people or ideas. These are the Affects and scripts that make racism worldwide so resistant to change.

Meet the Affects, Part 7: Fear-Terror

Are you aware of how often your habituated Fear scripts put limits on your life, liberty, and the pursuit of happiness? Rather than simply treating the symptoms of Fear, here is how to "move alongside" Fear to evolve your confidence and discover what freedom is all about!

Taking the Next Step

When we are aware of our images and Affects, they can serve as guides, providing the precise insights we need to reveal the patterns that keep us stuck. Before we go any further in applying this awareness, there are a few important things to consider as we start to apply what we've learned.

Fight or Flight – Freeze or Please
Conflict is unavoidable in any relationship that becomes vulnerable enough to be honest. If you're tired of having the same old arguments again and again, here's how to change that friction into transformative fire. We must do this in our relationships if we ever want to end the cycles of defensiveness — in our most intimate relationships and between cultures.

The Problem with Enlightenment
How were you socialized from birth to think and feel about yourself and others? We have each been shaped, outside of our awareness, by imagery and scripts we did not choose. Now you have the map and tools to do the inner archaeology required to be free to choose how you want to live.

Education, Justice and Accountability
It's time we reform how we do discipline and accountability with the understanding that people who hurt others are shaped and scripted by their own experiences. These are the tools that support real change for perpetrators — and real healing for those harmed — and we already have them!

Faith and the Evolving Image of God
Our experience of God relies on imagery that inspires love or hate in ways few others can. In exploring the role of emotional scripts in our experience of God, we'll gain new understanding of how imagery and habituation work in faith — and even in non-faith.

Institutionalized Imagery and Relinquishing Defenses
Choosing to Evolve involves transforming our own defensive individual emotional scripts, but sometimes institutions like schools and places of worship can reinforce the very patterns we're trying to change. Here's how to transform centers of mass dissociation into centers for healing and spiritual growth.

Meet the Players of Team You

Consciousness — a Team Sport
Do you ever wonder why some of your emotions always seem to dominate the others? Using a team analogy here, we'll combine the components of consciousness to explore this dynamic differently to help you learn how to create a whole new playbook!

Identity, Identification, and the Images We Own
How many ways have you been labeled? Can you let these labels go? We receive these images more by chance than by choice. We Choose to Evolve as we learn to practice the art of de-habituation and dis-identification to reconnect with our most essential identity: Learning Being.

Our Scripts at Work
Do issues of work and money rank at the top of things that trigger the most negative feelings in your life? In this chapter we will explore how to uncover the habituated imagery and emotional scripts that both guide and limit your experience of work and money.

Evolving Images of Intimacy
Are the recurring conflicts in your most important relationships making you crazy? While suggestions for applying this material to relationships are in almost every chapter, we'll focus directly now on the previously uncharted territory of intimacy when we Choose to Evolve as a couple!

All My Relations
We all live interdependently in a web of relationships with which we interact. We are not just Choosing to Evolve for our own wellbeing, but for the wellbeing of *all* our relationships — and for generations to come. Consider this your invitation to make *this* your Leap Year!

Introduction

Innerstate 55
Take any highway headed out of town
Past the empty billboards halfway falling down
They offer no suggestion for where you should be bound
But you only need directions
To where you are now
Just a little weary from the road
But a voice inside your head still says go
So you headed out for somewhere
But now you just don't know
If it makes a difference where you go
Make good friends with the silence in your head
Take good care of the one who shares your bed
If you're looking for a perfect world
Try not to forget
It's the walls inside your own heart
That determine what you get
On the billboard there's an image of a girl
Like a faded memory from a different world
Did she teach you anything?
Were you just too full to learn?
Is it too late to take another turn?
When you get to where the power lines are few
And a smart phone can't tell you what to do
There will come a moment
When you finally have to choose
To drive away the fears
Or let them keep driving you
Then you make good friends with the silence in your head
Take good care of the one who shares your bed

If you're looking for a perfect world
Try not to forget
It's the walls inside your own heart
That determine what you get

W̌hat follows is a journey into uncovering and transforming what Rumi called "the barriers" in our hearts that we have built against love. I know. That sounds a little fluffy, right? The thing is, love is a funky little word that often conveys almost no real meaning. So let's replace that word for the moment with "authentic interest."

If you tell your children that you love them but don't show interest in them, the words are hollow expressions, and they will not likely feel loved. If, on the other hand, you have *authentic interest* in someone — if you *really* feel that interest and show it — they will most likely feel loved whether or not you tell them you love them.

Of course, there is a difference between feeling loved and *being* loved. As a child, I may not recognize the scolding voice of my mother as loving concern for my wellbeing. In other words, how concern and care are expressed does not always make us feel good.

The opposite is also true. If you are less interested in your child than you are of your child not embarrassing you, your child will likely feel it. All of us have a tendency to delude ourselves about our intentions at times. Words are often used to obscure the truth rather than reveal it. Whatever you mean when you use the word, "love," is an expression of *your* own unique experiences. I may not share your memories of love or your particular emotional motivation in this moment. Your idea of love is unique to you. I do not know what the Sufi mystic-poet, Rumi, was thinking as he spoke of love. But I do know something about the barriers in our hearts that we have built against it.

We are directed to love by almost every spiritual tradition that has ever existed on the planet. So then why is our world so full of hatred, division, and hurt? Why are so many intimate relationships broken soon after they begin — and so many children left to figure out the world on their own? What will it take for us to transcend the endless cycles of sectarian violence between tribes?

Rumi was onto something when he wrote: "Don't seek after love. Instead seek out the barriers in your heart that you have built against it." Or, as I would relate it, *"seek out the barriers in your heart that have hijacked and squelched your capacity for authentic interest."*

What we will discover as we proceed is that habituation — and its byproduct, the squelching of "love"— is one of the central features of human consciousness. We can't change that. We can, however, learn how to participate with habituation in a new way. This is how we Choose to Evolve, and it is the greatest challenge we face — both as individuals and as humankind.

Evolving vs. Revolving

These are interesting times in which to be born — the information age meets the digital revolution. And *revolution* is exactly the right word for what's going on in our world today as we *revolve* through all of the same human activities we ever have, yet with greater capacity and frequency.

For the majority of the human race, digital devices have taken what we always did and made it possible to do it a whole lot more. The result? A growing discontent and overload with a side order of burnout. And, as this information revolution spins our conscious capacity to warp speeds, we begin to face the reality that regardless of the amount of data available *or* the speed of our communication, our struggles continue. We lose heart or we begin to look elsewhere.

Take intimate relationships for example. Let's say that the average person has some glitch in their capacity to "love" – some barrier within their heart. In the 1950s that person might have had the opportunity to date a few other people over the course of a year. Perhaps one or two of these would rise to a level of significance where the interactions became intimate enough to hit that heart barrier and leave them wondering what happened.

Today with all the popular dating apps, we can "swipe left" to mimic this process several times a day. The speed of the revolution itself may be creating a greater awareness of our patterns. You may not understand the cycle, but you have a nagging suspicion that you have been here before. As a result, we experience greater and greater discontent with whatever limits our capacity for love, to say nothing of happiness or success.

And, as we revolve ever more rapidly through the patterns of our life created by the dynamics of our own inner world, we begin to see that we're experiencing the same problems, the same dynamics, and the same outcomes, both individually and collectively, in our relationships, and in our world. These conflicts don't come simply from lack of information or connection. Our lives have scripts. Our thoughts and feelings have patterns. If you think back for a moment about the recurring issues in your own life, I think you'll see what I mean. So now the question becomes, how do we uncover and transform these scripts and patterns in ways that create less suffering and more peace and wellbeing?

In the coming pages we will explore the common thread that runs through many if not all of the issues we experience both personally and collectively. That common thread involves processes at the core of our consciousness that operate mostly outside of our awareness. They are the processes that evolved in humans in order to remember, to imagine, to automate, anticipate, and direct our attention.

The good news is that the "information revolution" is creating a new awareness in humankind that can actually lead to our Evolution. Our discontent and suffering are like rainfall at the end of a winter. The silent roots are beginning to stir.

The evolution of consciousness that we will be exploring isn't so much about *what* we think, but rather *how* we think about what we think. Do you believe everything you think?

It is also about how we experience our feelings. How do you *feel* about what you feel? If that sounds confusing, don't worry or feel embarrassed. The goal of this book is to offer some powerful insights from a variety of sources and make them accessible to anyone motivated to discover them.

The roots of this coming evolution of human consciousness have been growing deeper through our personal and collective tragedies. Our wounds have stirred a restless hunger for something better. While the revelations of science about the inner workings of our neurobiology may be fascinating, it's really our *application* of these insights into our day-to-day lives that we need most — and this requires something different from us, something more akin to art.

The reasoning behind this assertion is that a human consciousness is something of an image machine — and the arts offer us access to the most powerful images of all. If we want to program a computer we need to know how to write its code. If we want to operate our consciousness in a new way, the language we must learn is poetry.

So here we are at a crossroads, where we as individuals and as a species find ourselves confronted with our dysfunctional and destructive patterns. If we look closely, however, we can see that there is a common thread that runs through all of these issues. That thread is the basic engine of human consciousness, geared to habituate whatever we feed it.

As you learn the basics about how consciousness works, you will begin to participate in your thoughts and feelings in a new way. You will gain the awareness you need to be less manipulated by the world around you. You will uncover core dynamics to your life that have limited your personal power and freedom. You may also discover that the world is a much more beautiful place than you have imagined, and you are much more than you have believed.

SECTION I

Becoming Aware of
Imagery and Habituation

CHAPTER 1

Life Is But a Dream

"I don't know what's the matter with me. I keep making the same mistakes over and over, and even though I know what I want to do differently in my life, I just can't seem to do it. Every time I have a new opportunity, I find myself making the same bad choices — but I can only see that once the choice is made and it's too late. How can I break a pattern that has haunted me all of my life?"

— *"Greg"*

Like Greg, we all have dynamics that threaten our wholeness, both individually and collectively. To begin to face and resolve these issues, it helps to understand a few key things about how our consciousness works — and the role these processes play in the problems we face. The very processes that have given us our greatest abilities are also the ones that created our greatest liabilities.

Greg came to my studio feeling utterly lost. When you feel lost, it helps to find a supportive and caring friend who offers comfort. It also helps if you can get your hands on a map and figure out where you are. I believe the material we are about to explore is just such a map and that it can help you, just as it did Greg, to learn how to transcend the disabling patterns in your life.

But this is not just about our individual growth and recovery. You could say that human cultures are also struggling to transcend dysfunctional patterns. The rapid advance of knowledge and discovery strain the capacity of these cultures to manage change. As we will see, the solutions to our greatest difficulties can be found deep within the processes of our human consciousness, and gaining this new awareness is likely the greatest hope for our future as a species.

But before we enter this rabbit hole, close your eyes for just a moment and think of me, the author of this book. What do you see and feel? Though we may be strangers, you probably just got an image of me, just as I have an image of you, the reader. Where did we get these images? How do they impact our experience? Would you be experiencing this differently if you imaged me as female? Would your expectations of this book shift? Take just a moment to imagine that I am a woman speaking to you. How does that impact your experience?

The images we have accumulated impact everything we do. They operate automatically, framing our perceptions and assigning meaning to every single experience we have. If we want to address the many problems that threaten our wholeness, both individually and collectively, we must learn to pay attention to the images we carry inside of us. Once we gain this understanding and practice it, we have a new capacity for real and lasting change.

Imagine what you might experience if your image of me was already negative. If you have read a hundred books, and none of them helped you manage your problems, then you might have an image of me that was at least partly motivated by the frustration of your past experience.

Now imagine how your personal imagery might impact your experience of intimacy or job satisfaction. Past experiences, retained as memory images, are what we "know." Consciousness automatically uses these images to recognize similarities in the present moment and to anticipate the future. Just as remembering where you parked your car is the image you use to find it, your consciousness helps you recognize the similarities between current and past experiences and know what to do with this information.

Movement and Imagery

Consider the intelligence of a flower and a toad. How is human consciousness different from these? Every living thing must have some kind of intelligence to move toward its resources, and, if possible, to move away from its threats. One of the big differences between flowers and toads is their capacity for movement. Flowers send down roots and bend toward light. Toads jump toward prey and away from danger.

Humans, on the other hand, have a much more advanced capacity for movement, and with movement comes a different kind of consciousness. One very important component of movement is the extraordinary development of memory and the imagery of anticipation. An example of this process is how you remember where you live and anticipate what you will find when you go there.

Of course, the development of a system of memory/anticipation isn't in much demand if you are a tree. But it would seem that all mobile species exhibit the capacity to remember and anticipate, even if that process is somewhat instinctive, as it is in the migratory patterns of butterflies and hummingbirds.

Mobility is probably at the root of our development of abstract thought. Try closing your eyes and thinking about buying some groceries. Where would you go? In your abstract inner construction of the world there is a map. If you can close your eyes and then point with your finger in the direction of the nearest store, you have just accomplished abstract thought. You have an inner map.

Let me hasten to say that there is nothing bad about consciousness that has not achieved abstract thought. Flowers are beautiful. We love them in their simplicity. But there is an incredible difference between the intelligence that inhabits a flower and the intelligence that resides within a toad. The evolution of consciousness in humans is an even bigger leap.

The Basic Engine of Consciousness

This process of memory/anticipation runs within us all the time. And, because we have developed the capacity for abstract construction of the world, we are blessed with the ability to not only remember where things are, but to also anticipate what we will find there. And to make things even more complicated, we don't just carry abstract images of how to get places. We also accumulate images of ourselves and of others. These images, too, become quite automated.

What are we automating?

When we reach for a drink, we do so without much thought. We don't consider how much strength will be required, which direction to move or how much pressure it will take to hold the cup in our grip. We may even automatically anticipate whether the drink is hot or cold — and *how* hot or cold the drink will be to gauge the size of the sip we take.

All of this operates within us automatically, somewhere beneath our awareness. And most of the time, it's a big advantage. But it can also be a huge curse. Automation comes at the cost of flexibility and awareness. How you automate your experience of drinking coffee can be tricky. Sometimes we don't give it enough thought, and we spill or burn ourselves because the image is out of sync with reality.

It is even more problematic when what we have automated/ habituated becomes a dominant pattern of thinking or feeling — calling to mind the old saying, "when the only tool you have is a hammer, everything looks like a nail." Having your image out of sync with reality may not be a huge issue with something like coffee because we don't really identify with coffee as a part of us. But when we have identified something we consider to be part of who we are, these kinds of glitches can be disastrous.

Identification and Association

In addition to the imagery and habituation there are a couple of other dynamics to notice. One necessary part of our development that begins in early childhood is the process of discerning what *is* part of us and what *is not*. And, while this process begins physically, it continues throughout our lives as we continue to relate and resonate with the world we encounter.

Think for a moment about your favorite movie or novel. Which character in that story did you most identify with? I remember when the movie, "Jaws," first came out in theaters. There was a scene in the movie when the tough old sea captain was sliding down the back of the boat into the shark's mouth. It was at that exact moment when I felt a tap on my shoulder from the man behind me; he couldn't see the screen because I had identified so much with that doomed sea captain that I had climbed up the back of my seat to escape the shark.

What happened inside my brain for me to be literally crawling out of my seat? Well, first, the emotional stimulation in my immediate sensory world (the dark, quiet theater) had to be lower than that of the imagery I was experiencing (or my inner imagery) for me to fully identify with the action on the screen. For this to happen, I had to completely dissociate from my immediate sensory experience to connect with the much higher level of emotional stimulation happening in the movie. These dynamics of identification and association are happening within us all the time, even if displayed in less dramatic ways.

Your Mind . . . on Team You

Imagine your mind as a football team on which there are many players, and each player holds a set of images (plays) it will call up again and again in your life. After a while, these plays run almost effortlessly every single time your circumstances call for them. And, each time these "plays" are run, we *identify* with both the action happening on the field and the player carrying the "ball" —our immediate attention. The more effortless a play becomes, the more we turn our attention away from that play to give thought to the next one.

This is essentially how we learn lots of things. We practice and then habituate and then automate — and eventually each "play" becomes second nature to us and hardly requires any attention from us at all. Then one day the game changes, and the old plays don't work anymore.

When this "game change" happens, you may look around and notice that most of your team is sitting on the bench, and what plays you do still have are only for the players already on the field. You've likely identified with some of these players — and dissociated from others. Put simply, this is the kind of identification and dissociation that is very natural to the way our minds operate.

So what happens if one "player" becomes dominant? What if this dominant player is a memory image of being abused by an authority figure? Now imagine what would happen if this image was the only one your mind, automatically referenced any time you're in the presence of any authority figure. Your team is only doing what it is supposed to do — practicing the plays it has learned — but now this one player is running the game, and it is time you hired a new coach.

Whether or not you completely — or at all — understand football, stay with me here. This football imagery is the best description I've come up with to explain the consciousness from which we are evolving. Although we all experience this "dominant problem player" scenario in varying degrees, the same processes of habituated images (plays being run), identification (with particular players), and dissociation (with the rest of the team) are there in all of us, all the time.

On the low end, we may have a problem player that shows up so seldom that it rarely creates issues in our lives. For others, there's a problem player so dominating that it keeps messing things up. When a traumatic set of images becomes a dominant fixation, these images can become so habituated through practice that they continually define our anticipated future. This combination of imagery and habituation can make things easier for us or make our life very difficult.

What makes addressing these "dominant problem player" issues even more challenging is that habituation is something of a trance state. The very dynamics of habituation direct our attention toward identifying with some aspects of life and dis-identifying with others. We get caught up in this kind of play in much the same way I was when I crawled up the back of my seat in the theater.

Later on we will explore the many tools available to help us wake up from this trance. The good news is that attaining a basic understanding of how consciousness works can make all of this easier. Let's begin by getting really clear about what habituation is and how it works.

Girls and Guitars

When I was about 13 years old, my brother and I learned to play the guitar from a college student named Wendy. Wendy had long blond hair, bell-bottom jeans, and a voice like an angel. Italian, mysterious, and kind, she had my *complete* attention. Let's just say that if my interest in guitar was a slow drip before we met, it turned into a gushing stream once Wendy arrived. (But I digress.)

Wendy began our lessons by teaching us chords, placing our fingers in the right positions until we could make each chord sound right without buzzing and twanging. This required a good deal of effort and time, and I remember practicing until my finger tips were too sore to continue — and even more once my fingertips were calloused enough to endure.

Why did I go through all this struggle and pain? Reflecting on my motivation now, I see three main reasons. The first had to do with my self-image. I wanted to be like those musicians I saw and heard performing on the television. I *identified* with them. The second was simply the way music spoke to me. The combination of poetry and music seemed to resonate with me in a way nothing else did. Songs seemed to express my feelings in a way I couldn't. There is something powerful that happens when you hear poetry speak to the things you know in your heart but have not yet found the words to express. While I did not identify will *all* music (I had grown weary of my father's records), the music I heard on the radio spoke to me. I identified with music and with those who played it. Finally, I think Wendy's enticing air of sophistication and worldliness made me want to please and impress her. As a 13-year-old forging his identity, all three of these motivations came into play. I learned who I wanted to be as I learned to play the guitar.

Once we had a few chords properly learned, Wendy began to teach us to strum. It was a simple, eight-count pattern with a little bit of syncopation: Down, Down Up, Up Down Up (each comma denotes an eighth-note rest). I spent the whole next week practicing it . . . wrong.

I'll never forget how embarrassed I was when Wendy corrected me at our next lesson. The scene of her correcting me was not what I had imagined or expected. This image was completely at odds with my image of the two of us — a major issue in my desire for her affection. This was all made worse because I began the lesson feeling so proud of my work.

The more I learn about human consciousness the more I realize how important that moment was for me. It easily could have squelched my budding interest in music. In fact, embarrassing moments like this often become defining moments in our lives. Fortunately for me, Wendy had a way of making everything all right. She always seemed as interested in *me* as she was in my strum.

Once I got this basic strum right, we moved on to changing chords while strumming. Then we began playing songs and singing along with the guitar. I learned chord progressions for a few songs as well as fingerpicking styles —all in the course of one summer.

The Jaws of Humiliation

By the time I got to college, I was playing and singing for money in the local bars of Shreveport, Louisiana. This was a good gig for a college student. I can't describe the feeling of performing a song you love to a room full of people. The vulnerability and immediacy of feedback creates a sort of addictive communion, as does the experience of losing yourself in the expression of a song. But that is fodder for a whole other book.

During this time I learned hundreds of songs. Eventually I could play *hours* of music without much thought at all. It had all become automatic — the changing of chords, the repetitive patterns of strumming and picking — all of it was by then "second nature."

After college, I spent a little time writing music in Nashville and New York. It was the early 80's and the folk-rock musical imagery of my life was crashing headlong into Disco, Urban Cowboy, New Wave, and Punk. I realized very quickly that to make a living playing music in bars you had to play what people wanted to hear. Fortunately for me, I only owned one pair of parachute pants before I moved on.

During this time of music writing, I also returned to Shreveport as often as I could to play the haunts of my college days. One evening while I was working on a song in the studio, I got a call from the guy who lived across the street. He had heard me play in a bar the night before, and he said he wanted to play something for me. Intrigued, I headed across the street for my first encounter with John Troy, a guy I barely knew.

John was a big man in his 40s who had the interesting history of managing Billy Joel during Joel's early years. I didn't know any of this at the time, so you can imagine my surprise when I walked into his house to find a gold record hanging on the wall. As I was trying to ask him about it, John ushered me to a chair in the middle of the room. It was perfectly positioned for the stereophonic effect of his B&O sound system with Klipsche speakers. He placed a vinyl record on the turntable and cranked up the volume.

What came out of the speakers was indescribable to me. It was fast — unbelievably fast. It was an album recorded live in San Francisco with Paco De Lucia, Al Di Meola and John McLaughlan, and each was recorded at a distinct position in the stereophonic landscape. As they played their lightning perfection I was humbled.

These were not the patterns I had perfected. This was a whole different level of guitar playing, the likes of which I had never heard. I immediately felt that it was already too late for me to ever play like that. It was one of those defining moments that shapes your expectations — and quietly changes the course of your life without your even realizing it. My musical imagery was cracked and broken.

As I look back at this moment now, I realize, of course, that I was wrong. I could have learned. I was still plenty young enough to make that shift if I had the interest to do it. But I fell into the trap that many young people fall into when confronted with pure genius. As silly as it may sound, I felt a humiliation that shut me down and froze me up —

I never really progressed in my guitar playing after that.

I tell this story now to illustrate how running into ideas that challenge the images we hold of ourselves, the world we live in — and the future we imagine for ourselves — can crack us open. It's what we do next that makes all the difference. As habituating/automating creatures, we have a capacity to rehearse, perfect, and somewhat automate all kinds of functions. There is a great deal of beauty and genius in this because it allows us to think and move with greater and greater complexity. Just as I did with performing music, moving many bits of processing to the background of our attention frees our immediate awareness to focus on the next thing that gets our attention.

As neuroscientists say, "Where you fire, you wire," meaning that the more you do something, the more easily you can do it again until it becomes "second nature." We all have a million things we do every day without thinking about it at all. Even the way we talk is automated.

Among our most important automations are the ways we think and feel. As we will soon explore, thoughts and feelings are habituated in a way that is not unlike playing the guitar or riding a bike. In fact, each image we carry in our mind is charged with some degree of emotion. I never asked John why he thought I needed to hear, "A Friday Night in San Francisco," but to this day when I play that album I can still feel the sting of my inexplicable feeling of humiliation.

How Patterns Can Define Us

What has become clear to me in my reflections is that our wired/automated patterns are double-edged swords that both free us and limit us. What becomes "second nature" to us will also ultimately define our lives more than anything else, especially when it comes to the patterns we automate with our thoughts and feelings.

You may have a mental image of yourself as a rock star, but you are more defined by the habituated patterns you have practiced to the point of automation. If that effortless pattern is mostly drinking like a rock star as opposed to constantly practicing your craft, it really won't make much difference what you believe yourself to be... to some degree you are what you habituate.

Having a habituated relationship to your morning coffee seems of little consequence, but having a habituated pattern for how you experience fear, anger, embarrassment, or excitement will greatly define your personality and how you relate to everything and everyone around you. Habituated patterns of our emotions make choices for us without our even realizing it.

I suppose there is a risk in every exposure to something great — and how we react to a humbling experience can either inspire or debilitate us. When our cherished images come into conflict with something different, it can overwhelm us and call forth our need to defend against the damage to our self-imagery. This is where the challenging issues of our lives begin. And, as we will later explore, these defensive moves can rob us of our freedom and wellbeing.

Are you beginning to see the role habituation plays in the basic engine of our consciousness? It's also important to understand that much of our habituation also involves movement. From almost the moment of birth we will spend countless hours rehearsing particular movements, from typing on a computer keyboard to the graceful art of ballet — and all habituated movement in between.

We habituate how we cross our legs and wave our hands. We also habituate to a general *level* of physical activity. You may have heard the new slogan, "sitting is the new smoking." It would appear that one of the health risks of our modern digital life is our lack of physical activity. So as people are getting this message, treadmill desks and standing desks are becoming a "thing." Can you imagine how weird this would have seemed to people in the 1950s?

How you move your body is habitual. In fact, one way to practice some capacity for change is to regularly enter into new movements that are unfamiliar. When was the last time you moved your body in a way that was unfamiliar? I recommend that you try this now. Just try moving your body in a way that feels different. Use your non-dominant hand to do routine tasks. Walk differently. Bust a new dance move (If you do this in public people may stare.)

Human beings can also get pretty disturbed if other human beings aren't moving their bodies in the socially prescribed manner. Any unusual body movements immediately gain our attention in a crowd. This may be due to our basic need for safety, but it is also about emotion and communication. Body movement is connected to emotion, and emotion is a biological system that communicates without words. We will explore that system later in this text, but first let's review the territory we have covered so far.

The Keys to Our Leaping

Because the habituation/automation of emotionally charged imagery is the basic engine of consciousness, understanding this process provides the key to the evolutionary leap we are taking. Once you have this basic awareness of the processes of habituation and identification/dissociation we've explored so far, you will be able to unlock all the doors that lie ahead.

What I habituated at the age of 13 was so much more than chord progressions. I was automating a self-image, an image of self-expression, and an image of girls, just to name a few. Just as my automation of strumming a chord on the guitar changed my way of experiencing music, the images I automated for girls would become that by which I would compare all future females.

Without any conscious choice — and beyond my awareness at the time —, Wendy became a guide for measuring and comparing all my adolescent encounters with girls. Like so much of our experience, this imagery was automatically habituated without any intentional choice on my part. Only in retrospect can I see that I was looking for — and finding — Wendy in all of my subsequent encounters with girls.

As we will see next, this process of habituating is what very often gives our emotionally charged early life experiences a significant role in guiding our expectations. In fact, habituating is the process in our human consciousness that is responsible for much of our genius. However, it is the scripting that this habituation brings to our lives that can also become our greatest challenge.

We have begun this journey by bringing a new awareness to what usually goes unnoticed in our conscious experience. The goal of this awareness is not to become self-conscious, but rather to gain more capacity to *choose* what it is we automate/habituate. As we will soon explore, it is our habituation of emotional dynamics that may create our biggest blind spot as a species.

CHAPTER 2

The Images That Row Your Boat

The good thing about being creatures who habituate is the amazing complexity habituation makes possible. Just think about all of the things that had to become second nature to you in order for you to read and understand this book. Through habituation you have evolved many amazing capacities. And now, armed with this understanding we can continue to evolve by gaining the ability to choose whether and when to use those capacities.

We have all seen what happens when we habituate to patterns that mess up our relationships, destroy our health and the health of our world, and rob us of our happiness. Psychotherapy is one way to untangle these patterns.

As a therapist, I have spent many years listening and exploring the root causes of the suffering of my clients. The dynamics we uncovered, even those that caused their deepest hurts and destruction, were, quite simply, not their fault. There was almost always some significant challenge or trauma that caused them to develop some kind of coping script to get through. It was the best they could do at the time. After that, every situation they encountered that reminded them of that original challenge or trauma triggered that same coping script. After a while, this pattern became habituated, more like a reflex than an intentional choice.

Once their coping script became a dominant force in their thinking (remember that football team?), they had little choice in the outcomes caused by their habituated way of being. Our problems are almost *always* the outcome of patterns we have habituated years before.

Here's what most of my clients find to be the mind-boggling truth about all this: these patterns become so automatic that it is often hard to realize they're even there — or to recognize them for what they are.

Consider how you normally interact with others. The way you meet and greet others, the patterns of your conversations, and the way you deal with conflict are *all* habituated/automated. This is the absolutely normal processing of experience for humans. Unfortunately, the same process that makes things easy for us can also make it easy to retain our most dysfunctional dynamics.

Later in this book we will look at the way we enter into conflict with other people. Some of these patterns can be so problematic and pervasive that they impact every arena of our lives. Once we begin to see and recognize these patterns, we can begin to learn how to understand and change our public and even private discourse that mimics dysfunctional family relationships where communication is dead before it begins.

For now, however, I'll share only this. Whether you are a liberal or conservative, anti-abortion or pro women's rights, big government or small, peace activist or believe in security through domination, a trickle downer or a Robin Hood . . . no matter where you stand on immigration or guns or freedom of speech, gay rights, parenting, education, or the death penalty . . . whether you work on Wall Street or occupy it . . . whether you believe we are living in the end times or the best of times — your perspective is the result of whatever combination of memory images and anticipatory images you have habituated.

It's easy to take for granted the memory and anticipatory images we have habituated to provide us with a fairly automated way of being. What's more, these images, perspectives, anticipations, and expectations have become intertwined with the abstract images we have of ourselves. This entanglement is why we identify with our ideological perspectives in ways that become deeply personal. (And why the positions we take become so important to us!)

If we want to move beyond the heated rhetoric and growing distrust in our polarized culture with its constant pendulum swings, we have two challenges. The first challenge is simply that once we have done something once, it is much more likely we will do it again. Habituation/automated responses happen very quickly and are hard to change because our consciousness has evolved to retain them.

The second challenge involves how we tend to defend whatever images we have identified as "us." This self-imagery is crucial to how we perform our roles and responsibilities in our social context. Damage to a self-image can leave us struggling to know how to feel, act, and relate. The reason we feel the need to defend the images we hold of the self is because these very images offer us a stable platform in the sea of constant change that bombards us through our sensory and imagery experiences.

Now, I want to take just a moment to make something really clear. There is no singular image we carry of our "self." *Self-images* as I am describing them should not be confused with the kind of thing you post in your Facebook profile or the bio you share in a press release. The imagery that makes up your sense of self includes thousands of moments and experiences with which you identified at some point. Not all of these images are equal — some of them carry much more emotional energy than others.

Changing your attachment to some of these images is like changing your identity, and most of us are far too invested in our existing self-imagery to begin this journey until we run into a crisis. Sometimes the crisis can be dramatic — and sometimes it's just a gradual loss of wellbeing that feels "comfortably numb."

When I learned the wrong way to strum the guitar and was corrected by Wendy, it wasn't just my playing that was flawed. The larger issue I had to overcome was the crack that formed in my image of *myself*. If Wendy had been more critical, less supportive, or less interested in me, I might have stopped playing the guitar altogether. (Better to not try than to fail, right?). By not trying I could retain the self-imagery I was clinging to and protect it from being tarnished.

I hope you can see in this example how my image of being a guitar player was like a dream to which I had become attached. At the time, being a guitar player was not my present reality; it was still imaginary. However, this imagery had the power to define what I did with my time and how I felt about myself.

Most people are very protective of whatever self-imagery they have, even in the face of overwhelming evidence that it is flawed and dysfunctional. For personal growth to really happen, our self-imagery has to become less defended and more flexible and capable of continual transformation. We need the stable platform our images provide for us, but when our images become too rigid and defended we suffer — and so do our relationships.

It helps to recognize that the imagery we have of ourselves is never complete or "true." It is simply the sum of the impressions we have identified with and the models we have learned to imitate.

Consider Bill

Bill was a young man who came to me quite isolated and devoid of friends. His early memories included feeling displaced when his younger sister was born. Ever since he was young, his images from the past included feelings of resentment of *anyone* who got attention from his parents. He felt a constant need to impress others. It also seemed important to him that he had a grandfather who was a political luminary in the community. All of this worked together to establish within Bill the expectation that he was supposed to be important. He was driven to be a star.

For Bill, it was not enough to be a participant in things. He needed to be the source of accolades and attention. He needed to feel special and adored just to feel worthy. He wanted to impress people — and to always have the last word.

Though this mindset led to some limited success and skill development for Bill, there were inevitable disappointments including rejection by his peers, and of course, the resulting humiliation. His initial reaction to his sister's birth had formed the habituation of hypersensitivity within him that made him tend to overreact at times. Every time this initial scripted/habituated pattern ran into a wall of rejection, Bill, without knowing what was happening, felt he had no choice but to defend against the resulting crack in his self-imagery.

Bill's defensive responses, however, were always radically different. Sometimes he would withdraw and escape the situations, leaving him feeling isolated and helpless. Other times he would become manic and show off to escape his feelings of embarrassment. The defensive script that became most habituated for Bill, however, was to blame someone else. Eventually he succumbed to a persistent victim mentality, and he wasted years of his life focusing his anger on others who had become the stars he thought he was supposed to have been.

To say that Bill was choosing this outcome would be an overestimation of his awareness. For Bill to recognize and confront this habituated pattern within himself, however, would mean having to challenge the very imagery he held of himself.

It is a tricky thing for a therapist to help someone become conscious of defensive scripts. When someone is clinging to the imagery they hold of their "self," their habituated pattern of defending against any critique by attacking the critic can make giving them feedback risky. What is there to prevent the therapist from triggering the same defensive script? With Bill so habituated to defend what little pride he had left, anything that sounded like criticism would surely trigger one of his defensive patterns even more.

By the time I met him, Bill had habituated a way to defend against any humiliation. To feel embarrassed seemed impossible and overwhelming, as if having any flaw was to unacceptable as a human being, defective and worthless. The only path for therapy for Bill would have to include a sense that his therapist liked him even if he wasn't a star. (Remember how Wendy made me feel in my moment of humiliation?) Only through establishing new positive self-imagery could Bill possibly begin to explore the patterns that were robbing him of success.

Most people live their lives glued to a self-image that has become stagnant and well defended. Many people spend a great deal of their time and energy in habituated defensive scripts, trying to protect their positive sense of self. The images they hold of who they are must be perfect and finished.

But here's the question. What if we each begin to see our self as someone in constant transformation, someone capable of being both flawed *and* still learning? If the imagery we hold of our "self" must always remain stable, then how can we really experience growth and change? How can we continue evolving and freeing ourselves from the patterns that are limiting who we could be?

I know this feels a little complicated. Don't give up. It is incredibly important to your health and wellbeing. Would it be possible for you see yourself as imperfect — and yet still perfectly fine? Can you accept the idea that none of your experiences must be your *defining* experience? Can you see the value in others' experiences and what they may have to teach you?

The more we cling to our habituated imagery of our "self," the more we end up out of touch and limited by this imagery. We may even take pride in arrogantly asserting there is nothing new to discover about ourselves.

The more we imagine ourselves as complete, the harder it becomes when we encounter the limitations of our own experience. One of the main components of human consciousness involves memory images that are then projected within us as expectations. (That's how you find your beer!) All humans are limited in their exposure to life experiences, however, and our individual memory is just a random set of images to which we've been exposed because we were born in a certain place at a certain time to a particular family. No matter how much we have traveled and how richly we have lived, our experience is always going to be limited.

Take a moment to remember some of the moments in your life when you felt humiliated. How did you respond? How might those responses have become habituated? This is the first step in your evolutionary leap. Pay attention to the habituation of your consciousness and how you tend to defend your self-imagery. The good news is you are bigger than you believe!

Try spending a day believing you are a toad or a flower. Play with your identity. Try spending the day believing you are nothing but a student who is learning about life. Your name is Learner. Your identity is Learning. Your only goal in the world is to Learn. See what happens when you walk down the street with this new Learner identity. You may be surprised at how freeing it is.

As Learner you can be embarrassed and not feel overwhelmed. It is just a part of the process of learning. It is OK to be the fool. Fools often uncover the heart of things. The self you know right now is only a tiny glimpse of who you are and can be, so what if you were to live your life as confidently incomplete?

Our Images of the World

Just as we develop images of ourselves based on the things with which we identify, we also gather images of others — and the world around us. Like the images we hold of ourselves, the images we hold of our world are also never complete, *and* they are tinted through the lens of our own past experiences (our memory images). In other words, when you look at a tree do you really see *that* particular tree? Or are you simply picking up on the image of "tree" you have habituated?

What's more, even if you are looking very carefully at this one tree, you can only pay attention to the things you know *how* to notice, so you are still experiencing an image of the tree based on your own past images of "tree." The same is true for every "other" that we meet, including people.

It's also important to note that the abstract images we carry of the world and of ourselves are often deeply intertwined. How we see the world around us impacts the way we see ourselves — and vice versa, so it is important to include more than our self-imagery in this exploration. Not only can we gain awareness by seeing ourselves as "Learners;" we can also gain a lot of capacity for growth by looking closely at the images we have of others, our culture, our faith, and the world. This growth begins with acknowledging the source of our images and the limited experience that brought them to us.

In addition to our own experiences, the religious and ideological perspectives we adopt from our tribal culture provide us with a stable platform from which we can move around the world. Many of these abstractions then also become a part of our self-imagery. We include the images imparted to us by our tribal connection in the language we learn, along with countless other bits of perspective that tell us our place in the world. These images that are all we know of the world — and they can be very diverse — are "second nature" to us as if they were infused into our mother's milk.

Imagine the differences between the images carried by a nomadic people vs. a planting culture — or a culture of conquest vs. an oppressed or occupied one. Imagine how differently you might see yourself if you grew up in each of these. Also imagine what it would be like to think that your images were the only correct ones.

As the world shrinks through advances in communication and transportation, tribal images are being more rapidly confronted by the wide variety of alternative perspectives now available to us. Sometimes we may experience moments of cultural humiliation — and then defend against that feeling of humiliation by participating in actions that deny or resist the fractures in our cultural identity in much the same way Bill defended against the cracks in his identity.

Now don't get me wrong. I am not saying that taking pride in one's homeland or culture is wrong. Wave your flag high and proud. What I am saying is that in order to evolve our consciousness we need to be *aware* of how people — and governments — everywhere are humans who are also incomplete and limited in awareness. It's important to notice how we cling to the imagined perfection of our tribe as if our life depends on it. Remember, our images of our culture and images of our self are always connected. You can't experience a personal evolution of consciousness until you are ready to consider the limitations of your cultural inheritance.

So how can we recognize the positive and negative aspects of our tribal images? Can we see the limitations? Can we be Learners in this arena as well? Can we allow our tribal images to be cracked and humiliated without rushing to employ defensive scripts?

In his first volume of *Affect Imagery Consciousness*, Silvan Tomkins, a pioneering researcher in human affect theory, wrote, "The world is a dream we learn to have from script we did not write."

Taking this awareness back to Bill's story, now we can see that his self-imagery came not only from his perceptions of the events of his childhood. Bill's self-imagery was also shaped by his exposure to a cultural inheritance that valued celebrity over talent, rewarded vanity over transparency, and encouraged false bravado over vulnerable honesty.

Be aware that Waking Up is a process that may take a while. It took Bill a couple of months to become conscious of the habituated images he carried and to begin to experiment with them. It took him a couple of *years* to truly feel free of both his dominant script (I need to be the star) and the defensive scripts he employed when that dominant script didn't succeed (blame the critics). As his awareness grew, Bill began to evolve.

Did Bill still have moments when the old familiar scripts wanted to play their automated function? Sure he did. However, once he learned how to let go of his perfect self-imagery and return to being a Learner, these moments became fewer and farther between. Over time, Bill became quite successful and capable of engaging people from a wide variety of political, religious, and ideological perspectives without activating his old defensiveness. He even learned how fun it could be to just add his energy to a movement (without needing to be the leader). At last, Bill was truly free to make choices that were at odds with his indoctrinated cultural images.

Finding Freedom

I have often taken a string off of my guitar as an object lesson on freedom. I then ask, "Which is more free, the string in my hand or the one still on the guitar?" Many, if not most people will say it is the string in my hand. Then comes my follow-up question: "What is it free to do?" The string on the guitar is free to make music.

You will never be free to write a book unless you can commit to the tensions and the limits involved. Even when you were a child, you knew that you would only be free to read a book if you committed to the time and effort of learning the code. Freedom is not only the capacity for choice but also the choice of capacity. I have worked with a number of young adults who felt frozen in time. They had arrived at adulthood with a strong desire to be free from constraints, but like the guitar string in my hand their lack of commitment to something had left them with more limitations than freedom.

Though at any moment they could choose to go *any* direction with their lives, the indecision to go in a *particular* direction with their lives left them more limited than free. The uncommitted guitar string in the hand may be free to be used in many different ways, but the same is true for the string that is committed to the guitar. The only difference in these freedoms is that the string on the guitar is *doing* something now, *committing* to the tension of its limits, gaining new experiences, and letting new resonance come through it in the present moment.

So there is no freedom that doesn't come with the displacement of our other options. If I spend my time studying one subject, there will be a million others I will ignore. And in every case, making a choice creates the freedom of a new capacity, and indecision leaves you with more limitations. The existential truth that human life is limited flies in the face of advertisers who would prefer to make you think you can have it all.

Don't Buy the Image

I believe that you have been programmed by a barrage of daily messages and advertisements, to think that your life is supposed to be something it can never be. Your marriage is supposed to be romantic, exciting, comforting, and free from conflict. You are supposed to be both rich *and* good looking. You are supposed to be creative *and* unique. You should never be sad or lonely, and if you are, there's a pill for that. That's what commercials seem to tell us.

The newest trend in advertising is tracking your every click — and then feeding you what you seem to want. Before long, the artificial intelligence ad machine will be able to profile your identity better than you can.

The truth, however, is that even the most gregarious and intelligent of people struggle to arrive at what is defined by our culture as "success." And for most of us, any moment of failure in striving for this impossible self-image leaves us stuck in our defensive scripts. We hide or blame or distract ourselves with even more images provided by the cultural image machine.

Committing to these kinds of cultural norms can be quite a bit like being that string on the guitar, but this time with the tension tuned so tight the string breaks. Buying into the images provided to us by advertisers is like that. If you have fallen into that emotional trap, don't worry. You can still begin again in a way that will work better.

Opting out of the cultural clone factory isn't what sets you free, however. It's what you do *next* that counts. You will still have to commit to something — and you'll need to make sure that what you commit to isn't simply a way to avoid future humiliation.

Above all, know that it is OK for life to *not* be beautiful all the time. It is OK for you to not feel like you have it all together. It is OK to be in a committed relationship that has conflict. The issue is about becoming a Learner. Are you learning or are you stuck? More importantly, are you stuck because your life can never measure up to the image you have been given for it?

Just once I'd like to see a beer commercial that shows a guy getting off work looking stressed and frustrated. The voice-over would say, "Your job sucks. Your ex-wife thinks you're a jerk. You want to escape it all, don't you? Have a beer. You deserve a break!" Instead, the commercials always show all positive emotions along with images of pretty, happy people. That's what beer does. It makes you handsome and happy — for a few minutes.

When you combine the kinds of images we humans now see many times a day with thousands of movies with happy endings, you've only begun to get the picture. And, if we allow the images in our memories to become our expectations, how could the realities of our lives ever measure up to the commercial version?

Repeat after me: "Human experience is always limited. I cannot have it all. The only freedom to be found is in consciously recognizing the images I have filled my experience with because they tell me how to be and what to do. To be conscious of these images allows me to decide whether they represent what I want to be and do in the world."

There is a reason why impoverished third-world children often seem happier than wealthy first-world ones. They have not been programmed to expect more. Once I took a team of people to a poor area of Jamaica. We were helping to build a dental clinic. At one point a minister there invited me to a gathering of pastors. They were discussing an epidemic of local men committing suicide. Their take on the tragedy was this: Satellite TV had come to Jamaica a few years earlier and now the children of these men had become frustrated with their situation and longed for all the things they saw on TV that their fathers could not provide.

Living Authentically

The first step in playing any instrument involves accepting the limited nature of our skill. In other words, we have to start somewhere. If we approach learning anything with the belief that we already know it, then we are probably caught in a defensive script — the opposite of a Learner identity. The same wisdom holds true with how we access the instrument of consciousness, even though we may already believe that we know how to use it and that there is only one way.

We cannot change the fact that we are creatures with highly developed habituation processes. We also cannot change the fact that we operate from abstract images that have then become habituated and taken for granted as expectations. Our evolution of consciousness will not change these aspects of our life. The evolution we seek is about becoming *conscious* of these images and gaining the capacity to choose whether to listen to them or not.

I once got to know the poet, James Kavanaugh. At some point I remember him saying, "Every kind of life is a prison and the only true freedom is to live it authentically." I would say that to "live authentically" means, essentially, to *live less defensively*. What in the world does that mean? To live less defensively means confidently voicing your images/expectations with the *absolute certainty* that these expectations could be wrong or incomplete.

Once Bill worked through this first step of evolving consciousness, he was able to confidently speak his mind as he had in the past. Now, however, he was also quick to acknowledge that his was only one limited perspective. If others in the group saw it differently, he could acquiesce without feeling an overwhelming need to withdraw.

So this first step in the journey toward evolved consciousness is about overcoming our tendency to defend against any information that shows us that our images are incomplete. So we must accept this incompleteness from the very start. The evolved consciousness is able to let the imagery of self, other, and the world, be simply that — imagery. Where did I get mine and where did you get yours? This one simple shift changes the game! To wrap up this part of our discussion, here's a song I wrote that illustrates this game-changing step:

Hide And Seek
When you were young
You learned your lessons well
You won't get hurt if you don't let anybody
Get inside your shell
So you learned to hide your love away
And play the game all the other children play
It was hide and seek and keep away
Deep inside there's a little girl
Who wants to come out and play
Now the coast is clear and the time is right
Don't play hide and seek
With me tonight
You played it cool
From the day that you were
A kid in Jr. High
Acting so grown up
Impressing all the guys
Now you know that masquerade
And you do it so well
You can't even tell
That it's hide and seek and keep away
Deep inside there's a little girl
Who wants to come out and play

Now the coast is clear
And the time is right
Don't play hide and seek
With me tonight
Too many laughs are never laughed
Too many tears are never cried
Too many days of just pretending
Too many souls have been denied
Isn't it time we started putting
All of these silly games aside
Before there's no one left to seek
And all we do is hide
It was hide and seek
And keep away
Deep inside there's a little girl
Who wants to come out and play
But the coast is clear now
And you don't really need that shell
Isn't it time that you and I got to play
Show and tell

CHAPTER 3

The Secret of Going Gently

One of the questions I frequently get when someone begins to learn about all this is, "If the basic engine of consciousness is the habituation of abstract imagery, and my imagery is always limited to what little I have experienced, then I should be really humble about my perspective. Won't that undermine the confidence I need to succeed?"

Of course it is true that you don't hold the whole of creation in your memory. In fact, your memory is quite limited and dependent on the range of experiences to which you've been exposed. Once we fully digest this essential truth, it changes everything. This understanding requires not only a major shift in our self-imagery — and the many patterns that defend it — but also in our capacity to embrace ambiguity. We gain a certain kind of humility, but our confidence does not have to be lost in the process. There is an old term for people who possess the capacity for humble assertiveness. They are called "the meek."

Webster defines "meek" as: "having or showing a quiet and gentle nature: not wanting to fight or argue with other people." It offers synonyms like: demure, down-to-earth, lowly, humble, modest, unassuming and unpretentious.

Demure: modest and reserved.

Down-to-Earth: informal and easy to talk to, practical and sensible.

Humble: not proud: not thinking of yourself as better than other people.

Unassuming: not pretentious or arrogant.

Unpretentious: the opposite of making unjustified or excessive claims expressive of unwarranted, or exaggerated importance, worth, or stature.

Get the picture?

Now, just for grins let's take a look at what it would look like to be the *opposite* of meek. If I tally this correctly, the non-meek are braggarts who are hard to talk to because they think they are better than you. They arrogantly hide behind formality while claiming that they are more important than they are.

Now, before we judge those who exhibit these non-meek qualities too harshly, let's take a moment to reflect on our *own* defensive tendencies. Haven't we *all* wanted to feel important? Don't we *all* hate having our weaknesses exposed? Haven't we *all* been tempted at times to brag or feel arrogant? Most of what is described here would fall under the long list of ways we *all* tend to defend against threats to our positive self-imagery.

If we are all predisposed by past experiences to have certain sensitivities (or lack of sensitivities), then remembering the refrain sung by many various folk singers, "There but for fortune go you or I" can help us foster a meeker consciousness. Or at the very least, this awareness may help us step back from some of the dehumanizing rhetoric that seems to permeate modern culture.

There will always be those who want to gain advantage by using whatever insights into human consciousness they can find — and the worst way this material could be used would be for us to label others as flawed due to their lack of meekness. So as tempting as that might be, now that we know what we know, please don't go there. To label others as flawed is the exact *opposite* of meekness!

Once we really get the awareness into our bones that all of us are operating from a consciousness that simply picks up whatever experiences are available, turns them into imagery, and automates those images into expectations, we cannot judge others so harshly. Knowing this won't necessarily change anything, though. To change our habituated imagery requires one of two things: de-habituation or new habituation. I offer the concept of meekness as an image worth habituating.

Meekness in this context is all about our capacity to *accept* the failings of others and to recognize that their challenges may be much greater than our own. Or, to paraphrase a popular saying making the rounds on the Internet right now, "Everyone you meet is facing a challenge you know nothing about." This reality becomes much easier to embrace once you accept the habituation/imagery aspect of consciousness. For all of us, our personal history is automatically transferred into expectations unless we learn to manage this process — and you never know what people have been exposed to in their past.

If you look within every layer of society, every institution including marriage and parenting, and all the tragic scenes that flash across the news, even a small amount of meekness could make all the difference in the world.

The meek are assertive without being aggressive. They are quick to acknowledge their own weaknesses, limitations, and preconceptions. They are less defensive and therefore more open to considering criticism, which means they have a continuous capacity for learning. Aren't these the qualities we need in leadership?

Whether we are looking at police brutality, violence in schools, family violence, or the personal/political attacks on talk radio, it is not our *differences* that are killing us, but rather our lack of consciousness. Anyone who exhibits the qualities we describe here as "meekness" can be understood to be someone who does not need to defend against a threat to his or her self-imagery. This is clearly not the norm in our world, but it could be!

An Everyday Neurosis

If you have accepted that you are both a habituating creature and that you are carrying images in your memory that are likely impacting your expectations, then you are ready to begin applying what you have learned to your life. Let me take you on a little tour of how I experience most of these dynamics in people who come to my office for help.

The first thing I experience of a new client is their complaint. They tell me what isn't working in their life, what is causing them distress, and all about their suffering. We explore their memories and expectations, and I observe what they seem to be experiencing in the present.

Eventually a pattern tends to emerge that looks something like this: There was something that happened, usually in childhood between about ages 3 and 16. This event triggered a high level of emotion in them, and it also threatened some positive images of "self." This threat then became the impetus for the creation of a defensive script.

This defensive script, meant to protect their self-imagery actually only served to impede the growth of that imagery. Sometimes the script is a sort of hyper-vigilance that seeks to avoid a replay of the original event or experience. For others, it is a hypersensitivity to any particular situation that can trigger an enormous emotional response such as anger, distress, humiliation or panic.

These defensive scripts, once habituated, have often become a source of embarrassment. In many cases, friends and family have found my client's sensitivities or vigilance strange or perhaps even irritating. So once again, their positive sense of "self" is in trouble and must be defended.

As more layers of defensive scripts develop over time, my clients often discover that they developed *another* habituated image of the self — one of self-contempt or fear of being defective.

Finally, he or she may find a way to manage this fear of being defective through a sort of depressed and disengaged hopelessness and helplessness. To live as a helpless victim who has given up all hope for getting better is a terrible way to be. As Milton Erickson was fond of saying, "The symptom is a solution." Or in other words, the script is always solving something. In many cases, the script offers an escape from the confusing mess of negative self-images that have accumulated and then become habituated.

When it comes to understanding our own human consciousness, the only training we receive tends to be the modeling of our family and friends, and that can be pretty poor unless you were very fortunate. For most of us, the modeling we receive is a little bit like being taught to drive a car by someone who only knows how to operate the radio.

To be clear, in saying this I don't mean we should blame anyone. The simple reality is that we can only see what we have experienced, and some people have experienced a lot more than others. Imagine the difference between being raised by an alcoholic and being raised by a teacher of meditation. When faced with a moment where your positive self-imagery is challenged, one person might seek escapist distractions while the other has learned to rely on something completely different. Perhaps they have learned to rely on an image of the self that is about learning and transformation rather than one that must be perfect and complete.

It is an amazing thing to be born into this human experience and to develop all of the wonderful gifts available to us. We have a tremendous capacity for memory and anticipation. We can experience the beauty of the communion of resonance with another person. We have the capacity to automate so many functions that we are free to perform with artistic or athletic genius.

However, this gift of consciousness comes with a great challenge. It doesn't take much for a single moment in childhood to spark a pattern that can cause us a lot of trouble from then on. The attention (or lack of attention) of a parent can impact our images of self and others. Even birth order can influence some powerful emotional dynamics. In some cases even the mildest of traumas can be define our expectations in amazing ways. In almost every case, the biggest challenges seem to come not from childhood wounds but the defensive ways we learned to cope with them.

The good news is that it is possible, regardless of the circumstances or degrees of our issues, for our brokenness to open us to an evolution of consciousness that can transform our lives. It all begins with this simple idea we have been exploring, understanding the habituation of our imagery. With this new awareness we can learn to be less attached to our habituated images — as well as the automatic defenses we have built to cope with them.

"Until you learn to name your ghosts and baptize your hopes, you have not yet been born; you are still someone else's creation."–Maria Cardinal

I was five years old when a visit to the doctor revealed that something was up with my kidneys. This discovery eventually led to surgery, and my left kidney was removed. I can remember a fair amount of detail from that time period. You can imagine what a traumatic experience this ordeal must have been for a five-year-old.

I remember cold x-ray tables and big needles. I even remember going into surgery. A man in a white mask pointed at two black things and asked me which flavor I would prefer, Mickey Mouse or Donald Duck. (I said Donald Duck of course.) He placed the mask on my face and told me to count backward from 10.

There are many other memories of this time, of course. Visits from family, a box of Christmas cookies, something about the president being shot in Dallas, tiny wind-up toys, paint-by-number sets, a pretty nurse, pick-up sticks, and feeling dizzy in the car as we drove home. My clearest memory of all, however, is the day I met my scar.

I sat on the examination table on a follow-up visit to the pediatrician when he removed the bandages from my side. There it was — all 34 stitches — and it looked like I had volunteered for a magic act that went horribly wrong — like I had been almost cut in half. It was gross. Disgusting. I remember asking the doctor, "When will it go away?"

"It won't go away," he said, "but it *will* look a lot better."

Let me pause this story for a moment to comment on how this experience now seems somewhat metaphorical. Maybe you can relate. Think about the scenes you remember of *your* life that shaped who you are. Like me, you may have a serious scar — or maybe more than one. Sometimes our scars are from wounds that heal just fine and we are left only with a few painful memories. And sometimes our wounds, and the resulting scars, leave us with sensitivities and predispositions that become far more problematic than the actual event. They are the wellspring of our hypersensitivity — that big red button just waiting to be pushed at the slightest provocation.

Going back to my own scar story, my favorite summer pastime was swimming, and our family belonged to a club with a big swimming pool. I'll bet you can imagine my apprehension the summer after the operation as I found myself taking off my shirt to enter the pool. "How can I hide this . . . thing?" was my most persistent thought.

In an instant I decided on a plan. I would keep my t-shirt on and get in the pool. That is how a defensive script starts. The choice of what to do is secondary to the impulse of protecting the positive self-imagery. Of course, this strategy was doomed from the start. Wearing a t-shirt in the pool looked silly. Every kid I ran into asked, "Why are you wearing that t-shirt?" And of course, I lied. "Sunburn" I'd say.

I'm not sure how long this went on, but at some point I finally figured out a new strategy. Once I was in the pool, I would take *off* the shirt. As long as I stayed in the water and kept a little extra distance from people, no one would notice that I was disgusting.

Next, I discovered that when I took my shirt off in the boys' bathroom, I could put my left arm around the waist of my swim trunks and stick my thumb where the belt buckle would have been so that my left forearm would cover most of my scar, especially if I pushed my elbow in toward my back. So I learned to walk like Napoleon from the changing room to the water. This new strategy also allowed me to get out of the pool and go off the diving board, though that was still a bit awkward because I was exposed for the brief second when I had to raise both arms to break the surface of water.

Who knows how elaborate my strategies might have become —
and how automatic they might be to me, even now, were it not for my
grandfather. His mother's family was from the Choctaw tribe, and he
was a wise man with deep compassion. As I think of him, I can still
smell his pipe and see his kind and curious eyes.

Granddaddy worked as the Executive Secretary for the State
Board of Mental Health, and on several occasions I would go to
visit his office way up high in the Mississippi State Office Building
in downtown Jackson. In those days, the windows still opened; the
building was built before central air-conditioning. On at least one
occasion I remember how Granddaddy let me climb out of his office
window while he held onto my belt. It would not be unreasonable
for you to now wonder how he got the job with the Board of Mental
Health, but for me that memory just reminds me of the trust I had in
him and that he had in me.

On one particular visit to the office I remember Granddaddy
asking, "Would you like to make some money?"

"Sure!" I said,

And with that we walked down the hallway to another room
that must have been a typing pool, where maybe a dozen women
sat at little desks, typing. Gathering everyone together, Granddaddy
announced, "My grandson here has had an operation. He was very
brave and everything is fine now, and he has a scar to show for it. For
just 25 cents each, he will let you see his scar." (Keep in mind that this
was around 1965, so that would be like $20 now. Big Money.)

So I pulled up my shirt and held out my hand as a series of ladies
walked by, looked at my scar with admiration (Not disgust? Wow!),
and gave me a quarter. The following week I repeated this performance
at the birthday party of a friend. I never worried about the scar again.

It wasn't that the memory of the scar had disappeared — nor had
its constant presence on my body. However, the image of the scar had
changed from a source of shame to a source of courage and strength.
The meaning of the whole traumatic event had shifted.

What do you think would have happened to me if my grandfather had not intervened? Some moments have the power to shape the
rest of your life. One unfortunate moment can leave you in a shell of
defensiveness, distancing yourself from any contact that might expose
your hidden shame. Another can have the power to relieve you of your

need for defenses and free you up to be more fully alive. In my defining moment with my scar, my grandfather was my salvation.

I have watched many courageous people overcome devastating trauma and return to full capacity for self-acceptance and loving relationships. What could be more inspiring than to witness a person who is wrapped tightly within the cocoon of defensiveness begin to break out their wings and fly in the freedom of their own true being? Sometimes it's almost as if our trauma gives us an urgency to find our salvation instead of medicating our consciousness.

As I watch people moving through this process, I can't help but wonder if everyone hasn't been traumatized in some way. Aren't we *all* in need of a place where we can go to inspect our predisposed sensitivities and fixations without risking overwhelming judgment? A place where the relationship is more important than being right and where lovingkindness can support us as we heal our defensive strategies of distancing and hiding?

For all who suffer from trauma, my hope is that they will find someone whose genuine lack of pretense or defense can help open the door to healing and recovery. No book could ever substitute for the caring presence of another person; however, within these pages I hope you'll find some stories, experiences, and insights to help you open the door to that gift.

Wanda's Trauma

Imagine a woman who had grown up with a particularly challenging trauma. Her uncle had molested her in her early childhood. This is a story I have heard several times in my years of counseling, so I will blend the stories of several women to offer a broader picture. This story is made up, but it draws from many experiences I've had supporting women who are working through sexual trauma. We will call this composite woman "Wanda."

It surprises some people to learn that one of the most debilitating aspects of child sexual abuse is the way sexual shame is sometimes carried forward through the repetition of arousing memory images. Though this is certainly not the case for everyone, in my work I have found this scenario to be common. Depending on the specific nature of the trauma, a child who has been inappropriately touched or fondled by an adult may have had such an intense experience that the memory of it is arousing. As a result, sometimes the child will re-experience the memory of the abuse until it becomes a big part of his or her habituated imagery associated with sexual arousal.

In Wanda's case, even as an adult her sexual arousal usually involved some level of replaying this memory. Over time, the shame Wanda began to feel around this pattern compelled her to develop some elaborate defenses to hide it. Eventually, the layers of her defenses created more and more problems in her life and her relationships. Eventually, Wanda ran into a situation where her coping scripts failed her, and that was when she came looking for help.

It is also important to recognize that at the time a child is sexually abused he or she may or may not feel traumatized. Often, the child is completely unaware or unsure about what is happening. For a child, a trusted adult can seem to simply be playing a new game, doing something for the child's benefit, or showing them special attention. It is easy to see how a child could carry these images forward as a sexual reference for arousal and replay the memory for pleasure. Of course, to do this will almost certainly become a source of shame over time.

Wanda could have had a different experience. Depending on the perpetrator's approach, she might have memories of overwhelming fear or disgust. Those with these kinds of traumatic experiences often experience higher levels of dissociation, however, that make memories less clear. For Wanda, the source of disturbance was close at hand and not hard to recognize.

Situations like Wanda's are not rare. They highlight one of the terrible debilitating conditions that perpetrators initiate in their victims — the confusing split between having images that elicit both intense arousal and debilitating shame.

How much would you have to trust someone to tell them about that kind of experience? Can you imagine the courage it would take to even begin to face this aspect of your life, much less explore the ways it has impacted your choices and your relationships? My experiences have shown these people to be among the bravest you and I will ever know.

It was not my job in these cases to become involved in the mitigation or treatment of the perpetrators. In every case that person was deceased and there were no avenues for addressing their actions. My job was to support the healing of the traumatized.

The process of our work involved separating the natural experience of sexual arousal from the inappropriate nature of the experience of abuse. For Wanda, the imagery of her abuse had been replayed in her memory until it seemed all the more powerful. In other words, Wanda's journey involved learning to feel good about arousal as a natural response of her body. She also needed to work on the memory images that had become a source of shame and defenses.

Wanda discovered that her sexual shame was defining her life in many ways she had tried to ignore. Because of how consciousness habituates imagery, the arousal associated with the memory tended to happen whenever she experienced anything that felt connected or similar in some way to the scene of abuse. For some survivors of sexual trauma, this habituated imagery is triggered whenever sexual contact begins. Others may experience arousal triggered by some other aspect of their momentary experience, and this can be really confusing. For instance, if the childhood trauma occurred in a room that was painted blue or with a particular kind of person, encountering anything similar can trigger the same arousal.

For Wanda, the troubling experience involved authority figures that, like her uncle, had a particular kind of strictness to their personality. Encountering such a person in her normal, day-to-day life created a meltdown of confusion and embarrassment made all the worse by the fear that she might be crazy. The longer she carried this secret, the denser the walls of her defenses grew until everything about her felt fake.

Wanda's consciousness was simply doing what consciousness does — comparing her immediate experiences to past imagery in order to recognize and make meaning of the moment. Unfortunately for Wanda, her memory images being compared to her current moments had some pretty intense stuff attached to them and caused great disturbances for her.

Wanda cannot change the way her consciousness operates, but she can learn how to recognize these triggers in the moment — and then to dance through them. As Wanda works to develop this capacity she will also begin to learn how to extinguish the defensive scripts she developed to cope with those traumatic scenes — the destructive ways she tried to escape or control her unwanted responses.

With the help of Sensory Focused Meditation, Wanda learned how to manage the moments of being triggered. By practicing a sort of mindfulness that allowed her to shift her attention away from the imagery in her mind and toward her senses, she became better at managing those moments that triggered her shame. As these triggering moments became less often a problem, she no longer needed some of her destructive scripts that had caused so much trouble in her life.

The important thing for Wanda to realize was that she had done nothing wrong. Her arousal/pleasure was simply a natural response of her body. It was also natural for her to remember it, replay it, and experience the feeling of pleasure. Over time Wanda chose to establish new patterns around sex that include playfulness and face-to-face intimacy. Wanda experienced more freedom in her sexuality not because the old images were erased, but because their meaning had changed. She learned to shame the uncle instead of her own sexual arousal and then, freed from that shame, Wanda was at last able to explore her sexual experiences in the here and now.

I hope that describing this brave journey taken by so many women offers insight about how we *can* develop skills for managing the powerful imagery machine of our consciousness. (A little bit later we'll explore a few specific practices for increasing these skills.) The images we carry in our memory are unique to each of us —mostly a matter of chance rather than choice. What we are exposed to, particularly early in life, often sets us into a particular spin with memory images that set us up for hypersensitivities or hyper-vigilance that can wreak havoc in our lives.

When we become aware that these kinds of concerns may exist in the lives of the people around us who are "fighting battles we know nothing about," we become meek. We feel more compassion. We recognize that every conversation we have is taking place between two beings operating from their own unique memories and all the expectations associated with them. Any *real* conversation will seek to explore those images, and the *best* conversations allow for an open dialogue where both parties are able to question the source and completeness of their own images.

The Meek and the Mild and Girls Gone Wild

Humans are hard-wired to pay attention to action. This explains why our natural tendency is to prioritize an argument over a calm conversation. (In the next section we will explore this biological truth in greater depth.) If you live long enough — and you pay enough attention — you'll begin to sense that humans are almost addicted to drama. We don't tend to watch movies where people have conversations that lead to discovering great truths about one another. Those kinds of movies hardly ever make it.

The blockbusters, on the other hand, almost always include high-impact conflict between heroes and villains, with enough violence in their conflict to keep it riveting. How do these popular images play into our anticipatory beliefs and expectations? Don't they, too, contribute to the pantheon of memory images that help define our self-imagery and our imagery of others?

The time has come for the meek to "inherit the earth." News channels feed on polarization to create entertainment dramas where someone has to be good and someone has to be bad. The biggest ratings come when the bad guys (as defined by some limited perspective) get what's coming to them. As I see it, even the tiniest bit of exposure to the ideas I am presenting will help undermine the easy judgments of others.

Once we begin to ask questions about the villains in the black hats (What happened to them to make them do these things and think these ways?), we begin to evolve. The old ideas of what Walter Wink called "The Myth of Redemptive Violence" will no longer work in a consciousness that understands that we are all habituated to images we somehow identify with — and all of this is mostly the luck of the draw.

And, if you have been cast as "villain" in your own world, don't give up and give in to that expectation. The pain of your childhood *can* heal. We now have the knowledge to help set you free from this role. Don't hurt anyone else before you find someone who can help you see beyond your defensive scripts. I wrote this song a few years ago to articulate this important message.

A Song For Bernie
So the judge heard the case
And they gave you parole
Now you're headed down to Austin
To relocate your soul

The tabloids have some questions
That their readers need to know
They want to turn your story
Into a Broadway show
I heard they gave you mercy
Because you were abused
I hope you get some distance
From that ghost inside of you
But don't forget the brothers
Back on cell block number two
You can bet a broken childhood
Did a number on them too
Set the scene just right
and any man will break
seems we're always drawn to
the very thing it takes
The judge may hear your plea
and a jury may agree
but no matter the decree
Only love can set you free
Some bury the pain down deep
And fill that hole with hate
Or you can fill it up with kindness
And still dissociate
Either way you go
The feeling's gonna tail you
You can live with your defenses
Until the day they fail you
Set the scene just right
and any man will break
And it seems we're always drawn to
the very thing it takes
The judge may hear your plea
and the jury may agree
but no matter the decree
Only love can set you free
Imagine there's no prison
It's easy if you try

Little boys all grow up
Knowing its OK to cry

Meek people are not given to dividing the world into "good" and "bad." They know that far beyond the traditional white and black hats, *everyone* has been shaped and everyone has been programmed.

Being shaped and programmed, however, doesn't make us incapable of making judgments or taking action. To be meek does not mean you are a doormat. It actually means you have enough self-awareness to avoid the traps that many people fall into when they experience conflict.

We are living in an age where even the passing thoughts of a 12-year-old can be heard around the world almost instantly through social media. We are also living in a time where the distance between us is dissolving to allow for direct confrontation of conflicting ideologies, customs, and beliefs.

Conflict is inevitable. And, because this new world of multi-cultural experiences involves greater conflict and exposure to differences than ever before, now more than ever it makes sense to reconsider how we relate to one another when our differences emerge. Without an evolution of consciousness we have two choices, escalate or escape. When I say that human consciousness is the greatest threat to humankind, I am suggesting that, just as my traumatized clients had to learn, until we manage consciousness differently we are likely to only create a more dangerous and dysfunctional society.

This new consciousness involves taking particular care how we define "enemies" and "villains." While we do have to hold people accountable for their actions, an evolved consciousness retains the capacity to recognize the images and experiences that set suffering in motion.

Let me also be clear what meekness is *not*. Meekness has nothing to do with squashing our thoughts and feelings. That isn't meekness. It is repression. Meekness does not require us to give up emotional freedom, but emotional freedom also does not give us a monopoly on the truth or entitle us to having others agree with us. Meekness is not about denying our feelings, hiding our light, or playing small. It is about confidently approaching others with the humility and openness that makes it possible to learn.

I want a vibrant world to live in. I want sun shiny days to romp around in and foggy nights to make love in — and vice versa! Developing meekness gives us the capacity to be moved by others' thoughts and feelings. More than anything, as we will see, meekness is about the capacity to reflect on our own thoughts and feelings without dogma or defensiveness, even when we are really sad, mad, glad — or feel like we've been had.

CHAPTER 4

The Art of Waking Up

If your image of meekness is a mousy little person who never speaks his or her mind, I suggest you need a replacement image. Try picturing instead someone who exhibits a quiet strength. Imagine that person who listens without prejudice and speaks without defensive bravado.

I call this kind of imagination exercise "the draft." Going back to our football analogy, it's like you have a football team of a million players (images) in your memory, and yet *none* of them know how to throw the ball. What do you do? Draft a new player, of course! Recruit a new image and let that new "player" help you adjust your expectations. We will revisit this idea of "the draft" again a little later on.

For now, the important thing is this: The *evolved* consciousness is one that is not restricted to the narrow experiences of life to which it has been exposed. Nor does it let these images define identity, personality, or destiny. Choosing to Evolve is about choosing images *intentionally* rather than accepting only what life has brought your way. Rehearsing these images, especially when they are tied to a physical sensation, can be just as effective in our transformation as any random memory of an event we may have.

Self-Doubt and Ambiguity

If aliens from outer space have ever visited Earth, my guess is that they'd go home telling the rest of the galaxy about our human habit of banding together in our common beliefs just to reinforce our feelings of security and certainty with one another. Throughout the history of human experience, divergence and dissent have been solved by excommunication. We have literally driven dissent out of our presence. You don't agree with our belief system? Out you go! Problem solved.

And, when it was not possible to drive all the diversity away, we typically withdrew to isolated places where we could keep our children from exposure to alternative images. You may think that dissent and diversity cannot be so easily silenced today. With social media and the Internet, we are so much more connected to people around the world, so aren't we much more likely now than ever before to have to face the differences between us? With all of the diversity of human experience now at our fingertips, you wouldn't think that we would be struggling to manage the conflicts inherent in diversity.

Coming to grips with this unprecedented clash of diverse cultures worldwide *should* be one of the greatest challenges of the century. How will we manage this conflict? Fortunately or unfortunately we have been given a filter to keep this from happening. The Internet is programmed to feed you what you want. Complex algorithms track your every preference and then feed you what you "like" as the information age falls victim to marketing. While it may be easier than ever before to *believe* you are connecting with the whole wide world, you are actually being fed, not just the commodities you like, but the ideas you already have.

Are we this afraid of facing those who see and feel the world differently? Or is it possible that we are just not yet ready for it? Do we possess the relational intelligence to manage the challenges of such diversity? Maybe we are happy to stay in our comfy bubbles because deep down we know we aren't all that skilled at managing conflict. Most of the time we still tend to approach conflict like the NFL: We line up our best defenses and go at it until someone gets a concussion.

Let's face it. It's *embarrassing* to be proven wrong about something — and any conflict can bring about the possibility of that happening, so it's natural to want to avoid it. But that isn't the only reason we avoid conflict. Conflict can reveal the unknown and the unknowable within us. And, because many of us have built elaborate defenses against anything that could introduce ambiguity to our understanding of life, we tend to believe that it's a far better thing to avoid conflict whenever we can.

What's It All About?

Just as you and I carry images of ourselves, we also carry an image of what *life* is. This library of images includes so many things it would be impossible to list. For example, when you close your eyes and think of God — or your sense of purpose, your place in the world, your calling — all of these are a part of your imagery of life. These images operate automatically within our consciousness for the most part. And this automation keeps a lot of negative feelings away.

For example, you have an image of the universe that allows you to not have to think about it much. Even using the label, "universe," gives you a sense of knowing it. You look up into the sky without any sense of ambiguity. But if an astrophysicist were to tell you that you are not looking up at all, but rather you are looking out from your vantage point, you might feel just a hint of the vulnerability that comes when our dominant images confront new information.

Whether you follow a particular faith or see yourself as spiritual in a way not defined by traditional religion, or even if you are neither of these, you carry within your mind many images of life. Even if I were to say, 'I don't believe in God," I would still be expressing something of my imagery of life. From these images — and there are many — we form the expectations by which we live and judge our experiences. This is the basic engine of consciousness we have been exploring. It gives us many advantages. The problems we face, however, are often about how we cling to those images even as our experiences reveal that they are overly simplistic, or, in some cases, pure illusion.

When I was a young boy I could spend hours lying on the grass and watching the clouds go by. I loved to imagine that the clouds were standing still and that the earth was moving beneath me. I can still remember that cool feeling, sensing that movement, and thinking about the earth as a vessel traveling through space. Sometimes challenging the limited imagery we were given can be thrilling. It can even return a greater sense of adventure to our life.

The images we have of life create a system that we use to feel safe in the world by helping us name our experiences in ways that feel more manageable. In his book, *Sacred Eyes*, Robert Keck observed that humanity moved from childhood to adolescence thousands of years ago, and, like all adolescents, our species then began to test the limits of its power by trying out different identities and discovering how to control things (including other people). This quest for control permeated every arena of life: technological, philosophical, cultural, occupational, social, and really, just about everything. But gaining control came with a price — the automation of functions that include our imagery and emotions.

Keck believed that humanity must now enter into adulthood (or spend some time in rehab). The challenge of the adult is to know when to *not* exert control. Choosing to Evolve is about practicing an awareness that fully understands how human consciousness tends to automate and control, sometimes in ways that lead to destruction, dysfunction, and endless conflict. One way to practice this awareness is to be more intentional about the labels we give and the way they encourage us to take things for granted.

I have often found that labels serve to demystify the world. If you go outside at night and look upward, what do you see? If you said, "stars," I invite you to try something. Try looking into the darkness without thinking of any names for what you see. Just *experience* what is there. You may discover that there is more unknown than known out there in the darkness. Using the term, "stars," for just one of the things we see somehow serves to let us ignore that. Labeling and automating play a big part in removing the mystery and ambiguity from life.

The same is true for how we label ourselves. Using a label gives us a sense of familiarity and control that is just plain false. Now, labels aren't bad in and of themselves — they offer us a way to make the immense mysteries of life less overwhelming. It is the way we use labels to ignore things that has a significant dulling effect on our entire life experience.

The name given to me at birth is Charles Milton Gaby. It is a label I have sometimes felt unhappy about. Charles seems so formal, but the less formal, Charlie, never resonated with me. Chuck was friendly enough, but it seemed foreign also. Milton was a cartoon monster character of my childhood. Gaby was always being pronounced wrong — I can't tell you how many times my mother would say something like, "It's *Gāby*, like baby with a G."

Gaby is actually an old English word for "fool, minstrel, or court jester." As much as I resisted that name as a child I have come to accept that it fits who I am now. It feels like who I have become, or perhaps in some strange way I have become what I was called.

Once you understand the impact of the labels you use every day, you may want to change your name every year or two — and you may want to name others something different every day or two. (I'll leave it up to you whether you mention this to them!) It's amazing how changing a label, even in your own mind, can give you a fresh perspective on just about everything. I particularly suggest that you keep changing your name for God.

"I prayed that God would rid me of God."

— Meister Eckhart

"Religion is the best defense against a religious experience."

— C. G. Jung

If you seek a truly transformative relationship with the fountain of truth and life, I invite you to consider that clinging to our concretized images is something akin to idolatry. To reclaim the ecstatic child in your soul who yearns for that divine dance, you have to embrace both ambiguity and mystery. Labels carry with them a defined imagery that can become closed to any emerging insight or new experience. They seem to imply that we have the whole thing figured out. We don't.

One of the reasons conflict triggers so much intense emotion is that the images (and labels) we carry provide a defense against our fear of the unknown. Just like using the word "stars" seems to give us a sense that we know the mysteries of the great beyond, these images of God, or truth, or belief are defenses against feeling small, powerless, and afraid. Someday we will laugh at our insecurity and shake our heads at the way we let it define us. The next evolution for humanity, therefore, is an adventure in consciousness. And here's the important part: it is not about *controlling* consciousness. It is about *freeing* our consciousness from its current bondage, created by our clinging to habituated images.

If you want to Wake Up, choose to play with the labels you have for your self, your friends, and your big picture of life. Consider opening yourself to mystery and embracing what you don't understand, rather than trying to defend what you think you know. Try living for a few minutes with no answers, just questions. You may be surprised at how much more alive you feel!

"To be a mystic is the opposite of taking things for granted."

— Matthew Fox

"Life is not a problem to be solved, it is a mystery to be lived."

— Sam Keen

Of course it's likely that we will never be able to live without the guiding light of the images we have gathered along our life's path. But meek people are more at home with not having to know all the answers. The evolving consciousness may well tend to find more meaning in those moments where they remove the labels and experience the moment in mystery than they will in ordering the world via some dogmatic code of spiritual laws.

The work of Choosing to Evolve opens us up to experience life as big and wild — with far less of it conforming to our preset expectations. Even a little bit of this practice can reveal the great adventure of your life. In the movie, *The Evening Star*, there is a conversation on a beach between a retired astronaut (played by Jack Nicholson) and an aging debutant (played by Shirley McLain). Shirley is regretting the adventures she has not lived in her life, and Jack is encouraging her:

"That's easy for you," she says, "you have walked on the moon!"

Jack replies, "But you have walked on the Earth. It's a much nicer place."

Dialogue and the Meek

In addition to cracking open the mystery and adventure in your life's moments, doing this work will change the way you interact with others, especially when conflict emerges. Many of us have a close friend or family member, a sibling or a spouse whose perspective lands them on the other side of our own position in the debated issues of our times. These divisions are felt more deeply in some families than in others. For the most part, modern civilization provides us with ample opportunity to avoid those with different views. Or, if we absolutely cannot avoid running into the opposition, we know better than to talk about it.

If this description fits you, consider that being meek includes recovering your voice. I believe that the silent masses of gentle people are not apathetic or lazy when it comes to their concerns about the direction of their culture and their world. They suffer, as the world suffers, from a lack of good models for healthy conflict. Instead, we have habituated ways of managing conflict that fail to acknowledge the aspects of consciousness we are now exploring. Evolved dialogue is assertive without being *aggressive*.

How can we tell the difference between assertiveness and aggression?

It's easy. Look for defensiveness. Aggression and aggressive speech always carry a hidden message of instability and desperation — a need to defend the images that person carries. Assertiveness is actually much more powerful. Assertiveness makes its point without defending its own images. It speaks its truth without losing the capacity for listening and expressing empathy.

It's easy to see when you notice this difference how defensiveness is the death of openness and curiosity, to say nothing of empathy. Let me say that again: Once you start defending your images, you lose your empathy and real communication is dead.

This is why arguments — a classic clash of defenses — are useless. Real communication cannot happen unless both people have the ability and willingness to recognize and admit how and where they received their images — and what these images mean to them. Real communication also requires both people to be open and interested in the other's experiences. Questions to ask might include: Where did you pick up this expectation? What was happening in your life at the time? How has it served you to carry it as an expectation in life?

One of the most common patterns of communication I see in couples is exactly the same one I see in our polarized political climate. Couples start off by telling each other what they think and how they feel. And then, when conflict arises, they get defensive. It's not like this is a conscious decision on anyone's part. It is simply the way they have learned to protect their positive self-imagery — a habituated pattern they likely picked up from seeing it modeled throughout their lives.

Then, as the conflict escalates, they tend to begin blaming each other, which makes matters worse. Perhaps instead we should place our blame on whoever taught us to have conflict this way! Unfortunately, as defensiveness continues, the ability to feel any real empathy for each other's experience causes us to have the same fight over and over again in different situations.

Eventually this repetitive experience of escalating conflict begins to feel hopeless, so they stop doing it. You might think that this is a good thing but it's not. What this cessation of conflict usually means is that one or both of the people have emotionally detached from the other. At that point of detachment, they actually lose even more empathy, and they develop distrust and disgust. Often, they then find solace in the company of others who will not challenge their perspectives. They prefer to detach from their partner rather than to repeat the disastrous escalation of conflict.

I was holding a group meeting on the night Barack Obama was elected President. The group had been meeting for about eight weeks, and though they had shared many personal stories, no one had mentioned the election. I was certain that within the group there was plenty of passion about politics, so I asked the group if anyone else thought it was strange that we hadn't mentioned the election. The response was an audible groan of distress, followed by, "Let's just not go there. We don't want to ruin our new friendships."

Eventually, one by one, each person shared how he or she had voted in the election. So I asked a little more about why they had voted the way they had. I was taken with the response of one woman who shared that she had wanted to vote for one candidate, but she knew that her family and friends would hate her if she did.

As we continued to discuss the political polarization within our culture, it became more and more clear that for these people, the divisions over politics impacted both social and business networks. For any of them to change their mind about any number of "the issues" was more than just a personal decision. It was a relational, economic, spiritual, and identity issue. These are among the many reasons why dialogue between polarized perspectives is difficult. Our images are part of both our social fabric and our self-imagery.

The thing to remember here is that regardless of our differences, dialogue is important. Not because it is likely to bring us to complete agreement, but because when curiosity and empathy is replaced with defensiveness, all communication dies — along with our capacity to learn and grow. One thing I do know for sure is that whatever human interaction was meant to be, it is not the hateful and defensive rhetoric to which we have become accustomed. More often than not, I see people finding common ground through dialogue.

When couples learn to manage conflict non-defensively through this evolution of consciousness, conflict no longer divides and destroys their intimacy. Instead, conflict becomes a central part of their discovery together. *Productive* conflict opens us to larger experiences of the world.

Achieving this kind of intimacy with another person is qualitatively better than any shallow relationship that is full of harmony but low on truth. To have a really good relationship, we need to commit whatever time and energy it requires to build our skills for recognizing our own imagery and entering into conflict without defending our images.

It bears repeating here that the cornerstone of meekness is a lack of defensiveness. Some of the Christian Gospels include a saying of Jesus: "Blessed are the meek for they will inherit the earth." Whatever the origin of this saying, and regardless of whatever religious belief we may have, the saying is likely prescient. Without a meek, non-defensive consciousness we are doomed to cycles of violence at all levels of relationships. Whether we observe the way we relate to our own existence, other people, or the world at large, defensiveness undermines any real growth. It blocks our capacity to examine and question the source of our images. It creates impasses to communication and puts purposeful processes into stalemate.

Meekness allows us to hold our images more lightly. In doing so, we become far more adaptive to the ever-changing flow of life. We can communicate with empathy and compassion. We can learn and grow together. We can Choose to Evolve.

Summary

The next human evolution has already begun. Its roots have been growing for years, and all that has been missing is enough of our tears to water the roots. You can hear it in the rhetoric of public discourse, failing systems of education and justice, economic gaps, environmental crises, international conflicts, and broken intimate relationships.

There is a common thread that weaves through all of these problems. In a human consciousness where we are either unaware or unquestioning of our guiding images, that are so habituated they have become "second nature," we waste our time and energy defending those images. When we become blind to the incompleteness of these images, we lose our capacity for productive dialogue.

The first step toward this next evolutionary leap for humankind is recognizing how our capacity for abstract thought (memory/anticipation), combined with our processes of habituation/automation, has led to stuck patterns of defending the extremely limited images we have of our self, others, and the world. Our evolving consciousness will learn to balance our need for stable imagery with our need for embracing doubt and ambiguity. When it comes to self-imagery, we can learn to anchor our stability in our capacity for transformation — discovering how to be a Learner.

In anxious times the ambiguities of life can seem pretty scary. It's no wonder we tend to want to cling ever more tightly to whatever stability we have found and to surround ourselves with that. It's no wonder we find ourselves drawn to likeminded people and shun alternative voices. It is understandable that as many of us have become cynical and self-centered, we have lost hope for a future any brighter than the past. As I see it, the greatest threats to humanity are not global warming, nuclear proliferation, or human greed. The biggest threat to humanity is human consciousness at its current state. By "current state" I am referring to our human consciousness that habituates imagery and projects this imagery as its anticipation of future experience — without question.

The processes of consciousness that have evolved in us thus far have given us great power — and great vulnerabilities. These processes are not going to change. However, our *awareness* of these processes can create opportunities to work with them in ways that are more adaptive. This is Choosing to Evolve.

Practicing the work of evolving our consciousness isn't hard, but it takes commitment and consistency. Without both of these, how could we ever transform what has been previously habituated? Old habits may seem insurmountable, but that's all right. We now have a new map, and from it we can create new scripts. One of the great keys for creating a new script is a better understanding of our human emotions. Before we get to that, though, let's pause to digest what we have covered so far.

Evolutionary Practices

The practices involved in applying the ideas we have shared could fill a hundred books, but for now I will share just a few practices that I've found to be especially helpful in growing our awareness.

Playing with Habituation Awareness

Go to a crowded place and spend at least 15 minutes watching people. Make a list of the things you see that seem to be habituated. Watch how people meet up, how they speak, and how they say goodbye. If you pay attention, the list will be long.

Try something that you have not habituated, i.e. play an unfamiliar instrument, read something in an unfamiliar language, eat with the opposite hand, or try having a conversation with no words, only noises. These activities, while likely to feel a little bit awkward or silly, can really help us become more conscious of our habituated processes.

Practice tuning into your senses. See if you can avoid fixating on particular sights and sounds. Let it all in at once. Take in the totality of sound in a space.

Randomly choose something in your immediate presence to explore. Even if it is a familiar object, approach it as if it were strange. What do you *not* know about it? What might this thing mean to you if new information or awareness is different than what you usually think?

Playing with Imagery Awareness

Try visiting a familiar location. Before you enter, pause to notice your image of the place. What do you remember of it? What is your general emotional feeling about it? Notice whether you project that feeling as an expectation for what you will feel again when you enter. Do you feel anything different this time?

Try relaxing, as if you were about to nap, but before you sleep, take a little tour through your memory. Who have been the most important people in your life? Pick one of them and notice your image of that person and the way your image gives stability to the relationship. Then notice how the image is imperfect and incomplete. What do you not know about them? How does your image of them participate in what you ignore about them?

Try writing a few pages in your journal or simple spiral notebook to describe your self. Notice the positive or negative nature of your self-imagery. Where did you receive the images with which you identify? Can you see transformations of that image over the years of your life? Where is your growth edge now? A great place to start is simply making a list of the things, people, movie characters, books, and music with which you have identified over the years. You may be surprised at how these images have shaped who you are today!

Have a conversation with a friend about ultimate concerns. What is the meaning of our lives? What's it all about for you? Where do you get your images for this? Can you express these things in a way that embraces the limits of your experience? Can you allow yourself to seem foolish enough to learn?

Mindfulness

I would classify mindfulness as any practice that moves us to a greater appreciation of the uniqueness of the moment we're in — or that transcends the automated, "taken for granted," tendencies of our consciousness. Mindfulness can be as simple as consciously looking at our life itself as a miracle. The thoughtful songs of Minnesota's Peter Mayer may speak to this better than any other I know.

Holy Now
written by Peter Mayer

When I was a boy, each week
On Sunday, we would go to church
And pay attention to the priest
He would read the holy word
And consecrate the holy bread
And everyone would kneel and bow
Today the only difference is
Everything is holy now
Everything, everything
Everything is holy now

When I was in Sunday school
We would learn about the time
Moses split the sea in two
Jesus made the water wine
And I remember feeling sad
That miracles don't happen still
But now I can't keep track
'Cause everything's a miracle
Everything, Everything
Everything's a miracle

Wine from water is not so small
But an even better magic trick
Is that anything is here at all
So the challenging thing becomes
Not to look for miracles
But finding where there isn't one

When holy water was rare at best
It barely wet my fingertips
But now I have to hold my breath
Like I'm swimming in a sea of it
It used to be a world half there
Heaven's second rate hand-me-down
But I walk it with a reverent air
'Cause everything is holy now
Everything, everything
Everything is holy now

Read a questioning child's face
And say it's not a testament
That'd be very hard to say
See another new morning come
And say it's not a sacrament
I tell you that it can't be done

This morning, outside I stood
And saw a little red-winged bird
Shining like a burning bush
Singing like a scripture verse
It made me want to bow my head
I remember when church let out
How things have changed since then
Everything is holy now
It used to be a world half-there
Heaven's second rate hand-me-down
But I walk it with a reverent air
'Cause everything is holy now

While mindfulness can be a practice of noticing the sensory details of the moment we're in, it can also be holding the *big picture* in the context of that same moment. Yes, we may be having a disagreement, but hey, isn't it cool that we are two conscious creatures living on an amazing big blue ball that is spinning around a star?

Mindfulness, when understood in this way, is not about escaping our abstract thought, but rather employing a conscious choice to keep introducing yourself to life in a way that can eventually erase the stuck patterns of our habituated/automated tendencies.

If you pause right now and look around you, I think you can easily get a sense of what I mean. Just pick one thing to look at that you usually take for granted. Take a breath. Breathe in your experience of that thing/person/whatever. Now take away whatever name you have for it and consider how it speaks to you now in this moment.

Meister Eckhart once wrote: *"If I just studied a caterpillar long enough, I'd never have to read another word of scripture, so full of the word of God is one caterpillar."*

There is great joy to be found through entering the world with eyes that are not taking things for granted. This is something that has been a part of spiritual teachings for thousands of years. Human beings evolved to be creatures with a high degree of automated/habituated functioning, and this means that we take these functions for granted, which then allows us to turn our attention to ever-higher orders of function.

However, if that process of automation becomes too dominant, all of the pleasure of life is lost. We become slaves to our inner automation/habituation. We stop looking at sunsets because they all look alike. We have sex but we don't make love. Life becomes stale, adventure is lost, and, in the words of the legendary B.B, King, "the thrill is gone." That dynamic has rippling effects through every corner of our lives.

Spiritual practices in every tradition offer a counter to this numbness, but unfortunately much of the current religiosity is far too stuck in less evolved consciousness to explore them. We'll delve more into that later.

Mindfulness Exercises

Stepping Stones

Try journaling about the 7 transformations of your self-imagery. Start from infancy and choose 7 specific checkpoints in your life to describe how you saw yourself at each of these stages. Note the people, circumstances, and images that influenced your image of yourself. When you are done, read this as a story that offers you a sense of fluidity in your own self-imagery.

Labeling/Naming

Names and labels are one way that we lay our abstract images on top of the world.

Take all the names away.

Look around you with no names for anything and see what you would see if you didn't have a name for that. What does it feel like to just be with something without defining it?

Give new names to the things (even people) around you right now.

Giving yourself a new name is one way to play with the stuck nature of your own self-imagery. I once led a weekend retreat in which we gave each other new names. It led to some surprising new revelations for people.

Make it Strange

In *Dialogue: The Art of Thinking Together*, William Isaacs suggests that in order to have real dialogue with others we have to learn to suspend our judgments and enter the moment with curiosity and reflection. In those times where we would otherwise be tempted to assume we already know the truth, learn to "Make it Strange." This requires a disruption of our old consciousness and the capacity to turn off all our automation/habituation to enter the ambiguity of the moment. This is much easier said than done. Give it a try and you'll see what I mean.

Constant Reminders

Try setting the alarm on your watch or cell phone to go off at regular intervals. Each time the alarm goes off, take a moment to notice what you are *not* noticing around you or within you. What are you taking for granted and not really seeing in this present moment? What images are playing in your inner dialogue? How do you perceive what you are doing in relationship to your images of self, others and the world?

Mindlessness Exercises

Abstract thought and habituation so define the human race it is hard to even imagine life without either of them, and I am not suggesting that. What I *am* suggesting, however, is that while abstract thought and habituation are incredible assets, these two functions of our consciousness can also get us into a lot of trouble. By practicing and developing our ability to turn off habituation, we gain a capacity for greater choice.

"Lose your mind and come to your senses."
— Fritz Perls

Sensory Focus

There is a practice I teach in some of my classes where I invite people to close their eyes and bring all of their attention to the backs of their eyelids. Do this now.

Look at the light or darkness flowing through your eyelids.

Try switching back and forth from one eye to the other.

Time it with your breathing. Look left eye and breathe. Then look right and breathe. Feel your breathing as you pay attention to the sense of sight.

While you are doing this breathing, try also giving attention to the sounds around you. Don't worry about what the sound is. Just let the waves pass through you and give attention without definition. The sensory experience can be quite rich without giving any meaning to it whatsoever. It's like being a stone in a river of energy. Try to be present with all of it at once. Just be in the flow of it all without fixating on any one thing.

Now rest your eyes, but continue looking around and paying attention. Notice any other body sensations you're feeling as part of the mix of the sensory experience of the moment. After a time, you may find that your thoughts and images start coming in to distract you from your senses. Don't worry — just welcome them. Notice the feelings they represent and then release them, returning to your sensate focus. Try this for 10 minutes.

Meditation

Almost any practice of meditation can lead to gaining some capacity for quieting the inner dialogue that is sometimes called "the chattering monkey mind." But meditation can also be evocative if you have experienced trauma. The goal of meditation is emptiness — a mind that is completely still with no thoughts at all. Give your attention to *nothing*. (Trust me, this does get easier with practice!) I have found that the key to finding this place of emptiness in your mind is to not resist any of the images and thoughts that bubble up as you seek to be still. The more we resist, the more distracted we become. Instead, try to just observe what is coming up as it appears, without attaching any meaning. Practice flowing with your consciousness rather than resisting or fixating. Eventually the waters *will* become calmer.

As with the rest of the steps of evolving consciousness, the key to this first step is not to judge the processes of abstract thought (memory/anticipation) or habituation. It is to learn to manage them rather than be managed by them.

A Few Things To Ponder

There is much more we could consider with regard to the habituated imagery in human consciousness, much of which is beyond the scope of this book:

- Are human beings hell-bent on automating everything in our world because that is the way our own consciousness works?
- Is that a problem?
- How does technological automation of the world around us create issues for us?
- Can we choose what to automate and what not to?

The reality is, we have no choice about evolution. It will happen in one direction or another, whether we want it to or not. We already know that the constant availability of digital media is rewiring our brains. Can we now, with our current knowledge, decide to evolve in a particular way? Is it possible that we can consciously evolve our own consciousness by developing specific skills for managing or modulating both our images and our emotions? Is it possible, that we might evolve in a way that makes us less vulnerable to manipulation by political operatives and commercial advertising?

SECTION II

Becoming Aware of Scripted Emotions

CHAPTER 5

Shift Happens!

So far we have explored two dynamics of human consciousness: habituation and imagery. It is easy to see how almost all of what we consider our human experience is made possible by these two processes that run continuously in the background of our consciousness. The automatic way in which our memory images operate allows us to move through the world with a stable sense of knowing. Without this automated system for accessing the images stored in our memory, we could never feel at home with ourselves or with the world around us.

It is also easy to see how this automated functioning of our consciousness contributes to making our personal and interpersonal problems resistant to change. In fact, much of our suffering comes from habituated images that don't serve us. Habituation is not a bad thing in and of itself. Habituating can be great — until what we've habituated makes us lose our job, our relationships, or our sense of wellbeing. The same holds true for our imagery. Abstract images can create stability — until that stability becomes out of touch with our ever-changing present.

What's more, the longer we carry habituated images that create suffering, the more challenging it is to change the images we're habituating. And, once these dynamics become "hard-wired" in our brains, it becomes like an irrigation ditch into which water always wants to flow. For true change to happen, we have to "dig some new ditches" by creating new wiring. The good news is that knowing what we now know about this system of imagery and habituation, we can use the way our mind operates to create a shortcut. In other words, we can use these same processes of imagery and habituation to *transform* our habituated images.

The next evolution of human consciousness isn't about changing the way our consciousness works, but rather learning how to *use* the way consciousness works to create better outcomes. Through awareness and intentional practices we can gain the freedom to choose whether to remain in the easy flow of our current automation of habituated images, or whether to create changes to our imagery that will transform our experience. When we change our images we can change our life.

Have you ever tried to make a big change in your life, but failed again and again? Have you blamed your lack of "will power" for your inability to make true change stick? This is where many attempts to address the issues in our lives get bogged down. Relying on "will power" as a way to create lasting change seldom creates lasting results. Remember that will power is a temporary emotional response — and all emotional responses tend to fade.

What we fail to recognize when our will power fails us is the powerful role our emotions then play in our perceptions and responses. Emotions, you see, are actually a combination of *biology* and *biography*. And, because our emotions are just as habituated as our images, it is in the role of emotion to direct our attention from moment to moment that we can find the keys to our Choosing to Evolve. Awareness of the role of our emotions — and gaining the capacity to notice it — is a big part of our next evolutionary step.

In this section we will examine the unique role emotion plays in our consciousness — and *how* our emotions become scripted. Because we tend to see the world through the lens of our emotions, when we understand emotion better we can learn to recognize how our experience of the present moment can be blurred by our past. Let me show you what I mean.

Unpacking Our Emotional Lens

Let's say you just found out that your best friend has agreed to take a job in another city. How would you feel about that? Most of us would probably feel sad and disappointed. And, for all kinds of reasons, this experience may also trigger some other emotions. What if you were recovering from a divorce? What if your spouse fell in love with someone else and moved away just a year before? How might your recent experience of divorce change how you feel about your friend moving away?

In this type of situation, you might be embarrassed that your feelings are so much more than sad. You could easily find yourself feeling *angry* with your best friend, betrayed, and abandoned — as if your friend was intentionally hurting you. Our consciousness at its most automatic/habituated level wants to make meaning out of your present by calling up whatever memory images seem most similar in your past experiences. What's especially important to realize about these retrieved images is that they are also endowed with an *emotional charge*. And, because all of this is automated, it all happens beneath your awareness — and in the blink of an eye.

Now imagine that you only heard about your friend's new job because you were online and saw it posted on social media. Now your phone is ringing and you answer it. It's your best friend, telling you excitedly about her dream job come true. All you can feel is anger. How do you handle that? Can you *say* that you feel angry? Or do you hide your feelings, pretending to be excited and happy for her for the sake of your friendship?

It doesn't take a lot of awareness to recognize that your best friend moving away for a dream job is not the same as your spouse leaving you for another lover. However, even though there are big differences in these two experiences of loss, our consciousness tends to want to connect them. And, in the moment you hear the news from your best friend, it can be very difficult to acknowledge all these feelings. You don't want to rain on your friend's parade, but to *not* share your feelings creates a loss of intimacy in this friendship — like a part of you is no longer there. On the other hand, expressing your feelings, thanks to the emotional charge carried by your habituated images, can also be a big problem. Losing a best friend because you responded to her exciting news as a bitter betrayal is just one tiny example of how our emotional dynamics can create unwarranted and unrealized suffering in our lives.

Imagine you are a four-year-old with an older brother who seems to always know how to do exactly what your father wants. Your older brother gets attention all the time by pleasing others. He is so perfect! He is so much better at everything than you are. How can you *ever* get Dad's attention with this much competition?

One day you are both at your father's office and your older brother is happily helping in his usual pleasing way. You see a box of rubber bands and you start shooting them off of your thumb at him. Your father gets mad and makes you stand in the corner. This makes you feel even angrier. Pretty soon you start acting out in other situations, even though you don't really know why you do it.

Now imagine that you go to kindergarten. Things are going along just fine, but then you see another boy in your class getting attention from the teacher by showing off his skill at reading or writing. You don't even realize that you are feeling humiliated, but as that moment matches up with your previous experiences with your brother, you start doing things to disrupt the class.

At this point, it is very unlikely that being punished for disrupting the class will do the job of changing your scripted response of acting out. And yet, if that script doesn't get somehow transformed, it may well become a defining dynamic in your life and future choices. What do you think it would take to transform that script?

Punishment, as we will see, may only make you feel less understood and deepen your layers of defensive emotional scripts. By the time you are 15, you'll wake up every day looking for the next injustice that might be done to you. You'll spend a lot of energy observing the pleasers — the "posers" — whose very presence makes you angry. As you become even less willing to acknowledge your own mistakes and failures, you'll spiral downward into more and more failure.

Here's another example: Imagine that you are 10 years old and you are playing imaginatively with some action figures or dolls. Some older kids come into the room and make fun of you. You are embarrassed, and once you are alone again you decide to start tearing the arms off the dolls. Then you follow the older kids and start learning how to play sports with them.

Years go by and you find yourself the father of a 10-year-old. You walk into a room to find him playing with an action figure. How do you respond? Do you feel a compulsion to make him to go outside and play? Do you automatically see his imaginative play as bad? Do you feel embarrassed that he is playing with the "doll?"

A Continuous Projection

Every moment of every day we are experiencing the effects of our emotionally charged habituated images without even realizing it. In fact, these emotionally charged memory images are *always* being projected onto the action of our current moment, and it is through this lens that we create meaning out of each and every experience we have.

Sometimes this is no big deal. Quite often, everything works just fine, and the lens through which we are giving our attention isn't all that important. There are *also* times in our lives when our memory images carry so much intense, habituated emotional content that they can disable us.

We may think that the horror of a traumatic moment in our past is long forgotten, and then it suddenly resurfaces in a new experience your mind identifies as similar. And, if that traumatic memory happens to carry a strong emotional charge, you may even dissociate from your present moment and into that "forgotten" memory to replay it in your mind's eye. This can feel embarrassing if you happen to be in the middle of a conversation, because during this "instant replay" you are oblivious to what is happening around you.

While we may never fully understand how all of this works, what we *do* understand about memory images has the potential to transform a great deal of the suffering in the world. To accomplish that relief, however, we will need to don our Learner identities and dig deep into the world of emotions.

As we explore emotion in the coming pages, it should become clear why the simplistic notion of "trust your gut" can be problematic. Sometimes what we are "feeling" is something we have *learned to feel* in order to avoid what we really feel. I'll explain this more in a moment. For now, just consider that to "trust your gut" means trusting a scripted way you have learned to feel. And, for example, if you have developed an emotional script for anger that puts you into a rage with every disappointment, "trusting your gut" is probably not going to help you.

Here is the key to understanding this new twist on that old adage. The truth is, trusting our feelings is unavoidable. The attention we give to anything in any moment is always going to be motivated by an emotion. In fact, this happens so automatically you could say trusting your feelings is almost a given. Emotion lives at the very core of how we perceive our experiences. With more awareness of how our emotional system operates, we can learn to choose whether and when to step back and reflect on that emotional lens. By approaching our emotional dynamics with the same kind of meekness we have already discussed, we can learn how and when to "trust our gut" — and when not to.

Emotions are an amazing gift to human consciousness, but they also can be our greatest liability. Our emotions can make us vulnerable to our most destructive passions, and they can make us easy prey for those who try to use our emotions to manipulate us. This understanding makes it easy to see how political movements employ this knowledge to gain followers and to motivate their base of supporters. And, by exploring these specific motivational powers of our own emotions, we can begin to inoculate ourselves against the hucksters and hype that may surround us and gain the capacity to choose whether to flow with an emotional response and its corresponding imagery — or to meekly reflect on our emotion and perhaps choose a different path. We begin this journey of understanding emotion by exploring their biological origins, the innate system of Affects.

AFFECTS: Our first language

Long before you could talk, you were already communicating. Even before you had habituated images to provide a stable platform from which to operate, you were already interacting with the world. What made this interaction possible? An innate, universal system of communication evolved by our species that relies on the specific components of expression we call *Affects*.

Affects indelibly mark our experience of each moment of our life from the moment we are born. If you want to understand how to help people, how to work through issues as a couple, or how to fix our broken educational and justice systems, then you might want to dig in here as we begin to consider what *really* motivates people.

One of the best ways to understand emotions is to see them as the innate patterns — the Affects — we all were born with. Of course, I know that the term, Affect, is not usually capitalized. For our purposes, however, I use this capitalization to distinguish this word from its more common use. The psycho/biological term "Affect," is pronounced with the accent on the first syllable with a short A (like Abject or Asterisk). Affects are often reflected in specific facial/emotional expressions and psychologists refer to the lack of these facial/emotional expressions as a "flat Affect."

Please note that in this work, for the purpose of differentiating between the name of a specific Affect and the *feeling* that may be associated with or scripted as response to that Affect, the name of the Affects, sometimes expressed in a hyphenated range, will be capitalized. I know this sounds strange at this point but it will make more sense when we get there. Trust me.

Affects are like a palate of colors (nine of them, to be exact) that paint everything we think and say, whether we realize it or not. Imagine words coming from your mouth with different shades of blue or red or yellow. Imagine that everyone around you paid more attention to the color coming out of your mouth than the words you spoke.

Affects are like information we share about what to do with the information we are sharing. Think of the difference in how you might respond to someone who is saying, "There's a big wave coming!" Depending on whether the sound of their voice is angry, afraid, or excited, your response will likely be completely different.

Even though we are not always conscious of it, our Affects are always operating silently in the background of our consciousness, motivating us and directing our attention. As the universal language we know from birth, Affects are the biological roots of what we *experience* as emotions, which are actually scripted/socialized reflections of our Affects.

Think about it this way. A baby cries, right out of the birth canal. This is a biological response the baby never had to learn. Over time, however, that baby will learn how, when, where, and with which people it is OK to cry. We all know that some people cry more than others, laugh more than others, or get excited more than others. Some of us may feel embarrassed when we cry or become afraid when we're angry and vice versa. How did *you* learn to feel about how you feel?

Affects, Then Scripts

Our emotional response to any situation is actually our own, unique, scripted *version* of that experience, based on how we have learned to avoid, express, co-assemble, or otherwise manage whatever Affect has been triggered by that situation.

Let's stop and think about that for a moment. While the universal language of Affects we are all born with may seem simple or common sense, I challenge you to consider that awareness of these Affects and the powerful role they play in our lives is far from simple. And, despite their central role in our lives, the language of Affect is something not commonly known or acknowledged. In fact, it is often our lack of recognizing this important aspect of our lives that causes much of our human suffering. We suffer, sometimes unnecessarily, when we fail to recognize the powerful role our habituated emotional patterns play in our thoughts and choices — as well as in our conflicts.

Remember Bill from Chapter Four? Imagine that Bill, who has by now learned to manage his need to feel important, is now in a long-term intimate relationship. What do you think might happen as Bill's life becomes intimately tied to another person's? What kind of new conflicts might arise? I can tell you that if Bill runs into trouble, his partner may not be able to realize or provide the kind of attention Bill needs to keep his old fear of inadequacy at bay.

As this scenario unfolds, Bill will likely express his feelings of distress over that loss, and when his partner doesn't understand the intensity of these feelings, Bill will feel them all the more. If Bill's partner then makes the mistake of criticizing Bill's need for attention, even more defensive scripts will likely appear.

Should Bill trust his feelings and express them? Doing so could inevitably lead to more conflict and possibly damage or end his relationship. Bill's defensiveness over his feelings of distress could take any number of shapes, many of which we will explore in the coming chapters.

The best hope for Bill in this case is *not* to trust his initial feelings — or to ignore them, either — but instead to regard his initial feelings more as he would a warning light on the dashboard of his car. The more Bill learns about his own scripts, the more he can learn to respond differently when that warning light comes on, rather than immediately taking action upon those feelings.

Bill can choose the path of meekness by Moving Alongside his initial feelings (we'll learn a lot more about this key technique in coming chapters) and spending a few moments identifying which Affect has likely triggered them.

Tapping into this capacity illustrated by Bill will put you in good company. It is hard to pick up a magazine or newspaper today without reading about current research and discoveries regarding various facets of human motivation and emotion. By sharing what I have found helpful in my own work I hope to make some of these complex insights more easily accessible, understandable, and applicable to more people. At one point in my own personal quest, I was fortunate to be introduced to the work of Silvan Tomkins, an early pioneer in this field. My professional exploration and application of this work eventually led me to accept an invitation to help represent Tomkins' work from the institute that bears his name.

Tomkins' Innate Affects

I firmly believe that the work of Silvan Tomkins was ahead of his time. His masterwork, *Affect Imagery Consciousness*, reads a bit like quantum physics, so I don't recommend it as a place to start. Instead, if you're interested in diving deeper, I've included a list of suggested reading on this topic in the resources section at the end of this book.

In the mid 20th century, Tomkins used high-speed photography to capture the universal expressions of Affect on the faces of infants to provide unique evidence that illustrates this common human language that is the starting point for our interaction with the world. His exquisite study led to the recognition of nine innate Affects universal to neuro-typical humans.

From Silvan Tomkins' work we can see how infants are innately wired to communicate through this system long before any other language emerges. What's more, this innate language continues throughout our life as our central mode of communicating our experience with the world.

To see the role that Affects play in our communication, I invite you to search the Internet for *the Harvard Still Face Experiment* and watch the three-minute video showing a mother interacting with her infant daughter. I don't think you can watch this brief video without coming to the realization of how important Affects are to our experience of safety and connection in the world.

Tomkins also demonstrated that although all humans share this common emotional language, we each have our own individual *version* of that language, the habituated patterns that create the lenses through which we experience the world. Let me say that again. While we may all experience the same set of Affects (tears, fears, joy, etc.), we are each shaped by our life experiences to manage and tolerate each Affect differently. Over time, this shaping becomes just as habituated as the way you hold your spoon.

Tomkins called these automated/habituated patterns, "scripts." For example, although we were all born "crybabies," some of us got the message early on that "big boys don't cry." Later we will discuss what happens when that big boy meets a big girl who *does* cry, and why it is likely that they will have conflict. Unfortunately, they probably won't understand that one of the main dynamics in their conflict — the differences in their emotional scripts — is something beyond their control that set them on a collision course long before they ever met.

Let's take a moment here for some important reflection. Think for a few minutes about a conflict you have experienced with a friend or loved one. Sit with the images you have of that conflict for a minute, and review them in your thoughts in as much detail as you can. As soon as you are able to really feel that experience of conflict, I invite you to consider these questions:

What was the issue, or source, of concern?

Do you have any experience previous to this conflict that feels in some way similar to this concern?

What are the emotions that emerged for you in that conflict?

As you reflect, you may notice that your emotional experience of the conflict had a different tint from that of your partner. You may even get a small glimpse of the emotion that motivated the conflict. The Affect involved in the conflict is probably the one that made you notice the issue in the first place. Do you sense that your partner understands what you feel? How do you know that?

The Source of Attention

Affects, you see, are more than just our first language. As Tomkins demonstrated, another primary function of Affect is to *direct our attention*. Think about that for a moment. Out of all the things happening around and within you right now, what is making you pay attention to reading this book?

Let's face it. Moment to moment life is a bit like taking a sip from a fire hose. The amount of constant stimulation we experience makes it impossible to give our attention to everything, so Affects serve as a sort of triage system to direct our attention to what is most important in each moment of our lives. That's a pretty big job — and most of the time we don't even notice that it's an Affect doing it!

Affects are first triggered by the stimulation of our senses very early in life. Sounds and sights around us compete with one other — and with our body sensations such as hunger and fatigue. The stimulus that becomes our focus in any particular moment largely depends on the *intensity* of Affect triggered.

As we mature from infancy into childhood, the same Affects start to become triggered by *imagery* as well as sights, sounds, and sensations. (Just thinking about Mom can bring tears to the eyes of a young child at summer camp.) At this point in development, children also begin to imagine their future possibilities for success or failure. These images, too, are fueled by Affect and stored for future reference.

The fear experienced by a child arriving at his or her first sleep-away camp can be triggered by any number of anticipatory images. Past experiences of being without his or her family, even briefly, may define this anticipation. The more negative that anticipation, the higher levels of fear the associated images will trigger. At this point, Fear dominates the other Affects and begins directing his or her attention to look for danger.

Once we understand and begin to recognize that our Affects operate at this level of our consciousness to direct our attention, we can see even more clearly how our emotional scripts impact our choices. Our Affects are constantly directing our attention and calling up our scripts — or prompting new ones — without our even knowing it.

Two guys walk into a bar. One has been through a long series of losses and traumas. The other has experienced very little suffering. In fact, he is wearing a t-shirt that says, "Life's a beach — and then you surf." As both of these guys walk into this same bar, one is looking for the danger and the other is looking for the fun.

What's even more interesting here is that more often than not, they will both find exactly what they are looking for — and neither will be conscious that it is their emotional scripts that are defining their experience. Because the ways in which our emotional scripts define our experiences operate at the most rudimentary level of our consciousness, understanding this process — and the emotions and Affects driving them, is key to this evolutionary leap we are taking.

I hope you are beginning to appreciate how important this awareness is. How can you change something you don't even realize is happening? Going back to our previous exploration of how we habituate imagery, do you see how this new layer of knowledge about Affects and scripts is crucial to our understanding of this most basic engine of consciousness?

The automation of our functioning that has led us to the top of the food chain isn't just the habituation of abstract imagery and its projection into an anticipated future. That same engine of consciousness is also being pointed in whichever direction the Affect tells it to go, whether Fear or Fun, based on scripts formed from past experiences. It is by understanding the *combination* of these insights that we can transform many of the issues we face — individually, relationally, and culturally.

To put this knowledge into context, let's consider how emotion can impact our culture in the current debate about global warming. If you expose two people with different emotional scripts to exactly the same research, do you see how their unique emotional scripts will play a role in their responses?

Let's look at the many emotional dynamics of this debate. If you watch one of the movies, *An Inconvenient Truth or Truth to Power*, you may find that the images in these movies trigger fear. But we do not all experience that fear in the same way. Some of us have developed Fear scripts that are freely expressive and become motivation for action. Others of us have Fear scripts that manage the feeling with hyper-vigilance that means we would never even go to a movie that might frighten us. Others of us have been scripted to ignore our experience of the feeling of fear because we have been humiliated for expressing it in the past. We may then learn to see our own Fear — and the Fear Affect of others — as embarrassing or even disgusting.

With all this in mind it's much easier to see why dialogue can be so difficult. We each can have radically different emotional scripts around the same event or experience. Think about the last time you saw someone express fear in a group setting. Remember the wide variety of responses on the faces of everyone else? Some probably ignored their fear and wanted to attack the person expressing it as weak. Others may have moved more toward panic. Some will simply *feel* the fear and pay attention to it — and then become motivated to relieve the source of the fear by doing what needs to be done to alleviate it.

The many scripts Tomkins explored can get fairly complicated. For now, let's keep it simple by thinking of scripts in two main ways. Some are general, like "Big boys don't cry." These general scripts involve how we have learned to feel about what we feel. I may have been so humiliated for crying as a child that I developed a script that withholds all tears as a way to protect myself from embarrassment. When hiding my tears is not possible, I will then have to feel humiliation.

Other scripts are very specific to particular scenes, like a fear script that only emerges around going to the dentist. These scene-specific scripts can become more generalized over time; fear of dentists can evolve into fear of white coats in general. That's because the imagery involved in a traumatic moment where intense Fear Affect was experienced is carried in our memory. It may remain there, dormant, until something in our life reminds us of it. Then the same engine of consciousness that lets you do so many wonderful things without thinking about them will take over and do what it always does. It will draw up that traumatic memory and project it onto the current situation with all the intense Affect that was present in the earlier traumatic moment.

In both cases, our consciousness makes sense of what's going on in the present by calling up images of the past. Each of these images in our memory is endowed with the Affect that was guiding our attention in that original moment. Because we are primarily emotional beings, all of those emotions we experience in our life then become the *scripted versions* of our biologically inherited Affects. Let's take a look at the 9 Affects Silvan Tomkins first discovered on the faces of infants.

The Nine Affects

As we touched on earlier in this chapter, Silvan Tomkins observed nine different universal facial expressions on the faces of babies, and he called these "Affects." As Tomkins determined, these nine facial responses always showed up before babies could have learned responses. While some other theorists/researchers have claimed that there are more or less Affects, I like these nine because I find them both helpful and observable. In most of these Affects, two hyphenated words reflect a range of intensity from low to high. The nine Affects are:

Interest–Excitement
Enjoyment–Joy
Surprise–Startle
Distress–Anguish
Anger–Rage
Fear–Terror
Shame–Humiliation
Dissmell
Disgust

I invite you to consider these nine Affects as if they were nine ways to pay attention, each having evolved in our human consciousness to play a particular role in our survival. Like our physical sensations, Affects are each experienced to different degrees — sometimes only slightly, and sometimes overwhelmingly.

Just as little bit of salt seems to bring out the flavor in some foods while a lot of salt will define a meal, most of the time we don't even notice which Affect is guiding our attention, focusing and flavoring the moment we're experiencing. These nine flavors, some sweet and some bitter, are sometimes like the hint of oak in a fine wine, and at other times, they are more like limburger cheese, with a flavor so intense it is impossible to ignore.

Here are a few absolute basics about Tomkins' understanding of the nine Affects:

Affects are innate: No one had to teach you how to cry, laugh, or blush. Affects are almost like emotional reflexes, and they play a role in directing your attention.

Affects are analogues: There is some similarity between the frequency of a stimulus and that of the Affect it triggers. And, from a basic neurobiological perspective, the biological frequency of the stimuli that triggers fear is different from that which triggers enjoyment.

Affects amplify stimuli: Once a stimulus triggers an Affect, the Affect will then amplify it. For example, the growl of a baby's stomach triggers Distress and then Distress amplifies the stimuli leading to the expressive cry of the infant that helps to get the baby fed.

Affects Bias Cognition: Dave McShane, a long time friend of Tomkins, calls this the ABCs of Affect theory. Once triggered, Affects flavor our attention and bias our thinking.

Affects are our first language: Affects are our first form of communication and are basic to everything we say or write. Try talking with no emotion and see how others respond. It would be a very strange world without the Affects.

Affects are contagious: The human Affect system is an "open loop." It serves survival that parents feel distress when their babies are distressed. We are wired to feel what others feel. We also develop scripts to somewhat limit this contagion.

Now that you have some basic idea about what the Affects are, we'll take a look at each individual Affect. When we are finished, you will have a deeper understanding of these roots of your emotions. Along the way we will learn a little more about how each Affect becomes scripted through our life experiences. With that knowledge on board, we'll be ready to take the next step in the transformative work of Choosing to Evolve.

Are you ready to dig a little deeper? Let's begin our tour of the nine Affects.

CHAPTER 6

Meet the Affects, Part 1: Distress-Anguish

Let's begin with our tour of your biological emotional inheritance with where it all began. The first expression to take over the muscles of your face and body — and even your voice — was Distress. While your birth was likely the first, it certainly would not be the last time you experienced the Affect of Distress. Of course, you had no way of knowing this as a newborn baby, but throughout your life, Distress will emerge again and again — every time your hunger, fatigue or irritation reaches a level of stimulation high enough to trigger this Affect more than the others.

When was the last time you had something to eat? How do you know when you are hungry? The hunger itself may make itself known to you through the growl of your stomach or just a general feeling of restless distress. Some people get grouchy when they're hungry (some people call this feeling "hangry"), probably because somewhere along the line they learned that it is more acceptable to show a little anger when they're hungry than to cry like they did as an infant.

The cry of Distress, which happens whenever a baby is hungry or fatigued, serves as a signal that something doesn't feel good. Crying is how babies are able to communicate what is going on with them from the start.

What you may not recognize, however, is that feelings of restlessness or irritation you experience now (maybe even at some point as you read this book), are related to the same Affect of Distress you experienced as a newborn baby. You also may have been taught since then to ignore the discomforts of hunger, fatigue, or some other irritation.

What happens for you when the Distress Affect is triggered? Do you tend to ignore your feeling of distress until it gets too intense to disregard? And, when you *do* pay attention to your feeling of distress, will you likely respond by getting grumpy? Or sad? Can you identify the stimulus that is triggering your Affect of Distress and take care of the source of your discomfort? Or will you just ignore that funky feeling and let it infect everything you are doing and thinking? Some of us have scripts that tend to "flood" when triggered, meaning, in this case, that we get distressed about our Distress.

If you have ever had the opportunity to care for a small child, then you may have had the experience of trying to soothe a child who is crying. If so, how did you accomplish that? If you haven't cared for a child in Distress, then you probably have seen other adults in this situation. Visit any shopping center on a weekend afternoon. You'll get plenty of opportunities.

Most of the time when a baby or young child begins to cry, the parent will quickly attempt to distract the child. They may rock the cradle or carrier. They may give them a toy, a pacifier, or their car keys — anything that will stimulate a different Affect than Distress. Why is distracting a crying child with a shiny object helpful? The shiny object triggers the Affect of Interest (we'll get into that one a little later), which at least temporarily competes with whatever is triggering his or her Distress. Unless, that is, the stimulus for the Distress is too intense to ignore.

Now imagine what happens when this child gets older and has to sit through *hours* of being still and studying in a classroom. When his Distress Affect is triggered from fatigue in this situation, what if the soothing distraction is not offered? Training children to use distractions to process their Distress may help in early childhood, but as an adult emotional script distracting ourselves from Distress can become a disability.

Tomkins believed that while Affects *amplify* whatever stimulated them, scripts then sometimes *magnify* that stimulus even more. So for some people, Distress from hunger can trigger associations with other Distress experiences. With the escalation of one Affect triggering another Affect, the ensuing chain reaction can turn a momentary irritation into a lasting mood.

Another interesting quality of Affects is how rapidly they change in babies. We call this Affective plasticity. If you watch an infant closely, you may observe that infant going through multiple Affects per minute. Older children and adults, however, can sustain a particular emotional tone for long periods of time. This happens even more as our powerful capacity for imagery matures. Eventually, the images in our memory can be just as effective at triggering — and retriggering — Affect as any physical or sensory stimulus.

The Story of Dick and Jane

When I met Dick and Jane, they had been in counseling with another therapist for a few years. Most of that work had seemed to center around Dick's lack of being like Jane. Dick had developed prototypical male scripts, which means that he was not at all in touch with his feelings of distress or fear. Over all, however, Dick was a good guy and cared deeply for Jane, and he was doing his best to work on being more sensitive. Still, their marriage continued to have problems, and their conflicts continued to escalate into intractable defensiveness.

Jane was gregarious and creative. She also had a tendency to "flood" emotionally, which means that once a negative Affect was triggered, her creative intellect would continue to feed more and more imagery into the furnace of her hurt. That endless supply of fuel could keep her crying for a whole day.

When Affect Biases Cognition

The way Jane expressed her Distress as an adult wasn't all that different from the way she expressed it as a child. The only difference for her as an adult was that she had so many more memories of being upset that could magnify her experience of any Distress. To make matters worse, their previous couples counseling had left Jane with the impression that all of her feelings of distress over not feeling connected to her husband were his fault. So when she became distressed, she also felt victimized and entitled to her emotional flooding.

In Dick and Jane's first session with me, Jane was already flooding with Distress before she spoke the very first words of her complaint: "After thirty years of marriage," she said to Dick, "you would think that by now you would know that I need you to be more connected and engaged with me!"

Given Dick's immediate defensive response, Jane's criticism was never going to get her what she wanted. But that didn't stop her from trying it — over and over again. I suggested that rather than play the blame game over her needs, Jane would do well to take responsibility for them. Eventually she learned to notice her feeling of distress when it first emerged, identify the memories and meanings associated with that feeling, and then to shift her own focus to what it was she really wanted.

When Jane learned to simply ask Dick for what she wanted, rather than to attack him for not providing it, their marriage took off like a rocket. Jane learned from all this intentional work that she had to give up her need to punish Dick, or to try to make him more like her. She also learned to limit how much she allowed her emotions to "flood."

Dick became much more interested in responding to and anticipating Jane's needs as he felt relief from the blaming and shaming that had become a stuck pattern that was on the verge of destroying their marriage.

Blaming others when our needs go unmet is only one way that we can get stuck in our Distress. People don't just eat when they are hungry. Sometimes we eat to manage our emotions. The baby cries so she can eat, but as adults sometimes we eat so we don't have to cry!

Eating in response to Distress is common because eating food triggers good feelings, offering us quick relief from our bad ones. In using the term, "bad," of course I'm not saying that any Affect is bad. Far from it. We need *all* of these Affects. By "bad" I am simply referring to whether our *experience* of an Affect feels more rewarding or punishing.

When a child shows Distress, parents often use whatever is at hand to soothe him or her. As we discussed earlier, we are often taught from birth to modulate our Distress by additional stimulation. Once we learn to use food to relieve a negative Affect, this choice can become habitual. Avoiding negative Affects with food or drink or drugs is the fast track to addiction.

As a general rule, anything we use to avoid experiencing an Affect is a slippery slope. The better we get at avoiding an Affect, the more likely we are to also ignore the source issue that triggered the Affect in the first place. We then develop and habituate scripts to deal with the *feeling* associated with the Affect rather than what triggered it in the first place — the real problem. Avoiding our experience of an Affect that doesn't feel good is like having a warning light on the dashboard of your car come on — and then turning it off because you don't want to deal with your engine trouble.

A person who is addicted to food may eat to temporarily manage Distress, but the more he or she eats, the more he or she creates a scenario filled with even more feelings of distress or shame (we'll get to shame a little bit later). These kinds of scripts often become self-ful-filling prophecies: The more we escape, the more we *need* to escape.

The Distress Affect is usually triggered by the constancy of some irritating stimulus, though there are other more complex triggers that are beyond the scope of this book. The facial expression of Distress is universal as are the vocalizations and body postures that accompany it. A low level stimulus like hunger may only trigger a slight sense of Distress, but a stimulus that seems to linger and intensify may trigger the upper end of the spectrum of this Affect, which Tomkins called Anguish.

Very few people have any difficulty picturing Distress. However, few of us are conscious of how our experience of Distress has become scripted over the years. So before we explore the remaining Affects, let's reflect on the *experience* of this one. Here are a few questions that can help build our awareness of the Affect of Distress.

Who was the most expressive of Distress in your family growing up? Who was the least? With which one do you most identify?

Do you tend to repress Distress or do you tend to flood once it is triggered?

If you cry, what usually triggers your tears?

How do you experience other people's Distress? Do you feel empathy for the Distress of others, or something else? (Depending on how you were socialized to experience Distress, you might even feel embarrassed or angry when someone near you cries.)

Do you have any early memories of crying and how the people around you responded to that? What messages did *you* receive about how you should express your feelings of Distress?

Exploring these questions can help you become more aware of your unique emotional scripts around Distress. Why is that so important? What if every time you experience Distress you get mad? What if every time your partner cries, you feel embarrassed? Can you imagine how this might cause some issues in your relationships?

Enhancing relationships isn't the only reason to do the work of exploring your emotional scripts. As we have discussed, one of the roles that Affects play in our consciousness is directing our attention. This happens quite automatically, and that's usually a good thing — that is until our scripts direct our attention in ways that cause us suffering and failure.

Think of the nine Affects like a car that has nine pedals and no steering wheel. The direction you go depends on which pedal is getting the most gas. Then imagine that the "gas" is some combination of your body sensations and your inner habituated imagery.

Babies only have their sensory world to push their Affect pedals, but as we get older, the imagery that passes through our consciousness is equally capable of pushing them. The power of our imagery can cause us to cry from remembering something or feel fear from imagining something.

Though this all may seem a bit complicated, if you spend some time with these concepts you will begin to see the power that lies within these insights. I also realize we are skimming over a great deal of information here — and you probably have many questions. That's OK, and it's also OK to just let some of it remain a mystery. Having been born and raised in Mississippi, I have always loved grits. I have received a great deal of sustenance and enjoyment from grits, despite the fact that I don't really know what it takes to make them out of corn. I really only need to know how to cook them and enjoy them!

In the same way, while there is much more you can learn about Affects and scripts, you really only need to know enough to apply this knowledge to your life. I have seen how even the most rudimentary exposure to these insights can make a profound difference for people willing to consider the basics:

> Our thoughts are motivated and flavored by Affects
> Since those Affects are scripted, so also is much of our thinking
> Conflict is often about the collision of two people's emotional scripts

Our Big-Picture Life

Myths and stories play a part in how we may make meaning out of life. If consciousness operates through a hierarchy of images (images of self, other, the world, etc.), then you could say that each of the myths and stories we carry in our memories provides a kind of backstory to the action in our lives. These are high-order abstractions — our own big picture.

What are your personal myths that give meaning to your day-to-day experiences? What are the stories you heard from childhood that told you what life was all about? These images operate in their habituated/automatic way to give meaning to our experiences, telling us how to feel about things and what deserves our attention. And, as with all habituated images, these "big picture" stories are taken for granted, unquestioned, until they fail us.

Perhaps, like me, you were told the old stories of "The Boy Who Cried Wolf" or "Henny Penny," who ran around saying that the sky was falling. It is hard to miss the hidden messages of these stories: Any over-expression of our Distress or Fear is foolish and shameful. The underlying messages about processing emotions we find in so many stories are just a few ways in which we socialize children to acknowledge or deny the Affects with which they were born.

We will explore more of these big-picture images later, but for now it is enough to acknowledge that they exist. You and I operate in the world, making sense of what it all means, based on our sense of stories, symbols, myths, and legends. Sets of images live in our consciousness to help us assign meaning to our experiences as we progress through our life. Joseph Campbell explored some of these images in his most famous work, "The Hero's Journey."

If human consciousness has evolved in such a way that our habituated abstract imagery provides us with the framework for our experiences, automates our functioning, and creates a stable emotional platform, then our continued evolution must be to learn how to *use* that imagery in a new way. Not just any way, mind you, but in a way that adds to our wellbeing and our capacity to face the challenges to our survival. Some of the questions we must face include: How do we manage the destabilizing of our imagery when myths change? How do we manage the cultural conflicts that occur as we experience the collision of alternative myths and stories? How can we become more adept at navigating the inevitable moments when our own mythology loses its capacity to inspire or heal?

Enter the Labyrinth

Stories like those I have mentioned have played a part in shaping our experience of the Affects and therefore have determined a great deal of our perspectives. So perhaps we now need a story that will serve as a guiding image in our Choosing to Evolve.

If you are familiar with the Greek myth of Theseus and the Minotaur, you will recall that King Minos of Crete prayed to Poseidon, god of the sea, to send him a bull from the sea as a sign that the gods supported his assumption of the throne — and thereby enhance his power. In response to King Minos's prayer, Poseidon presented him with an exquisite white sea bull — with the understanding that the bull would be sacrificed. King Minos, however, was so impressed by the creature that he decided to keep it in his herd, and he sacrificed another bull instead.

As punishment, Poseidon caused Pasiphae, the queen, to fall in love with the bull. Soon Pasiphae longed to consummate her passion, so she recruited Daedalus, a very smart Cretan, to construct a hollow form to deceive the animal. I'm not exactly sure how all this worked, but somehow Pasiphae conceived and gave birth to a Minotaur, a being with the body of a man and the head of a bull — and an appetite for human flesh.

This dangerous creature had to be managed, so Daedalus was called upon once again. This time, Daedalus constructed a labyrinth to protect the people from the beast.

To feed the Minotaur, King Minos required that Athenian youths be sent from time to time into the labyrinth. On one of these occasions Theseus, the prince of Athens, decided to travel to Crete with some of those ill-fated youths. He planned to kill the beast in order to spare their lives.

So Theseus was trying to solve the problem for his people, but solving this problem was complicated. For one thing, even if he had the power to slay the beast, how would he find his way back out of the labyrinth? Fortunately for him, Ariadne, the daughter of King Minos, had fallen in love with Theseus, and it was she who provided his solution. She offered Theseus a spool of thread and instructed him to tie one end of the thread to himself. She would hold the spool so he could find his way back out of the labyrinth after killing the Minotaur. The plan worked, and Theseus emerged victorious.

Ariadne left Crete with her beloved Theseus as he returned to Athens, but along the way Theseus decided to abandon her on the island of Naxos. I guess some heroes don't really want their glory shared. Perhaps in his egotistical revelry, Theseus also forgot to raise the sails that would signal his success on his homecoming and as a result, believing Theseus to be dead, his father committed suicide.

Can you imagine Ariadne's grief? Abandoned by the man she loved, she was exiled on an island for life. But then something amazing happened. Her tears were interrupted by the appearance of Dionysus, god of the vine, who announced that he was in love with Ariadne, and he then took her as his bride.

Why am I offering you my brief retelling of this myth? I suggest that this strange story is similar to our journey of Choosing to Evolve, and this ancient myth may offer us some special wisdom if we can hear it. Let's try reading this story as if all the characters were metaphors for different aspects of our own life experiences. What we may discover is a powerful image for our journey toward a new level of consciousness.

We are all tempted at times, like King Minos, by a desire to cling to an image of perfection. The Sea Bull was a possession of great value. But what the king was also clinging to was an image of *himself* as perfect and powerful.

All forms of fixation come with a price. Pasiphae's fixation with this perfection and power was equally great. Metaphorically, Pasiphae may represent the aspect of our lives that is always creating something. Whatever you adore defines what you create. The nature of consciousness is that we are always birthing new scripts — and somewhere along the way we all have given birth to a Minotaur.

The Minotaur in this story represents the primary emotional scripts that result from our fixations. This is the inner dynamic that becomes the source of great unrest and destruction in our lives. It eats up our energy in our attempts to keep it satisfied. We find ourselves serving it all the time, like a drive that is always present just beneath the surface of our thoughts.

In an earlier chapter I mentioned the story of Bill and how growing up with a luminary grandfather had created in him a fixation on needing to feel important. This script was his Minotaur. I say this not to imply any guilt. The development of this script happened early in Bill's childhood, and the unnatural creature that emerged came from his natural sense of adoration. The fixation was likely a response to a fear of not measuring up to family expectations as he perceived them.

Over time, Bill's fixation got him into trouble, destroying his relationships as other people responded poorly to his need to feel important. This triggered other emotions and led to other scripts.

Daedalus is the aspect of our consciousness that is always doing the bidding of our dominant script, always constructing a way to solve the problem. Daedalus is intellectual, but not at all rational, always in service to the scripts playing out in the moment.

In Bill's story, Daedalus' construction of Bill's inner labyrinth created layers upon layers of defensive scripts as he sought to either hide the Minotaur or to feed it more covertly. By the time I met him, Bill had been cycling constantly amongst his labyrinthine layers of defenses; however, just like in the myth, none of these scripts had really protected him from his monstrous core dynamic of insecurity. With any exposure of his need for importance, his well-worn scripts of withdrawal, attacking others, or self-disgust came into play. Finally, Bill had adopted his overriding script of hopelessness and helplessness.

It is important to note here that it's not like Bill hadn't tried to change his scripts. He had. Many times. Like Theseus, he had mounted numerous heroic expeditions into willing himself to be better, strive harder, and willfully make his life better. And also like Theseus, Bill's fixations on power and perfection made his heroic efforts to address his scripts into nothing more than new expressions of the same old scripts.

The labyrinth, you see, is by definition a tricky solution. It can be very hard to see how our fixations on our core script are constructing and maintaining their own elaborate defenses to secure our core issue and keep it stable.

Eventually, our entire consciousness begins to operate in service of this security system we've created. In other words, what begins as a way to escape an emotion becomes a kind of slavery to a system that eats up all our energy. Over time, this all comes to feel both unavoidable and familiar. Gradually, our inner kingdom falls into the kind of malaise of hopelessness or helplessness Bill was experiencing.

At some point in our own story, an inner voice may urge us toward the self-help bookshelves or some other source of advice. We may even find some insights in these places that will help us for a while. More often than not, however, the labyrinth of our defensive scripts will prevail, and we discover that our toughest warrior is just another expression of the same old scripts we used to gain control of that original triggering issue in the first place.

As Bill eventually discovered, everything changes in this story when we realize that the hero of the story is not so much Theseus as it is Ariadne. Like Bill, we may find a much simpler answer to our distressing problem when we begin to examine what it is about Ariadne that fuels her heroism.

Ariadne falls in love with the foreigner at great risk to herself. She knows that to love him is to be willing to reject all that she has known and to embrace whatever unknown may come. In other words, Ariadne is not fixated on her indoctrinated images. Vulnerable, transparent, and without guile Ariadne has to love who she loves.

Ariadne fears for Theseus, but her fears do not become a fixation that blinds her from seeing the simplest solution to the problem. Her solution is all about connection. She Moves Alongside the labyrinth, observing its layers without judgment, and maintains her belief in a positive outcome.

To adore anything is to risk disappointment. Ariadne risks her security without a second thought, and while this choice then leaves her abandoned and grieving, in the honest vulnerability of her grief the gods fall in love with her.

Some might call Ariadne a representation of the "observing ego." I simply say that it is possible for us to develop this capacity for Moving Alongside the threatening experiences of our life and consciousness to enhance our ability to reflect, question, and then alter dominant emotional dynamics.

Because it is Ariadne's love that motivates her, not some need for power and control, she is able to avoid becoming invested in the system that created the problem in the first place. By being invested only in love, Ariadne was able to betray the system and set free the energies that serve it.

Once we finally muster up the courage to face the failings of our scripts — and the fixations within ourselves — we can discover that our realizations and good intentions can't do it alone. We need to develop Ariadne's thread of connection — the "observing ego" that will enable us to find our way.

The idea of Moving Alongside embraces both the capacity to participate in *and* to observe our experiences — and to do that for one another. Of course, it really helps to have someone external to us who can Move Alongside *us*. This capacity for Moving Alongside is something we will explore in much greater depth in the next section of this book.

For now let's allow this image of Ariadne to set the stage for us, making it safe to take a look at our shadows. When we're holding onto that image of Ariadne, there is no judgment for *having* darkness — and Moving Alongside doesn't mean someone is fighting our battles for us. Rather, Moving Alongside means holding the space we need to both participate in *and* observe our experiences.

To *Move Alongside* is to be present in the moment with another human being without falling into habituated patterns of thought and speech. It is to embrace the awkward silence and to look again at the experience as if it were brand new. It is to let conflict be, without rushing to resolve or deny it. It is to faithfully hold fast to the connection even when it leads through anger, fear, shame and loss.

The thread we follow out of the darkness is a combination of insights. The first strand within the thread is an awareness of the basic engine of consciousness. Tightly wound around that strand is the awareness of our emotional scripts. By following this thread we can gain the capacity to recognize our stuck, defensive patterns. The last strand in the thread leads us to the practices we need to develop in order to continue evolving how we participate in these components of consciousness.

Pulling on the Thread of Distress

In all my years of counseling I would say that the dominant emotion expressed by my clients in our first session is distress. In fact, more often than not, and whether expressed or not, their driving motivation for seeking help was a sense of hopelessness or helplessness, often accompanied by tears.

In many cases these clients have been through other therapies and treatments, most of which seemed to be aimed more at *treating* or *labeling* their distress, rather than addressing its root cause.

Once we understand the scripted nature of our imagery and emotions, we begin to recognize that the distress is only the current expression of a larger system — the outermost layer of their labyrinth of scripts. Without the thread of awareness, there is little to empower them to safely explore the hidden passageways of their defenses, treating only their distress leaves them stuck outside the labyrinth, trying to paint a happy face on the wall.

The more you take in this material, the more you will see how to follow the distress, holding fast to the thread of enlightenment, and observe what is happening in the process. As we do this work, the layers of our scripts will become visible, and with loving eyes we can face the traumas and other influences that created the need for whatever defenses we constructed. But if we continue to look at this process with a more critical eye, we will only send the truth scurrying back into the shadows of our labyrinth of defensive scripts.

Our inner Ariadne is unaffected by the layers of defenses and fixations we have formed over the years. Ariadne is like the child whose natural vulnerability and Affect plasticity have yet to be complicated by the need to protect self-image to survive a traumatic moment.

If you are feeling helpless, the most important thing you can do is to listen to your distress without judgment. By listening to our tears we can begin our path of discovering the layered defensive scripts we've constructed for protection in the creation of our own inner labyrinth. In almost every case, the hopelessness fueling our distress is merely signaling the failure of a defensive script. So this time, rather than simply treating the distress — or creating a new script — we can choose to follow the thread.

The insights I am sharing with you in this book will help you learn how to, draw a map of your own labyrinth. In guiding so many people through the careful process of unraveling the layers of failed scripts that comprised their own labyrinth, the consistent discovery is that the hopelessness and helplessness that brought them to me was the result of a defense formed earlier in life to alleviate an initial distress.

This book will show you how to follow this thread through your own labyrinth of scripts — and how to hold that thread for others. Before we set off on this journey, however, we will need to equip ourselves with the understanding of a pivotal set of scripts almost always present in every human life. These are the scripts we develop as a way to protect our self-imagery from any experience that calls our self-imagery into question. The Affect most responsible for these moments of life is called Shame-Humiliation. The way we manage this one Affect may be the most important component in Choosing to Evolve.

CHAPTER 7

Meet the Affects, Part 2: Shame-Humiliation

In our earlier example, we met Bill, who felt incredible pressure to live an extraordinary life. Even as a child Bill was jealous of any of the other boys in his class at school who received more attention than he did. He was always quick to show off any success he had, and he was always competing to be the leader in any game or activity.

Eventually, Bill's fixation on being extraordinary became his liability. When he found himself excluded from his peer groups, he felt an urgent need to try all the harder to impress, and that only made matters worse for him.

Bill didn't realize any of this, of course. He was just doing the only thing he knew how to do. Because of his core script, all other options and possibilities were invisible to him — and inaccessible to his awareness. None of this was his fault, but that didn't mean he didn't experience feelings of shame about it.

What we will be exploring in this chapter is the Shame Affect and the defenses we use to avoid or silence it. When Bill's urgent need to be special was rejected by some of his peers, it triggered Shame-Humiliation. And, because Bill's Shame-Humiliation was actually triggered by the failure of his earlier script, feeling humiliated is very natural. Nevertheless, for most of us, including Bill, the feeling of shame is hard to handle. So what do we do? We defend against it by developing more scripts to manage it. Thus begins the elaborate construction of our labyrinth of scripts that we develop over time.

Shame-Humiliation

Whether you like it or not, Shame is a part of every human being's biological inheritance. The ideas around Shame explored and brought to light by Tomkins have been among the hardest aspects of his work for me to understand. The idea of exposing our Shame is absolutely repugnant for many of us who have grown up with religious or family traditions that relied upon guilt for motivating (and sometimes manipulating) us.

I would encourage you to see the information in this chapter as incredibly important to your awareness. Of all the material I present in my lectures and workshops, the following insights about the Shame Affect is what people often tell me was the most transformative.

Shame-Humiliation — At First Blush

In the same way we recognized the innate nature of Distress as a part of the human neurobiological system (you don't have to teach an infant how to cry), we can also easily see that the same is true for the Affect of Shame-Humiliation. You don't have to teach an infant how to blush — nor is a blush something that is easily concealed. But the blush visible most clearly on light-skinned faces is only a part of the observable aspects of Shame-Humiliation.

Most mothers and fathers have, at least once in their parenthood, said to their child, "Look me in the eye and say that again!" Why do we say that? It's simple. We know intuitively that people tend to avoid eye contact when their Shame Affect is triggered. I must emphasize here that confronting a child in this way may trigger the Shame Affect even when they have done nothing wrong!

We experience the Shame Affect in a spectrum from an almost imperceptible sense of disappointment, to embarrassment, to an almost dissociative sense of "being mortified." When Shame is triggered, we have trouble thinking clearly, we avert our eyes, and we drop our head as if the muscles in the back of our neck have lost all tone. At the more intense level of Shame, Humiliation, we want to go hide under a rock.

If you want to experiment with Shame, it isn't hard. Walk up to another person, and look at his or her face for 60 seconds without saying anything. Notice what happens. (Try it now if you can, before you read on to discover my take on it.)

OK. I know you didn't do it. Fine. I am not the boss of you. I get it. You think that you can understand this without practicing anything weird, right? But I can't help but wonder if even *thinking* about doing what I suggested triggered a defense you often use to protect yourself from Shame.

One of the ways we deal with Shame is to withdraw from experiences in which something might happen to cause us to feel shame. This is a big issue in our world. In fact, many people who have come to see me with a diagnosis of depression could actually be described more precisely as being hyper-vigilant about anything that might trigger Shame. If you don't try anything, you can't be embarrassed, right?

Have you ever had one of those moments when you were going along thinking everything was fine, chatting away with a friend, and then suddenly the friend drops a "bomb," saying that he or she is angry about something you said or did? You may recall not being able to think of anything to say. Or maybe you stammered out something and then looked for a quick escape.

It is likely that in that moment you were experiencing Shame. Shame seems to serve the purpose of amplifying any impediment to our good feelings, making it difficult to continue whatever positive Affect you were experiencing before.

Just as Distress amplifies the stimulus of hunger in a baby so that the baby and others around the baby are conscious of that need, Shame amplifies the loss of good feelings. And most often, the way in which Shame amplifies our loss of good feelings leaves us a little dazed and confused, maybe staring at the floor or off into space, avoiding eye contact.

What's interesting about Shame's amplification is that it is almost always proportional to the intensity of the good feelings present *before* the impediment. In other words, if the positive feelings we were experiencing previously were fairly low in intensity, Shame may pass quickly and go pretty much unnoticed. With the Affect of Shame, the higher the high, the lower the low it leaves in its wake.

If Affects are the primary motivators of our thoughts and actions, then the motivation of Shame seems to be to motivate us to turn inward and evaluate — to stop, pause, and reflect in a moment that is challenging our positive imagery or experience of ourselves, others, or the world.

It is important to distinguish between Affect and emotion here. The Shame *Affect* is triggered by an impediment to our positive feelings. It operates within us as a biological response, regardless of what images we have accumulated or habituated. *Emotions*, on the other hand, are the socialized and shaped *experiences* of those Affects. Emotions *are* triggered by the habituated set of images to which we have been indoctrinated. Shame is an *Affect*. Guilt, however, is an *emotional experience* — a scripted response we may have that *includes* the Affect of Shame, based on our earlier exposure to particular images.

Here's another example to illustrate this a little bit further. If you were indoctrinated to carry an image of poverty as laziness, you might be somewhat driven to financial success. Losing your job and being unemployed, then, would likely cause more than a little Distress. Because of your indoctrination, losing your job would also trigger Shame as your positive feelings about your self-image were impeded. The feelings of shame you experience are an emotional response, defined by your particular set of images and scripted over time. The body would still experience the Shame Affect even though it is triggered by your unique imagery.

For someone clinging to a very static image of self, the experience of Shame may feel overwhelming. As a result, rather than absorb the new information and grow from it, many of us learn early in life to defend against criticism or other feedback that might challenge our positive image of self. Just as some of us adopt generalized scripts for the Distress Affect, (Big boys don't cry) we also develop specific scripts to defend against the Shame Affect.

Dr. Donald Nathanson is a renowned psychiatrist who has done more than anyone else I know of to explain the dynamics of Shame-Humiliation. His treatise, *Shame and Pride, Affect, Sex and The Birth Of The Self*, is the defining work to which I direct all of my peers in psychotherapy.

Nathanson was struck early in his career by the fact that none of the dominant models or theories in psychology or neurobiology were effectively addressing Shame as an aspect of the human experience. In fact, most research completely ignored Shame as a factor in human behavior.

Nathanson will be remembered for his brilliant mind — genius on par with that of Tomkins — and more popularly, for his envisioning the primary ways in which humans respond to feelings of shame. Calling this model the Compass of Shame, Nathanson clarifies four families of scripts that are most often involved in the scripting against Shame. You could say these are the attempted fixes we automatically employ to try to hold onto some semblance of good feelings when the moment of Shame occurs.

It is important to note here that *all* of these defensive scripts work in the short-term. Their effect, however, in addition to often being short-lived, is problematic. We all use these scripts from time to time. They are so common that once you learn about them, you will likely begin to notice them all around you. What you may also begin to recognize is that when repeated often enough, these scripts can become dominant players in a person's life. And, the more they dominate, the more these scripts create problems of their own. It is our Shame response scripts that tend to play the largest roles in relationship conflicts, political conflicts, employee relationships, school bullying and violence, domestic violence, addiction, depression, terrorism, and even international conflict.

Second Blush of Shame

Are you able to feel — and then acknowledge — the Affect of Shame-Humiliation? Can you feel embarrassed and then immediately recognize what you are feeling? If you are like most people I have met, you have some mixed success with recognizing and accepting this Affect for what it is. So let's look closer at the defenses we use to escape those humiliating moments in what Nathanson describes as the four poles of the Compass of Shame, the four families of scripts we develop in the face of Shame.

Four Poles of the Compass

What are our best options once the Shame is triggered in us? Ideally, you can simply acknowledge the embarrassment, feel it, and then learn whatever lesson is there for you, if any. Or, you can recognize that only a part of you has been exposed as "wrong" or "imperfect" and redirect your energies into making whatever changes are needed to address the issue of the moment — i.e. study harder, find a tutor, or join a study group.

Most of the time, however, instead of these ideal options we find ourselves locked into scripts that are all about "fixing" the feeling instead of addressing the problem that triggered the Shame in the first place. Let me repeat: Our defensive scripts are all about dealing with the *feeling* of shame — not the issue that triggered the Affect of Shame. For example, if you felt shame about failing a test and you ran home to hide in your room, you were escaping the *feeling*, not dealing with the *source* of the problem, such as signing up for tutoring.

Some of us are fortunate to have teachers who have become sensitized to Shame-Humiliation and the issues it can create. These teachers create a classroom environment that makes it possible for us to risk making mistakes while still acknowledging them. Unfortunately this is not the norm, and many children and adolescents quickly develop one or more of these Compass of Shame defenses.

Deepening our exploration of the Affect of Shame, let's take a closer look at Nathanson's Compass of Shame, the four poles of which include Withdrawal, Attack-Self, Avoidance, and Attack-Other. Keep reading and I'll explain these polar progressions in greater and more accessible detail.

Withdrawal Scripts

This script seems to mimic the natural shame response, but it becomes amplified into something much more. What may begin as shy withdrawal from a specific interaction can become an automatic Withdrawal script for *all* future situations that might become embarrassing. Many of us have had the experience of embarrassment in a public speaking class for example. Remember that moment when every word of your carefully prepared speech suddenly seemed much less interesting as it came out of your mouth? Maybe you froze up and someone laughed. Maybe your mind went blank and you couldn't continue at all. These moments happen to everyone at one time or another, and the emotional wounds from these experiences are deeper for some of us than others.

The important thing to notice here is that it's not the *wound* of the Shame that stays with us. It's what we do next that counts. How do we cope? Will that coping process turn into a script? Will the way you cope *now* become habituated in the future? Will it eventually become so automatic that you don't even notice when you're putting that script into play?

Consider this scenario: Sara raises her hand in class. She gets laughed at for having the wrong answer. So Sara stops raising her hand — and she doesn't volunteer for anything from then on. That is a simple example of a Withdrawal script.

How many things did you try out as you were growing up? How many sports, musical instruments, or hobbies? If you think back about all of these, you may recall a moment when you experienced feelings of shame and decided to give up rather than doing the hard work of perfecting your skills. This is a normal process of discovery that can also turn into a lifetime of giving up at the first sign of failure.

In order to commit to the hard work of practicing a new skill, we usually have to have an attachment to the image of ourselves as someone who has acquired that skill. Any crack in that image caused by a failure or lack of talent will trigger our Shame-Humiliation. We have to be dedicated to reclaiming our path to positive self-imagery in order to stay committed to our skill development.

It's important to recognize that Shame is a necessary part of the human learning experience. In fact, Shame is often how learning happens; however, it is when we expose ourselves to the limits of our knowledge, running headfirst into what we do not know, that Shame is most often triggered. Pretty much any real learning we accomplish involves how we manage our Affect of Shame-Humiliation from there.

Imagine a kid showing up to baseball practice for the first time. She doesn't really know how to throw the ball very far, she strikes out every time she's at bat, and catching the ball is still hard for her because she hasn't learned to trust herself yet; she ducks every time the ball comes her way. She's going to have to deal with a lot of embarrassment if she wants to get better.

After particularly humiliating moments such as these, many a kid has given up baseball. Giving up is a natural thing to do. The question is, can that kid gain a new image of her self to replace the now defunct one? In the worst case, will she now develop a script of Withdrawing from *anything* that requires developing a new skill?

In my experience, a Withdrawal script is often diagnosed as depression with an anxious component. In extreme cases, there can be hyper-vigilance over anything that might trigger Shame. When the focus of our consciousness becomes centered on *preventing* more cracks in our self-imagery, we continue to Withdraw from any situation where we might be exposed as imperfect. With Withdrawal as our script our world shrinks, making it all the more difficult to retain our positive sense of self.

A teacher may not even notice that Johnny isn't raising his hand anymore. But imagine that Johnny ends up failing a class due to his script of Withdrawal, or "checking out." Isn't he likely to experience even more Shame on down the road? The more he uses this script of

Withdrawal to manage his Affect of Shame, the more Johnny finds himself diminished.

Now imagine the teacher *confronting* Johnny about his lack of engagement. Now he has even more Shame and a greater need for a defensive script. So he Withdraws yet again. This line of inquiry becomes even more interesting when we pause to consider what the teacher may be feeling, because in many cases, whether the teacher recognizes it or not, he or she may be feeling Shame too. Johnny's Withdrawal script has become an impediment to the teacher's positive self-imagery as well.

This scenario is one reason why these insights can be so helpful in the classroom. Teachers who can recognize scripted responses to Shame can develop skills at managing Shame more productively. They can make better choices aimed toward retaining positive self-imagery in the face of Shame both for themselves and for their students.

So now imagine that Johnny is hanging out with other kids who have similar Withdrawal scripts, and he gets involved in stealing a car for a joy ride. The joy ride ends with Johnny facing his parents — and a judge. His response to this will likely be a desire to Withdraw, but when this script continues to fail, it is just as likely that he will move on to developing one of the other scripts we are about to explore. Where in the system will he find the encouragement to deal with the root cause of his problem?

Now let's imagine that Johnny gets out of jail, meets a girl, and gets married. A few months go by, and Johnny has an issue at work and quits his job. He's done this before, but this time he has another person depending on his choices, and she starts pointing out how he is always quitting things.

What his wife has no way of knowing is that she is attacking the very coping mechanism Johnny has used all his life to deny the Shame triggered when his self-imagery is in trouble. Johnny's new wife has no idea that criticizing his quitting is like sweeping the legs from under Johnny's fragile self-imagery. So what is Johnny likely to do in response to the new Shame now triggered? What would you do if you were Johnny?

From my experience, it is unlikely that, given his history of avoiding Shame, Johnny would be able to suddenly change that script. The dynamics of the relationship with his wife will be impacted deeply because of it, and much will depend on how his scripts interact with those of his wife. What will his Withdrawal script trigger for her — and *her* habituated images? Will she have so much empathy that Johnny is enabled to continue his Withdrawal script? Will her own Shame then be triggered? How is her Shame scripted to automatically respond?

I wish with all my heart that someone could have taken that young boy's hand from where it lay motionless on his desk and show him how to raise it up again. I hope that, like me, you want to say to him, "Johnny, it's OK to make a mistake as long as you don't let it define you." I want to say to Johnny, "This is only one moment, and you will do better as you learn more." There is only one way to help someone in the midst of a Shame-Humiliation script, and that is to Move Alongside that person and hold tightly to that precious thread of human connection.

Moving Alongside is exactly what we all need in order to manage our experience of Shame. And, if we can't do it for ourselves, just the presence of someone who is there — not to fix the issue or raise our hand for us — but someone who will, by their very presence, say to us that we are still worth being around.

Attack-Self Scripts

Have you ever made fun of yourself in a moment of embarrassment? If you have, you already know that making a self-deprecating comment in a moment of embarrassment accomplishes a couple of things. First of all, it communicates to those around you that you *know* you messed up. And second, if we criticize ourselves it is less likely that others will join in. Instead they may feel compassionate or sympathetic, and they may even offer encouragement. It works!

Maybe you remember a moment where you spilled coffee on your shirt at a meeting and without even thinking you said, "I am such a klutz!" What you may not realize in that moment of embarrassment is that you are managing your Shame-Humiliation Affect by criticizing yourself. And, while the Attack-Self script often works very well for taking charge of our Shame in the moment, its effectiveness is a slippery slope.

Because Attack-Self scripts tend to work *too* well, the relief of our momentary humiliation keeps us from giving attention to whatever triggered our Affect of Shame-Humiliation in the first place. Learning to move more carefully, gracefully, and mindfully might be a new growth area for us to explore; however, that growth is highly unlikely if there is no impetus — no Affect — motivating us and directing our attention to practice this new way to manage our feelings of Shame.

In the most extreme cases, a person may become so habituated to the Attack-Self script that his or her life becomes defined by it. This definition may include chronic patterns of failure as well as masochistic relationships. Locked into the Attack-Self script, we may seem incapable of learning from our failures. The more we attack ourselves as a way to deal with our feelings of shame, the less we allow our Shame to motivate us to learn and grow.

Examples of the Attack-Self script abound in the classroom. The early elementary student who passes gas in class may simply bow his head and hope to disappear. But by the time he is in the 7th grade, if he has not gained better control of his flatulence, he may make a joke out of it. Making other people laugh at us sure beats having them laugh at us without our control or permission. "Yea, I meant to do that!" feels much better than "Oops. Excuse me."

Unfortunately for this kid, the long-term prospects of the Attack-Self script are pretty dismal. This script may help him fix his immediate feeling of shame, but it does not address his root issues. Let's be real. Making a joke about farts in a *college* classroom is unlikely to get the same response from his peers.

This is not to say that it's easy to accept a moment of Shame. Because Shame seems to want to tell us we are totally flawed, we'd rather run from it than let it teach us what we need to know. Students who struggle with certain subjects are likely to say things like, "I'm just no good at math. My brain is broken." This is often an invitation for their teachers to show mercy, and while mercy always feels nice, it can cripple us. The best teachers seem to know this already. Whether they know the term for this or not, they find a way to Move Alongside a student dealing with Shame with their support for a more positive self-image *without* ignoring the failure.

David Bolton coined the term, "mind shame," to describe the malady faced by millions of students who, when faced with learning differences that trigger Shame, develop a sense of inferiority or defectiveness about their own minds. This often happens around the third grade, because that is the point in school where students shift from learning to read to reading to learn. In Bolton's work, *Children of the*

Code, he exposes the very real challenges for students who do not easily assimilate written language. In each case, it's easy to see how their defenses on the Compass of Shame develop. Chief among these defenses is the Attack-Self script.

I find the same thing to be true in the consulting work I do. When someone tells me they are "just no good" with women, or money, or computers, I ask what they have been doing to remedy that. For many therapists, this can feel like we're shaming the client/patient. I disagree. By acknowledging the failure while affirming the person, we are teaching our client that his or her feeling of shame is normal and has an important role to play.

We all want to live lives free from the ugly feeling of shame. But freedom is not found in these Compass of Shame scripts. These scripts, while providing momentary relief, ultimately limit us more than they free us. They are temporary fixes to our experience of the feeling of shame, but over time they can become habituated defensiveness that take their toll on our capacity for learning and growth.

At best, these scripts can be temporarily helpful in the same way going into shock during a traumatic experience numbs us to the trauma. But once an Attack-Self script has become habituated, we may stop learning and settle for being the class clown. It's like saying; "It's OK for me to be a failure if I know that I am."

Imagine what this mindset would be like in a long-term intimate relationship? Once habituated to this "class clown" script, we would likely become difficult to live with. While we would tend to take responsibility for our failures, we never address the root cause.

But hold on for a second. Before you go telling someone you think they have an Attack-Self script, please remember what I shared about Johnny. What happens when we decide to "call out" the habituated scripts that each of us may carry? The new Shame evoked in these kinds of confrontations most often only serves to further harden the scripted defenses being used to protect fragile self-imagery.

So how can we support someone whom we realize is in the throes of a full-blown defense against what might be layers of Shame scripts? We learn how to Move Alongside them with patience, humility, and encouragement. This knowledge is powerful, and trying to help someone become conscious of their scripts by criticizing them is more likely to push them toward other points around the Compass of Shame.

You see, the tricky thing about our emotional motivation system is that I can't Shame myself, or anyone else, into stopping a Shame script. Maybe that's part of what makes the labyrinth of our human consciousness feel so complicated.

The defensive scripts we are using to manage our Shame will only fall away in the presence of what Carl Rogers called "unconditional positive regard." When I can look within and *accept* the source of my Shame without an overwhelming sense of failure and brokenness, I am able to let myself simply feel the momentary passing of the Affect of Shame, give attention to its source, remind myself of what needs to be done, and then move on.

Avoidance Scripts

An Avoidance script is very different from a Withdrawal script. Rather than to *withdraw* from the scenario where our Affect of Shame is triggered, an Avoidance script *ignores* the Shame by distracting others (and mostly ourselves) from the Shame Affect itself. While the Withdrawal script removes us, usually somewhat pre-emptively, from whatever might put us at risk for more Shame, the Avoidance script *immerses* us in the situations that trigger our Shame. We can then become so oblivious to the Shame that, in a sense, we become shameless.

To become shameless through an Avoidance script, we experience a kind of dissociation with the Affect of Shame in ways that often involve stimulating a positive Affect. In other words, rather than avoid raising our hand in class, we become numb to the experience of the Shame Affect itself. This may be most easy to see when you consider the many different shapes of addiction.

Consuming alcohol in order to grease the wheels of ambiguous and awkward social interactions is pretty common. But alcohol can easily become a substance in the service of an Avoidance script that is functioning to dissolve Shame in situations that are Shame/Fear producing. Now, that is not to say that everyone who takes a drink is doing so to reduce Shame. Tomkins noted that we use substances to increase positive Affect as well as to reduce negative Affect. It is the latter that he found more prone to creating addiction.

Having a drink at a party where we are already having a good time might have little consequence other than enhancing our Affect of Interest-Excitement. However, having a drink or two at a party when we are feeling self-conscious (Shame) can be so effective at reducing the Shame Affect that it becomes an entrenched script.

Drugs and alcohol are not the only vehicles for avoiding Shame. There are thousands of ways to stimulate enough alternative Affect to avoid our feeling of shame. Any Affect can be recruited, but more often than not, it is an Affect that feels good that comes running onto our mental playing field, distracting the crowd — if only for a moment. Showing off skills, knowledge, or possessions to draw attention away from our failures is a common example of an Avoidance script. Nathanson describes this as an attempt to get the spotlight to shine on something else besides whatever is triggering our Shame.

In the classroom, when Becky fails her math test she might find a need to show off her body, or find some other way to gain the attention of a boy. When Mark, a financial analyst, loses a million dollars of teachers' retirement investments in the stock market, he takes his friends sailing on his new boat. I have worked with many men and women who have used the experience of spending money as a way to manage Shame.

Let's admit it. We all feel a sense of power and authority when we purchasing something, even if it's a cup of coffee. You may feel shame over being unable to support yourself financially, but in the fleeting moment when you are ordering a decaf vanilla latte, you feel some relief. Of course, when the cup is empty, so is your wallet — and the Shame comes roaring back.

In all the cases where we call on the script of Avoidance to manage Shame, the feeling of shame is prolonged until relief and shame may even become cyclical. And, if this Avoidance script becomes dominant, it can become toxic, quite literally. Alcoholism is an example of an Avoidance script that often seems to follow this same cycle. The drink temporarily relieves the Shame — and then creates even more Shame as you act out your shamelessness. This is not to deny that with many drugs the addiction is equally biological. Because Affects are also biological, they play a big part in the cycles of addiction.

I can't leave this description of Avoidance without mentioning a personal theory of mine. I wonder if Nathanson's Compass of Shame can also help us better understand some of the most extreme mental health issues.

Maybe you have seen those greeting cards that say, "There is an amount of wine that will make you think, *Damn, I'm a great dancer.*"

Funny, right? With the script of Avoidance at play, delusions of grandeur aren't just for crazy people anymore.

The only difference between someone having a momentary flight from reality and someone diagnosed with a serious mental illness is probably only a matter of degree. In some cases, what we call mental illness may develop in proportion to the experience of Shame or other Affects that must be defended against. In other words, the more fragile our self-imagery, the more intense is our need for defenses against Shame.

Meet Dan

For a number of years I worked with a man, I'll call him Dan, who came into my practice during a period of his life when he had suffered from intense delusions that ranged from believing the police were watching him to moments when he felt everyone was working against him. Having grown up in the shadow of a father who was both extremely strict and widely respected, Dan had many memories colored with intense Shame–Humiliation.

We all have issues from childhood that create in us certain hypersensitivities for situations that trigger our emotional responses. Remember that this sensitivity is simply consciousness operating normally. As Dan encountered new experiences, he was automatically making sense of them by comparing them to his previous experiences and then projecting those previous images onto the new moment. So Dan's past set him up to have a hypersensitivity to being ignored. We eventually began to explore his delusions as an Avoidance script that provided an escape from the feeling that he was not important and possibly defective. His intense hypersensitivity to being ignored/abandoned was continually being triggered as he tried to navigate his life experiences.

Dan was smart, affable, and happy when given a role to play in a shelter or outreach center. But if that role was changed or if someone else was asked to work with him, any diminishment of his role became a trigger for Dan's extreme and dissociative response.

I believe that for Dan, the Affect of Shame-Humiliation had become so toxic that Avoidance was automatically scripted. And, when showing off or impressing other people failed, his Avoidance script intensified into delusions of grandeur or at other times, paranoia. In working with Dan, I came to see that sometimes paranoia could be the flipside of a delusion of importance. Feeling important was the only way Dan had learned to keep his feelings of humiliation at bay, and his paranoia was the dark side of this need. If no one else saw him as important, at least he could perceive that every police officer he saw on the street was concerned about him.

The intensity of Dan's Shame-Humiliation was overwhelming to him because of his past experiences that created his hypersensitivity to feeling ignored. The more we were able to reduce Dan's sensitivity by processing his memories of Shame in a safe and gradual way, the less need he had for the defensive script of Avoidance to manifest as delusions of grandeur.

As Dan did the work of facing the monstrous images from his past, he also learned how to do for himself what I was doing for him, which was to *observe* those feelings of shame that emerged when he felt ignored or diminished without automatically needing to Avoid them by reinforcing his importance. Dan now lives independently, has developed new friendships, and has also recovered old friendships he treasures.

It is important to note that sensitivities to emotional dynamics can also be biological in nature. Because Affects are also biological, anything that impacts a person's biology will impact them. Modern medical science has provided treatments that range from serotonin reuptake inhibition to changing the amount of helpful bacteria in the lower intestines. Scientists, however, aren't the only ones doing the experimentation. Drug and alcohol abuse continues to be rampant as many people seek ways to medicate their emotions.

While I am *not* saying that all people with severe mental illness can be cured without medical treatment, I *am* saying that many of them can. Even with my somewhat basic understanding of Tomkins' and Nathanson's work, I have learned to Move Alongside my clients to offer them a thread of unconditional positive regard to help lead them through their own labyrinth of defensive scripts that were the source of so much of their suffering.

So what can we do for someone who is caught up in an Avoidance script? Well, the first thing *not* to do is to pull them aside and tell them about the Compass of Shame. As we have already discovered, *any* criticism of a person who is caught up in a defensive script to avoid Shame will probably trigger even more Shame and therefore accelerate their need for more defensive scripts. I have been amazed at times at how little some therapists understand about the tight rope we must walk as we support people caught up in cycles of Shame without triggering more of it.

Without a stable connection to a sense of unconditional positive regard, a person is unlikely to face the Shame that he or she is avoiding. This is especially true when that person is already employing an Avoidance script to elude the feelings of shame he or she already has.

Helping someone who is using a particularly destructive Avoidance script is especially hard to do when that person is someone you depend upon for your own needs. For instance, having a partner who is caught up in a Shame spiral will likely cause a great deal of chaos in your life, disrupt your own needs, and often behave in ways that are quite hurtful to you. Your personal feelings of distress can make it very difficult to be helpful in healing his or her need for a defensive script.

In times like these, imagine that your partner has his or her foot stuck in some sort of trap. It doesn't help either of you to blame your partner for stepping in it. The scripts we are discussing are ones that promise relief but deliver slavery. When these defensive scripts become so second nature we don't even notice them, we are also blind to their impact on others — even those we love the most.

Take heart. Change is possible, and the key to breaking through these destructive relational dynamics is an Ariadne, patiently waiting, holding fast to the magic thread of connection. She knows it's not up to her to do anything except to be present, hold that thread and, say, "Don't be afraid to face your darkness. I won't lose you."

Attack-Other Scripts

Before we move into our exploration of this final point on Nathanson's Compass of Shame, it bears repeating why understanding this way of recognizing our Shame scripts is so important to evolving our consciousness. Human consciousness requires a stable platform from which to operate, and we have evolved that stability through our capacity to form abstract images of ourselves, others, and the world. These habituated images allow us to take for granted a massive amount of stimuli, offering us freedom to focus our attention on ever more creative and refined experiences.

So in this respect, having a stable self-image is a key to success in life. But what if that stability is threatened by something? Will we experience this threat to our stability as an opportunity to learn and grow, expand our perspective, and become more than we were before? Or will we defend against the feeling of shame that is triggered in these moments by following a defensive script we have learned somewhere along the way to temporarily eradicate the bad feeling rather than to face the source of our instability?

Perhaps the most destructive of all defenses against Shame is the Attack-Other script. The more common Attack-Other scripts can be seen in the way we gossip about others or celebrities as if somehow exposing their flaws and failures helps us feel better about our own. Think about that for a moment and consider how commonplace it is.

The Attack-Other script seems to work from a premise of, "If I can't feel better about me, then at least I can make you feel worse about you." And, while gossip may seem funny and harmless at times, there is really nothing harmless about it.

Those who gossip are usually in denial of their own Shame, and the Attack-Other script often involves dissociation of personal Shame altogether. However, gossip sometimes combines the Attack-Other script with an Attack-Self script. For example, Judy may say, "Did you see that pic of Jennifer Anniston? She is brave to show so much skin for her age! I should talk, though. I have a two-piece I wear to the beach every summer even though it looks like I've been hog tied!" Relief of interpersonal Shame can be a major source of humor, but as we have discussed, these scripts that provide humor on occasion can be incredibly destructive when they become a more dominant dynamic in our consciousness.

This kind of humor has become more and more prevalent in all arenas of society. Its rise may be another side effect of urbanization or the depersonalized nature of social media. Attacking another person on faceless Twitter is much easier than when we are in direct contact with someone's with human facial expressions. Perhaps it is harder to dehumanize and objectify others face to face.

While it is hard to pinpoint the cause of this rise, it is easy to see the consequences. When we adults model these Shame scripts for young people, we are teaching them that these scripts are an acceptable way to manage feelings of shame. If it is OK for a moderator to bully a panelist, why isn't it OK for a 12-year-old to bully a peer? If it's OK for television personalities to make fun of a politician, or vice versa, then why isn't it OK for teenagers to make fun of an outcast?

This still might seem like much ado about nothing if it weren't for the strong likelihood that this one family of scripts is behind some of the most extreme violence in our communities. It should come as no surprise, given our new understanding of this biological aspect of our consciousness, that domestic violence — and even extreme cases of violence like Columbine, Aurora, or Sandy Hook — are *all* likely motivated at some level by Shame. In each case we can see a person experiencing toxic levels of Shame and defending against it by acting powerfully against those who represent, in their minds, the source of that Shame.

Try reading the backstories on any of the stabbers, shooters, or bombers in the media and see if you don't notice Shame. They all had something happen in their lives that was a major trigger for Shame, way before they began planning their attack. Many developed Attack-Other scripts from some childhood trauma or some kind of abuse. At some point the Shame felt far too heavy, toxic, and destabilizing. The Attack-Other script offered a way out. They picked up the script from their parents or their peers or the media, and they learned to automatically resort to blaming anyone who seemed to be succeeding where they had failed.

At Columbine, for example, it was the popular kids who were targeted — the ones who seemed to embody the success these boys lacked. Because of their seeming success, the popular kids were an impediment to good feelings for these young men, and somewhere along the way, an Attack-Other script was modeled for them to follow.

It isn't just homicides that flow from the Attack-Other script. Some suicides are Attack-Other scripts playing out as well. I remember a teenage girl, Gina, whose boyfriend broke up with her in order to date her best friend. Gina confessed to me that she had thoughts of suicide, leaving a note that would tell them both how much she loved them. She imagined how guilty they would feel reading it after she died. As weird as it may sound, if Gina had gone through with her plan, I would classify it as an Attack-Other script. It was Gina's defense against the Shame triggered by the fracturing of her self-image.

Gina didn't follow through with her plan. Instead, she did the work required to feel her way through her shame and grief. It wasn't easy, but soon she was developing better intimate relationships. Eventually she was able to talk about the betrayal as a wake-up call to the shallowness of her past relationships.

Looking at bullying in schools from this perspective creates a pathway to new understanding. Some children learn early on to avoid Shame by putting others down. This scripted Attack-Other response to Shame is even more likely when they have received negative feedback or criticism that feels overwhelming to already fragile images of self. Bullies are very good at hiding their fragile self-images by making sure that others feel what they feel. Over time, bullies often begin to have intense fears of being defective or unlovable. The more they bully, the more they prove to themselves that they posses fatal flaws. Then any Shame-triggering experience is so toxic that it must be denied, and the script continues.

Sometimes we pick up Attack-Other scripts by observing parental interactions. Just watching parents attack each other in arguments may be enough to model that script for their children, who take all of this in as "normal." (How many of us grew up with parents who could acknowledge their embarrassment without using one of the scripts we have been exploring?)

The fact is, most families tend to normalize one or more of these scripts, and most of us grow up having these scripts modeled for us, so of course they seem absolutely normal. Far beyond all of the "life lessons" parents want to teach their children, it is actually how parents manage their own emotions and defenses that will teach their children the most about how to live.

A Comedy of Errors

The "class clown" is most often a great example of a person using an Attack-Other script, but not always. Sometimes the joke is on them, which is an Attack-Self script. Think of all the comedians who make fun of their weight or their relationship dysfunctions.

When Jeff was called on by his teacher to answer a problem on the board, he replied, "Mrs. Jones, I think we should let Betty answer that. She is, like, an academic *goddess* and I don't think we worship her enough."

This kind of response is a mild form of Attack-Other that is likely to elicit laughter. However, as Nathanson points out, if the class clown or a comedian steps over the line, inflicting too much Shame on the other, his audience will think of him as cruel and no longer funny. Much of what we tend to find funny is very close to that line.

Watch any comic or sitcom and you are likely to find yourself laughing at someone else's expense. The reason why we tend to laugh so easily at comedy that exposes Shame in others is that it relieves Shame in ourselves, and that relief triggers Enjoyment for us. But Attack-Other scripts can become very dangerous when they create an extended dissociation from any sense of Shame.

We live in a time when school violence remains on the rise. Bullies in the school, at the workplace, or in the home seem to be extreme mimics of the Attack-Other scripts found in the public discourse, talk radio, and even some newscasts. The Attack-Other script is modeled for us through cartoons, video games, and the media so much that it seems more of a *given* than a choice to make fun of others' shortcomings.

Most of the clients who have come to me who think they are suffering from anger issues are actually suffering from Shame avoidance issues. Imagine that you are a boy who grows up being criticized constantly — and often punished physically. (Hitting a child is a great way to teach them the Attack-Other script.) Let's say you are in the seventh grade and someone makes fun of your clothes — and so you just do what you know how to do — you hit the other kid. Now *you* have become a bully others fear. Being the bully may feel better than the weakness of humiliation, but it's important to realize that those who get their sense of power through being feared often fear themselves as well.

So now imagine that you (as this kid who became a bully in middle school) are growing up, and now you find yourself running with a dangerous crowd. Always quick to escalate an argument to violence, now you can't seem to be able to control your temper at all. In fact, you react so quickly and violently at times that it scares even you.

At this point we begin to see the image of Daedalus, building yet another layer to the labyrinth of defenses. First there was a core issue of abuse that was normalized. Then came the Shame when that normalized reaction didn't work in other relationships and situations. Then came the layer of defenses to deal with the Shame. Then, as one defensive script led to another, a seemingly endless cycle of Shame and defense began. Eventually this cycle triggers Fear of your own responses.

("What if I can't stop this?") These are the kinds of layered scripts that I have often encountered and helped others to navigate through.

Eventually anyone — friend, therapist, or any authority figure, can trigger your Shame. Anyone having more success than you do becomes an enemy to be attacked. The Shame triggers a script and then the script leads to more Shame. In an escalating cycle that leads eventually to a sense of being really messed up, and anxiety comes to call — and nothing creates anxiety faster than the fear that you are out of control.

A Summary of Shame

The Shame Affect is a natural experience that feels bad. What makes it even worse for many of us is that we have been taught to feel embarrassed about being embarrassed. In those periods of life where our self-image is most fragile, we are most likely tempted to try to escape Shame-Humiliation when it is triggered rather than to acknowledge and to learn from it.

The scripts we use to escape the feeling of shame are commonplace. They are often even a part of our entertainment. But these same scripts, when used to a higher degree, can cause great suffering in our lives and relationships.

Learning about Shame scripts is not just an academic exercise. To be aware of these scripts can help us to find our way through the layers of defenses that are at the heart of many issues in our lives and in our world. Few of us grew up in homes where we felt safe enough to recognize and acknowledge our embarrassing and humiliating moments. Families often normalize one or more of these four defensive scripts, and teen culture is even more given to Shame avoidance. In the critical culture of middle school, there is a minefield of opportunities for Shame to be triggered. The same can be said for our political culture — and even most marriages.

In my experience, our scripts can only change when we feel safe from judgment, both outwardly and inwardly. Otherwise, we are most likely to simply layer one script upon another. Perhaps an "Ariadne" will find the way to your labyrinth to hold that string of human connection and remind you of your value, even in your moments of humiliation. Your "Ariadne" will then say to you, "Everyone has a Minotaur. The important thing is to face it. Only then will *your* Minotaur lose its power."

In other words, rather than try to "fix" our Shame, I think we need to first normalize it — and then allow it to teach us. Because we are committed to becoming Learners, we can do this best by learning to, in the words of Paul McCartney, "Let it be."

So how do we "normalize" Shame? When I suggest that we "let it be," what I'm really saying is that if we can cultivate a simple willingness to embrace the experience of our Shame — just allow our Shame to be a part of us, rather than something to defend against, we allow ourselves to be open to learning from our critics and our failures while retaining our value as a person. This practice is harder than it may seem, and it offers us another good glimpse at what it means to be meek.

Every time we give in to the temptation to defend against Shame with Compass of Shame scripts, we end up creating *more* Shame down the road. The answer, then, is to live a little bit broken open, a little bit vulnerable — with a sense of meekness in which our real growth can begin with an element of facing the truth of where we are. How good are you at acknowledging your own hidden Shame? How good are you at helping those around you acknowledge *their* hidden Shame?

I have taught the Compass of Shame to thousands of people, and the responses I hear to this information are often quite similar. People who have previously attended my workshops remark about how often they can now see these defensive scripts in their own lives and in the world around them. That is why I have come to believe that even the most basic knowledge of the Affects and the scripts we use to manage them can transform lives. This knowledge is a key to learning to live more fully in the moment, to be less manipulated by others, to grow more capable of deeper intimacy, and to be more willing and able to learn from the Affect of Shame. To be this kind of Learner is truly evolutionary in scope.

Pulling on the Threads of Shame

If you identify with one or more of these scripts, I want you to know that it's OK. Almost always as I am supporting someone in their journey into the labyrinth of their defensive scripts, one or more of these Shame scripts turns up. This just makes sense, because Shame is the Affect triggered when things don't go the way we want them to. I also believe the scripts described by Nathanson are a secondary, complicating factor for almost every diagnoses ever made.

The good news is that the *knowledge* of these scripts provides an important strand to the thread of awareness we need to find our way through the key parts of our personal labyrinth of defenses that may have confounded us before. Using what we've learned about the Compass of Shame can help us find our way through a deeper layer of our own neurotic dynamics. It is impossible to change your life when your consciousness is stuck in a defensive script. Now that we have this thread, a whole new world can open before us.

It is important to be aware that we can't shame ourselves into changing a Shame script. The more critical our inner dialogue, the more we feel the need to defend our self-images. So, if we want to grow beyond our Shame, we have to become aware of our defenses against it — and then learn to live without these defenses. This can only happen when we begin to accept ourselves for the beautiful fools we are.

We all have our flaws, but we also have our gifts. We may have made mistakes, but given that we now better understand how consciousness works, it's much easier for us to see our moments of embarrassment as pathways to learning rather than threats that must be denied or avoided.

Given the traumas and the training (intentional and not so intentional) that we experienced growing up, as well as the scripts these experiences created, it is easy to see why we all have our challenges. With creativity and commitment, our new awareness can begin to transform those scripts into learning.

Are you ready for that? Have you had enough of the same stuck cycles? I invite you to consider the possibility that you will always have the impulse to stay the same, respond the same, and think the same. The scripts you have will never be *unlearned* any more than you can unlearn what you know about riding a bicycle.

Choosing to Evolve is more about becoming aware of the scripts that create problems in your life and relationships — and then gaining the capacity to choose differently. This evolved capacity begins with acknowledging Shame, and then embracing a self-image that includes both the fool and the Learner.

Desperate Shame

Before we leave this brief treatment of the Shame Affect, there needs to be some acknowledgment that many people reading this are desperately stuck in one of the scripts we have described. I use the term, "desperately" because it clarifies the dynamic of what we feel when a script is not working to alleviate an overwhelming sense of failure and defectiveness.

If you happen to be stuck in such a place, I hope the material we have explored here offers enough insight for you to find the help you need. Do not waste another week, month, or year of your life in this little corner of hell. We may not be able to change the way our consciousness works, but we can transform the scripting that has become our personal Waterloo.

So what does that kind of transformation require? Well, first you'll have to commit to learning much more about the system that runs your perspectives. Even though you now have some awareness of your scripted response to Shame, to begin this change will require more knowledge about the complexities of how Shame works. Sometimes it is the very relief that your escape script brings that keeps you trapped in this dynamic. And, as you will soon discover, sometimes even the part of us that recognizes and reflects on these stuck patterns can actually be part of those patterns.

One day you are going along just fine, and then you encounter something that impedes your positive image of self. Maybe it comes in the form of comparing your body shape to another person's. Maybe it begins with some sense of rejection. Maybe it appears as a loss of a job, a broken relationship, or a financial setback. The Shame triggered by this event feels pretty crappy, so you say to yourself, "It's time to get my shit together!" So you start a diet, begin to work out, update your Tender profile, consult a financial planner, or whatever else seems like a way out of Shame.

Everything you do now seems to require more effort, and, at least initially, triggers more negative Affects than positive ones. Eventually, you skip the gym and gorge yourself on tacos. Tacos are so tasty! Unfortunately, those tacos are going to come with a side of Shame, and the Shame is associated with a lack of control. The more you experience this Shame of your loss of control, the more you'll need a new way to escape that Shame.

Then when you go home your wife rejects your sexual advances, and you storm back out of the house to get a beer. You drink shamelessly because you are now caught up in an Avoidance script. The next day you feel even more Shame for the way you acted, so you switch over to an Attack-Self script.

So you say to your wife, "I'm just not attractive to you anymore. You should find someone else now that I am no longer young and pretty."

Then, when she admits that the way you slurp your coffee is annoying, you begin to attack whatever quirks and habits *she* has. Attack-Other.

Pretty soon, there you are back at the bar with an even greater need to rid yourself of negative emotional imagery. The pattern has now become a loop. The more we try to escape Shame, the more we seem to have of it.

So whatever it is that begins your need to escape Shame — whether it's rejection, a loss of connection, or a lack of living up to someone else's vision of perfection — your *experience* of Shame is not the problem. Shame, regardless of what caused it in the first place, simply is what it is. The problem with Shame is how we develop layers of scripted defenses against it. As you begin to see Shame through this new lens, you may also begin to recognize that the messes you are experiencing in your life aren't coming as much from your moments of Shame as they are from the defenses you have developed to escape them.

If this information resonates with you, now is the time to stop playing this "Shame game," and reset your system. Now that you are aware of these dynamics, it is time to practice owning your Shame, regardless of what it is or where it originated. You will never know what freedom feels like until you break free of this cycle — or what you might accomplish if you stop running away from Shame and let it play the part in your life it is meant to play. Keep reading to learn more about navigating the experience of Shame-Humiliation without letting it overwhelm you to the point of needing defensive scripts.

CHAPTER 8

Meet the Affects, Part 3: Two Ways to Feel Good

As depressing as it may sound, of the nine Affects Tomkins found on the faces of babies, only two of them feel good. If we happen to have been shaped by our life experiences to limit, deny, or repress these two positive Affects, then it's high time to break free of that prison and make the most of them!

Silvan Tomkins believed that we are healthiest when we maximize positive Affect. However, as my friend and mentor Dr. Gary David reminded me, a "positive" Affect does not necessarily mean it feels "good." Writing this book, for example, is a positive, but not necessarily pleasant, experience. In my experience, sustained Interest in a creative project over a long period of time is indeed exhausting.

According to Dr. Carroll Izard, an American research psychologist best known for his contributions to differential emotions theory (DET), "The affect or feeling that sustains productive work and creative activity is positive but not necessarily pleasant in the hedonistic sense or in terms of pleasurable sensory stimulation." To this Gary adds, "Such work is positive, as in *rewarding*. Even the positive Affects have to be limited to some degree. Too much intensity — positive *or* negative — can trigger Distress."

For our immediate purposes, however, let's focus on our capacity to experience the two Affects that feel good: Interest-Excitement and Enjoyment-Joy.

Interest–Excitement

Watching, tracking, attuning to movement, exploring things with the eyes — these are the kinds of things you see when something triggers a baby's Affect of Interest. Of all the Affects, Interest-Excitement is probably the most abundant; however, it is also the least noticed. Until, that is, the degree of Interest increases to Excitement.

For a baby, the range of Interest-Excitement starts, at the low end, with simply glancing at something. At the high end, the baby is experiencing heart pounding excitement that seems to take over his or her whole body.

Because Interest is most often triggered by novelty, perhaps this Affect evolved to make humans notice change. So it's the novelty of a stimulus that at first triggers our Affect of Interest. With repetition, this same stimulus becomes no longer novel, and eventually it doesn't even trigger enough Interest to compete with other stimuli in the room, in the mind, or in the body.

As we discussed earlier, it is habituation that allows our consciousness to automate function so we can then shift our focus to other things. (Remember Wendy and the guitar strum?) Research on babies has shown how quickly they habituate to new things. For instance, a new picture may elicit a fairly long visual exploration the first time it is presented to a baby, but this responsiveness recedes rapidly with each successive presentation of that same picture.

While we might think the baby is just getting bored with the new picture, it is actually the function of *habituation* that is coming into play, brought about by the Affect of Interest/Excitement. If you can think of Affects as nine different gas pedals on the vehicle of our attention, it's easier to realize what a powerful role they play in consciousness. Whichever gas pedal gets the most stimulation directs your attention.

Once novelty fades and a stimulus begins moving toward being habituated, other stimuli may surpass those triggering Interest, and our attention will be directed elsewhere. Look at it this way. When there are a whole lot of different stimuli pushing on those pedals all at once, whatever is intense enough to trigger an Affect the most wins our attention.

Excitement, which is the higher expression of this same Affect, feels good. Babies sometimes just bounce around, trying to keep their Excitement going. Children go crazy waiting for holidays or "the next big thing" they'll get to do. For adults, Excitement is often the product of our anticipation. Images stored in our minds of what we are most interested in doing, being, or sharing can enhance any immediate moment just by thinking about them.

Since the range of Interest to Excitement is one of only two ways humans feel good, I think now would be a good time to check in with your memory and see how excitable you are. Some people are intensely excitable, and others, not so much. When have you been excited lately? What was the pattern for excitement in your family? We will come back to Interest-Excitement in a moment.

Enjoyment-Joy

Like Interest-Excitement, the Affect of Enjoyment-Joy is also experienced in a range from low to high. At its lower level, Enjoyment may be expressed as a passing smirk or giggle. High-level Enjoyment can be that "Ahhhh" that happens when someone rubs your aching back or the "Ha Ha!" of a joyful belly laugh. Babies innately love to smile and laugh, and then they begin to learn from their environment when, where, and how much to express this Affect. Remembering what we learned earlier about how response to a triggered Affect gets habituated, what do you think would happen if a baby grows up with parents who never smile?

As I'll bet you're beginning to see, Affects play definite and particular roles in our human consciousness. And, because one of those roles is that of directing our attention to the most intense stimulus (sensory or imagery) in our immediate experience, Affects instigate the formation of emotional scripts once Interest fades and our response becomes habituated.

Once an emotional script is developed, that script operates at this basic level of consciousness. In my experience, people who grow up in a joyless environment simply don't pay attention to the aspects of their lives that would likely trigger that Affect in others. Instead, their attention is directed by other Affects to give attention to other things. If you grow up in an environment that rarely or never smiles or laughs, you probably won't even notice the funny little things that happen around you every single day. It is as if you have a filter on your experience that makes you pay attention to other Affects, or triggers, instead.

I think it goes without saying here that this is precisely why it is so important for parents to keep a great deal of emotional connection going with a baby. If you are a parent of a young child (or even thinking about having children), I highly recommend you learn more about this — and how best to keep that connection strong. No parents are perfect, but think of what an amazing thing it would be if all babies could grow up in an environment that seeks to maximize the good feelings and minimize the ones that feel bad.

As a parent, you are more than just a provider and caregiver. You are that baby's Ariadne, holding the thread of emotional connection, without which a child can get emotionally lost in the labyrinth of their own consciousness, especially in the area of Enjoyment-Joy.

Isn't it interesting how some people laugh all the time and others hardly laugh at all? What do you think makes that difference, given that all babies are born with the Enjoyment-Joy Affect? If you were a child whose parents rarely laughed with you, you likely learned — and habituated — not to express much joy. And then, throughout your life when you have found yourself in the presence of joyful people, you've likely felt somehow defective for not being able to join in with them emotionally. The fact is, we are basically brainwashed by our environment as to how much of the Affect of Enjoyment-Joy we will experience. It is that socialization that will define more of our lives than any bit of knowledge we acquire.

When was the last time you had a really good laugh with a friend? Who modeled playfulness and joy for you growing up? Are there people in your life who never smile and laugh? How many jokes do you know? Take a few minutes to just survey the territory of your Enjoyment-Joy. As you do that, let me share a few things about good feelings.

No matter what you do to relieve your sadness, worries or embarrassments, they won't necessarily help you feel good if you don't have scripts that allow you to feel excitement and enjoyment. You will probably feel less bad, but you just won't feel good.

Traditional psychotherapy has tended to focus on relieving bad feelings and helping people to cope with their bad feelings enough to be functional. As we now see, this is helpful, but only to a point. The diagnostic manual, developed in a medical/disease model, typically allows insurance to only pay for returning a patient to functionality, not happiness. However, there are bright spots now appearing in this field that you should know about.

Martin Seligman, the father of Positive Psychology, approaches therapy from the perspective of creating and enhancing *good* feelings rather than focusing on disease. This research-based field is showing so much promise that it makes me wonder if many of the diagnoses that have defined psycho-pathology are less about an over-abundance of negative Affect and more about the loss or impediment to positive Affect.

For example, if I have been raised to adopt emotional scripts and behavior patterns around Excitement and Enjoyment that are repressive or conflicted, it won't matter how much work I do on relieving the negatives. I still won't know how to feel good.

Remember my example of two people walking into a bar? One came from a scary life and the other not. One comes in looking for the danger and the other comes in looking for the fun. Both of these people may be completely unaware how their scripts are paving the road ahead of them with whatever they are anticipating.

Now imagine that these two people get married. One has been raised with scripts that deny or repress Enjoyment, and the other has been raised to feel joy regularly and for no particular reason. What do you think the conflicts in that house might look like?

Dirty Harry Meets Sally

Drawing from some familiar Hollywood imagery, imagine that a young Clint Eastwood marries a young Meg Ryan. Both of them are pretty cool, right? Wouldn't they be great together? Personally, I think it would be fun to get to know both of them, even though they are very different. The Clint of his movies (and in this imaginary scenario) expresses excitement and enjoyment in a very narrow way. Dirty Harry is always looking for danger — not joy. The Meg of her movies, on the other hand, tends to bounce like a child when excited and always seems eager to laugh and play.

Let's say these two figments of our movie-fueled imagination are married for about a year when one day a friend comes to visit. Meg is bouncing around and excited, and Clint is being . . . Clint. For some reason, today Meg begins to feel irritated that Clint isn't as excited as she is about their visitor.

Without thinking, Meg says something critical to Clint: "Why can't you just hang out with us without looking at your phone?" While of course this isn't the real issue, it will do as an opening salvo. The real issue of course is that Meg is feeling a loss of communion, no thread of connection, no match of her excitement. For Meg, this interruption of her excitement has triggered Shame. And clearly, her mode of managing her feelings of shame is an Attack-Other script.

Because *most* criticism is an impediment to the good feelings of its recipient, now Shame also has been triggered for Clint. The question now is whether Clint will resort to a defensive script as well. Let's say that for years Clint has habituated a Withdrawal script to manage his Shame, so he will more or less automatically say something to make nice for a moment and then find an opportunity to escape the situation — and the criticism.

Clint's Withdrawal script has always helped him in the past to relieve and prevent his feelings of shame by removing himself from the scenes in which Shame is triggered. But now this no longer works. As Clint withdraws, Meg feels rejected — and then she comes after him, criticizing him now all the more for his Withdrawal.

Notice that now we have moved to another layer. Meg is no longer criticizing Clint for his lack of enthusiasm, excitement, or enjoyment, which was the actual origin of her discomfort in this situation. Meg is now criticizing Clint for the way he is Withdrawing. She is unaware that this is the way he is dealing with the Shame of her initial criticism.

As we discussed earlier, it is seldom productive to attack the very coping mechanisms a person is using to deal with the cracks in his or her self-image. So now Clint Withdraws even more. Maybe he even slips into a new Attack-Other script: "Why are you always nagging at me about these kinds of things?"

Eventually, as this conflict repeats itself many times, Clint and Meg are getting stuck in the same arguments so often that Meg now Withdraws, too. They begin to become emotionally detached from one another, but from time to time the conflict still emerges, and it seems even more frustrating and intense each time.

Meg cries about it now. Clint is angry. Both are responding — not just to the conflict, but also to their repetitive cycle and their inability to fix the problem. Each time the conflict rears its head again it causes an additional layer of Distress and Anger. As a result of all this conflict, Meg begins to squelch her Excitement-Joy. After all, "Why cast your pearls before swine?"

Clint hardly notices that Meg isn't as excitable as she used to be. In fact, for Clint, everything now feels better, and, for him, more normal. For Meg, however, it is like a part of her has grown numb. This goes on for another year or so.

Then one day Meg is at a Hollywood party and runs into a young Robin Williams. Robin is in his element, holding court, improvising characters, and being silly. Meg gets so caught up in this wonderful feeling of enjoyment that suddenly her playfulness returns and she is excited and laughing again. It almost feels as if she is coming back to life.

So she goes home and tells Clint that she is moving out. She just can't live this way anymore. She is done!

Sometimes conflicts and scars grow so deep — and awareness so thin — that leaving is the only choice we see. I have found, however, that often it is possible, with this knowledge on board, to approach these kinds of conflicts differently. The differences in how "Clint" and "Meg" express their Affects of Excitement and Enjoyment aren't really that big a deal. They are both still cool. There is no bad guy in this scenario. The real villain in this story of conflict isn't the difference in their expressions, but rather their lack of awareness of these defenses and the loss of connection their defenses can create.

What I mean by this is that neither person recognized the toxic way the other was experiencing Shame — or how their defensive patterns were creating more harm than the initial difference. This is because defensiveness is almost always automatically accompanied by a loss of empathy. Both Clint and Meg assigned meaning to the other's words and actions based on their own habituated images.

For Meg, Clint's lack of Excitement "meant" he wasn't interested or caring. His Withdrawal after she criticized him only seemed to offer Meg more proof of Clint's lack of interest. For Clint, Meg's criticism "meant" that other people were more important to her than he was. Her continued criticism as he withdrew seemed to only confirm this meaning.

How could all of this have gone differently with the evolution of consciousness we're exploring in this book? Let's start with Meg. In the initial throes of her Shame, triggered by Clint's lack of excitement about their guest, Meg would take a moment to become mindful. Then, upon discovering that she was about to criticize Clint with an Attack-Other defensive script, Meg would decide to Move Alongside that feeling of shame for a moment instead. She'd realize that just because her Affect of Shame was triggered it didn't mean anyone was doing anything wrong. It only meant that her good feelings were being impeded.

Let me repeat that and emphasize it. *Feeling shame does not necessarily mean that anyone is being bad or doing wrong. It simply means that someone's positive Affect around something has been impeded.* In this case, the impediment was to Meg's Excitement about the day.

So Meg's evolution of consciousness involves her developing some new practices. She learns to take a moment, take a breath, and slow down enough to suspend her judgment of Clint rather than to defend against her feelings of shame. She might even be able to breathe *through* the moment of Shame without letting it define the whole situation. She could remind herself that it is OK for people to respond differently to the same situation. In fact, most people do.

Ideally, Meg could retain some empathy for both her feelings and Clint's: "What's going on?" she might then ask him.

"Oh, I've got a problem with lighting on the movie set," he might reply.

"I'm sorry. Can it wait?"

"Yes, I think so. I just need to make one quick call."

"OK, but hurry back. I want us to share this time together, you know it's important to me."

"OK, baby, that would make my day!" (Yes, pun intended)

Notice how retaining empathy did not prevent Meg from asserting what she needed, nor did this process repress the Affect of Shame triggered in her. What mindfulness and empathy did in this scenario was to put the Affective experience into the context it deserves.

To do this required Meg to manage some of her emotion inwardly rather than outwardly. In fact, she did a little trick that I sometimes teach couples. If you want to increase positive feelings you may find it helpful to notice that there are almost always positive desires hidden within even the most intense negative feelings.

Picture in your mind the Taoist symbol of the Yin and Yang — you know, it's that circular symbol with the curvy, interlocking black and white sides. If you look closely, there is a small white dot in the fullest area of the black, and a small black dot in the same area of white. Think of this ancient symbol as a metaphor for finding happiness in relationships: the seed of one side is found in the fullness of the other. In much the same way, tucked within the height of my anger may be the seed of desire for my greatest joy.

If, like Meg in this example, we can follow the thread of awareness of our images and emotional scripts, we can *Move Alongside* our irritation or humiliation. Then we can ask the basic question, "What is it that I really want here?" Then, rather than express our irritation through criticism or complaint, we can ask for more of that positive thing we want.

Sometimes words are unnecessary. You may remember Dick and Jane, the couple I mentioned in an earlier chapter who learned to do this well. They had suffered regular escalating conflict over the need for touch. They were quite different in their upbringing around physical contact. His family never hugged, while hers was very "touchy-feely."

The arguments between Dick and Jane always began when she, out of her feelings of frustration, criticized him for not being more affectionate. This may sound obvious, but it took some time for Jane to learn that if she could Move Alongside her feelings and pinpoint what it was she really wanted, she could get a lot more affection from Dick by simply giving what she was hoping to get. So when she felt touch deprived, she would reach out and stroke his arm or put her arms around him. He welcomed all of this and gradually became more physically connected with her as well.

I am not suggesting that we can always do this. We need to be sure to first develop enough safety in our relationships that we can openly tolerate and digest our feelings of anger, fear, distress, and shame. However, building that emotional safety is impossible when there is an overabundance of negative feelings and a lack of positive ones.

The key to turning this corner in our relationships is learning to first notice, then Move Alongside, and then process the negative emotions within us and transform them into positive assertions. This is very different from repressing our negative emotions by refusing to give our attention to our negative feelings.

How we deal with emotion at different stages of consciousness is dramatically different. Infants feel anger and express it immediately and directly. Children feel anger and do whatever script they have learned to express or not express it. Adults often have a whole library of memories and scripts for when they previously felt anger. They also have a pile of images to throw onto the fire to escalate the intensity of their feelings.

Consider the difference between letting emotion be the headlights of the car rather than a warning light on the dashboard. Though we know it is impossible to stop Affect and emotion from guiding our attention, we do have the capacity within us to notice it — and redirect it.

Evolving our consciousness is about making these choices. We may choose to be direct with our anger if that seems most productive, or we may choose to notice the warning light of our Affect-driven emotions, listen to that feeling deeply, digest it down to its simplest form, and then look for that dot of the positive we desire instead. When we do this work consistently and well, we have great opportunities to create positive relationships.

By Moving Alongside her emotions, Meg pays attention to this warning light, and she is meek enough to allow the possibility that its meaning isn't all that clear yet. She then allows herself the time and space to enter into a time of discovery, not defensiveness. Inwardly, she asks herself, "What am I really wanting here?" And, once she has a fix on that, she tunes into the positive feelings she wants to have. Then, meekly acknowledging to herself that her feelings, wishes, and needs are never an entitlement, but rather something she must assert and negotiate, Meg makes the choice that leads to that negotiation rather than alienation. Once Meg learns to manage her Shame in this way, she will no longer have to squelch her excitement and enjoyment when Clint doesn't meet it equally.

People who have the scripts to easily express excitement and joy are the most likely to run into relationships where others are not equipped to match this vibe. Of course that doesn't mean either of them is right or wrong; it just means that they are different. And, if they Choose to Evolve, they will learn to use the many opportunities their differences present to learn how to let their momentary experiences of Shame pass through without causing or escalating conflict. "Meg" can learn how to stay her usual bubbly self, even though Clint may never dance with her in that emotional bubble.

Now of course, we'd all like to see Clint dance and get playful enough for a belly laugh. However, we don't *need* Clint to do that in order for us to still love his character. Still, our imaginary Clint could learn a thing or two from this little vignette. When you can notice that your partner's Affect of Shame is triggered and he or she attacks you, even mildly, and that this triggers your Shame in return — as it was in this story for Clint — you, too, can take the journey I just described for Meg.

That's not to say any of this is easy or comes naturally. No one is perfect in their capacity to digest the negative affect within themselves. We will often find ourselves confronted with angry or shaming words by those we love. In these moments we would do well to at least learn to Move Alongside our emotion rather than lose our empathy by becoming defensive.

If you recognize that you have a tendency to become defensive in the face of Shame, there is a simple trick I learned to help you begin to create better dialogue. When you are criticized or complained about, *let your very first response be in the form of a question.* Seek more information. Ask for clarity.

At first you may have difficulty asking a question that doesn't sound defensive, but with time and practice you will improve. Asking requires that you set your defensiveness aside for a moment to tune into the other person more fully and carefully.

I have seen couples become so good at this that their conflicts became more like a love dance than a wrestling match. Once they learned to give attention to what is needed for each of them to feel better in just about any situation, these couples arrived at a state of deep intimacy that is rare in this world.

Now that we have explored four of the nine Affects, I hope you are beginning to develop your understanding of the scripted ways in which we learn to experience our own Affects — as well as the problems created by the ways we defend against them. Why is this awareness so important to the thread of hope we are following? One reason. Affects direct our attention. Let's now turn our attention to the Affect of Anger.

CHAPTER 9

Meet the Affects, Part 4: Anger-Rage

As we continue to move through our discussion of the nine Affects, we now turn our attention to Anger. Take a moment to explore your imagery around Anger. How do you experience Anger? Where have you seen it in your world and in your life? How do you generally feel about Anger?

Given what we have just discovered in our exploration of Shame, it will not surprise you to learn that much of the Anger we experience in our lives is actually a scripted response to Shame.

As we learned in our previous exploration of the Compass of Shame, and particularly with the Attack-Other script, the vulnerable experience of Shame-Humiliation is very often covered over by attacking whoever and whatever left us exposed. In this scripted response, the Shame Affect is completely ignored, and the Anger Affect then displaces the Shame in much the same way Excitement can displace Shame in an Avoidance script. In both cases, the Shame Affect is fleeting, if we even feel it at all.

By paying attention to this dynamic, we can begin to sense the subtle difference in how we express *feelings* of anger when they are actually a defense meant to cover our Shame. For the most part, we can sense this difference by noticing a lack of capacity to *feel* Shame or *hear* feedback from others.

That being said, now let's look at the *Affect* of Anger that is *not* a response to Shame. Tomkins saw the Anger Affect as a close cousin to Distress; in both Anger and Distress there are nagging steady-state stimuli that continue over time. The difference between Anger and Distress in this context is that the stimulus triggering Anger is more intense. To be more precise, Tomkins believed it to be the *rate and density of neural firing over time* that determines which of these two Affects is triggered.

If all this seems a little confusing, don't worry about it. The important thing to understand here is that Anger is a natural part of the human emotional landscape. Babies are born with the capacity for Anger, and this Affect usually gets triggered when the stimuli that trigger Distress are intensified — or not being managed. For instance, if you see an infant displaying Anger, you can bet that something in his or her experience has gotten too intense and stayed that way for too long.

Like all of the Affects, the experience of Anger changes as our consciousness changes. Infants roar and scream, because, having little or no imagery to enhance or inhibit the flow of Affect, Anger takes over the entire body and consciousness.

Children, on the other hand, usually show somewhat more refined scripts around the expression or repression of Anger, depending on what they have seen modeled by parents and other adults, teachers, or peers — which is how their own expressions have been socialized. They also have acquired enough abstract processing (memory/antici-pation) to have more highly developed expectations, which amounts to more opportunities for Anger to be triggered.

A New Game

It's Saturday morning, and Jack promises to take his six-year-old son, Bobby, to buy a new video game. Bobby looks forward to this treat all morning long. By late in the afternoon, Bobby has asked Jack repeatedly when they would go, but Jack is still busy with a project in the yard.

Jack becomes irritated with Bobby, and this frustration grows as Jack becomes more fatigued from his work and Bobby grows more frustrated the longer he waits for the promised excitement. Can you feel the emotional collision coming? Bobby's mother describes it as "watching a train wreck in slow motion."

So Saturday does not end well for Bobby *or* Jack. There is no trip to the video game store for Bobby; Jack goes to bed feeling angry. (And Bobby's mom, Jill, stays up late researching family therapists.) Given what we have discussed so far about habituation and Affects, it isn't very hard to see how this debacle occurred.

Infants respond with Anger to sensory stimuli that are intense *and* prolonged. A stimulus that is brief, like a stabbing pain, is more likely to trigger Fear (More on that Affect shortly). If the stimulus is less intense, but more prolonged, however, it will likely trigger Distress.

While this progression holds true for both children and adults, Anger in children — and even more so in adults — is more often triggered by the broken expectations of their imagery. By the time we are adults, we are likely to have developed more elaborate scripting for our responses to the Affect of Anger, including hair-trigger sensitivities related to our particular history. In our example with Jack and Bobby, Jack's sensitivity came from growing up in a family that valued hard work and delayed gratification. Though he enjoyed seeing Bobby excited about his game, deep down Jack felt angry when his son seemed focused on excitement and enjoyment when Jack was busy with the demands of home ownership.

To intensify Jack's feelings of anger, Jack's memory image of his own little brother who never pitched in to help with chores is leading his consciousness to automatically put Bobby into that category any time Bobby complains about work or wants to interrupt it for play. Although Jack is generally a nice guy and a good father, these are moments when his Anger, fueled by his habituated images and scripted emotional responses, tends to erupt in ways that feel inappropriate to the situation and frightening to Bobby and his mother.

This scenario provides us with a great illustration of how scripts form in layers. First there is a sensitivity that triggers an Affect. A script, usually formed in childhood, sets us up for the hyper-arousal of the same or another one of the Affects. Over time, as that script is triggered, the hyper-arousal becomes apparent to the people in our lives, and this usually leads to more embarrassment.

In this example, Jack could see the Fear on Jill's face as he erupted into Rage at Bobby. Later on, Jack would get an earful from Jill about how he was verbally abusing Bobby. The Shame-Humiliation then triggered in Jack is something he had experienced before in other situations that seemed similar. Over time, the script he had developed to deal with this Shame was Withdrawal.

There are a couple of things that are important to note here. First, Jack's Shame script of Withdrawal would not be necessary if not for the *earlier* script formed from his hypersensitivity and hyper-arousal of the Affect of Anger. That earlier script was his primary one

— all others were layered on top of it. Second, Jack's shame script of Withdrawal is now likely to create even more layers of issues and responses. The more Jack withdraws, for example, the more his family will respond to him negatively. He may experience this response from his family defensively and develop more scripts from the Compass of Shame to manage his Shame-Humiliation.

Eventually, with no intervention, Jack may develop yet another layer of scripting — an anxiety about his anger. This script usually happens when the defensive Shame script layer fails. Many people I have worked with had begun to distrust their responses in this way. They had become so filled with self-doubt and fear that they could not trust their perceptions of reality.

I began this book describing how our habituation of abstract imagery is the evolutionary leap that provided humans the capacity for creating stability in our lives and relationships. Our images of self, other, and the world around us serve as guides that allow us to operate with incredible efficiency.

So imagine what would happen to you if suddenly you couldn't trust your inner compass. It would be disorienting to say the least, right? For many if not most people, there is no more debilitating experience in life than this, and no greater Fear trigger than fearing that we have lost our capacity to perceive the world correctly.

If you happen to find yourself in this place, and you have become anxious about some aspect of your emotional responses, please read on. In the coming chapters we will explore the experiences of Fear and Panic — and how you can learn to trust yourself again and gain the stable sense of self that will allow you to thrive. The evolution of your consciousness has already begun.

Summary

- Anger is a natural part of human emotion.
- Just because a particular situation triggers Anger in one person doesn't mean that it will or should trigger Anger in others.
- Our past experiences can create sensitivities that predispose us to certain expectations.
- Becoming conscious of these sensitivities is not only possible, but also essential to our learning to Move Alongside our emotional experiences when they become hyper-aroused.

More on the Formation of Scripts

Birth order can be one dynamic in our scripting. I grew up in a family where anger was almost completely avoided, but my brother and I fought with each other as most siblings do. Younger siblings automatically come into the world as an impediment to the older child's good feelings, robbing them of their parents' undivided attention. The older child is often further burdened with requirements to look after the younger, and sometimes this can be a trigger for a boatload of resentment.

This dynamic of birth order is only one of the many reasons why siblings who are raised in the same house with the same influences can develop radically different scripts. Because older siblings have to learn to control their play around the more fragile younger ones, they often have to learn to control both their excitement *and* their anger. In fact, some older siblings develop scripts where they fear their Anger.

Fear of Anger can happen with younger siblings as well. All it takes is being punished — or witnessing a sibling being punished — for expressing feelings of anger. It doesn't take very many of these kinds of experiences for us to begin to associate Anger with Fear.

The same kind of script can emerge for a person who has actually *hurt* someone in a moment of anger — and especially if this action triggered Shame. For all kinds of reasons, many people experience fear every time their Anger is triggered.

Still others experience the exact opposite: They *feel* anger whenever Fear is triggered. This script has probably been a part of military training since before the days of Sparta. It makes a huge difference in battle if your warriors are trained to transform the freezing and fleeing impulses of Fear into the pure power of Anger. In our times, training in this script may still be a part of basic training, but that doesn't mean it isn't also promoted within families.

How this Fear script impacts the general culture is something worthy of many pages. For now, however, I will only suggest these questions:

Is the ideological polarization of a culture increased more by the clash of habituated images or the clash of emotional scripts?

Is it possible that at the heart of our disconnection in our public discourse we can discover the differences in how we have been taught to feel?

As we continue to glance over the myriad of ways Affects are scripted, it is important to understand that many of these scripts are simply in the air we breathe and the landscapes of our childhood. Our scripts play a major role in making us who we become.

And, speaking of landscapes, we should also consider how the natural environment around us influences our formation of imagery and scripts. How might we experience life differently if we are raised in a desert rather than a forest? My father's earliest years were on the dusty, wind-swept plains of Oklahoma. This is a natural environment that offers a solitary experience in which the emptiness of the landscape tends to put one's focus on the self and survival. This was not the case for me, as I grew up in the gardened world of Mississippi, where the abundance of life and color in my childhood likely kept my focus more outward than my father's.

Does a lack of external stimuli, as my father found in the desert, somehow create more space for our internal imagery to take precedence? I have often found that to be true, and this is one of the reasons I often prefer to visit the high deserts of the Southwestern United States. There is great beauty there, to be sure, but there is also an emptiness that turns me inward to the whispered dialogue of the heart. I face my inner labyrinth every time I visit there. In the desert where there are few external sources to trigger Affect, the images of my inner world have less competition.

The Evolving Consciousness and Anger

I hope by now it has become pretty clear that our emotional experiences can be pretty screwy. Unlike infants, no one reading this book is able to express these nine innate Affects directly. By early adulthood we all develop our own scripted versions of each Affect. That means that when we simply "feel what we feel," what we are often *actually* feeling is a combination of biology and biography. We have *learned* to feel what we feel.

And sometimes, these "feelings" we have learned to feel can be a complete distraction from what is *really* going on in our inner and outer world. Even worse, these learned emotional responses might be destructive or defensive scripts that are keeping us stuck in spiraling and escalating dysfunction.

The evolving consciousness we're now seeking is emotionally savvy. Within it we have the capacity to either flow with a feeling or to Move Alongside a feeling in order to observe it, question it, and learn from it.

The Gift of Getting Pissed

Where would we be without all those called to bring about justice because they were angry about something? Anger is often the catalyst for making a difference in the world. As such, Anger can be as much a force for good as for destruction. Do the meek ever get mad?

I once heard psychologist and author, Bill O'Hanlon, talk about finding a "calling" in life. He said what "calls" us in our life are the times when we feel "blissed or pissed." What I think O'Hanlon was suggesting with this quip is that finding our sense of purpose and passion in life most often involves listening to those things that either trigger our sense of beauty and awe — or to those things we find frustrating and enraging. I believe that in many ways these two feelings are pretty much two sides of the same coin.

Before we talk again about the Yin and Yang, however, we must acknowledge again the importance of listening to Anger and how the clear and direct expression of it can bring salvation to a situation. By salvation I mean a return of wholeness and wellbeing. I could share many examples of this, but for our purposes let's explore what happens when Anger is repressed.

A couple came into my office smiling more than most couples you would ever meet. Their life together seemed to be beautiful. They had everything they ever wanted including a new baby. They were very attractive and dressed in nice clothes. They spent the majority of the session talking about nice things. Only when I pressed them about their reason for coming to see me did I learn that there was a problem.

There was a concern about the baby. She cried a lot. And the crying seemed to be uncontrollable. I gave them a few ideas they could try, and they were very appreciative. Then, just as they were about to leave, the woman confessed that there was another issue. Once, in a fit of desperation and anger, her husband had grabbed the baby up and seemed to want to shake her. That is how we began the journey of exploring the husband's anger issues.

In the interest of time I will say that his story was one of both great success and great disappointment. He had gone from the heights of professional athletic achievement where he met his wife, to being injured, being forced to retire, and choosing to go to work in his father-in-law's business. All of this had happened in the year before they had this baby.

There had been no time for him to mourn his loss and disappointment, and he believed that to even acknowledge his anger would be too upsetting to his wife. He had spent most of the last 18 months trying to be supportive to her in her pregnancy and birth of their child. As he talked about all that, he was smiling; but when we went back to discuss the loss of his career, it was clear that his anger had only been repressed. His need to express his anger had been overruled by his need to be a good husband and father.

Unfortunately, their child's nonstop tears and screams challenged his capacity to continue hiding his feelings. The Anger then triggered was like a thread to his dark feelings that had been covered over with a slightly over-active smile. This repression was not new, he acknowledged. He had grown up in a family that never expressed anger. The few times he remembered his father as angry had also been in sudden outbursts. For him, Anger was utterly shameful.

Once he had a clearer understanding of the scripted nature of his emotions, he was agreeable to making a safety plan for his interactions with their child and to practicing some mindfulness techniques to use whenever the baby cried. And for a while, he kept me on speed-dial just in case he needed backup.

It took a few months of processing the challenges in their lives, as well as his extreme disappointment, in order to get in touch with and release these feelings of anger. Though he would always miss his professional athletic career, he discovered new ways to channel that feeling into youth sports, and soon his new career as a contractor took off. But none of this could happen until the feelings of anger could be released.

Given what we explored about Shame scripts, it would be easy to believe that he was transferring his anger to the baby because the baby was impeding his good feelings — or that the baby had become symbolic of *all* the disappointments he felt in his life. However, after looking into his repertoire of emotional scripts, I am convinced that this is not the case. It was his repression of his own anger and the explosive anger modeled by his father that had shaped his responses.

The further we explored his experience of anger, the more we discovered dynamics in his marriage that were triggers for Anger he had also repressed. Finally, he gained the capacity to confront these issues, and both of them learned that anger was an important part of their intimacy, because their only alternative was emotional detachment.

Having grown up in Mississippi where anger is always boiling and always denied, the issue of repressed anger has always been my Achilles' heel. In my intimate relationships I am always given to seek harmony, having learned early on that anger is crazy — or at best, impolite. All of the people I have ever loved, including my children, were more open and direct with their anger than I was. I can count on one hand the times when I felt that anger was a productive response to a situation. I can now say without hesitation that my experience of Anger has been truly dissociative.

I can also say with some certainty that this dynamic had a great deal to do with the demise of my first marriage. Dissociation of my anger resulted in an emotional disconnection to intimacy. Our scripts define more than our own expression; they also tend to define our expectations of others. When others in my life expressed their anger, I was ill prepared to accept it. Why couldn't they just repress their feelings of anger like I did?

It is hard to underestimate the damage that can be done by emotional detachment in an intimate relationship. It seems clear, though, that long before people seek a legal divorce, at least one of them has become emotionally detached long before.

Now I am angry. I am angry at the repressive culture I grew up in, where even Jesus clearing the temple of the moneychangers seemed inappropriate and over-the-top. I am angry at spiritual traditions that somehow perpetuate a kind of pseudo-humanity devoid of passion, where detachment and self-sacrifice are the only currency, and repressive emotional scripts masquerade as enlightenment.

Here's the thing, though. Before you can learn to Move Alongside your habituated, emotionally charged imagery, you must first be able to feel your Anger. What I see happening in so many spiritual movements, including the many practices of yoga, are teachers who want to arrive at a constant state of blissful detachment and teach those who are already repressed how to be at home in their repression.

This is not Choosing to Evolve. It's really just more of the same repressive bullshit that has been fed to the masses for centuries. True freedom and wellbeing don't come from repressive emotional scripts. I will hasten to add, however, that having no capacity to modulate your anger doesn't tend to create wellbeing either.

Control does not mean repression to the point of dissociation. Nor does control mean any static level of emotional discharge. Control means having a choice. Once we recover our connection to this passionate Affect we can learn to Move Alongside it or choose to express it directly, depending on the situation. This is what it means to Choose to Evolve.

Remember, we cannot change these basic elements of human consciousness. But we *can* learn how to work with them in a way that allows us to transcend our most destructive scripts and gain the freedom of greater choice.

If, like me, you have developed scripts that repress your anger, consider that these scripts go largely unnoticed, operating like a filter to your attention. With this filter in place, you simply don't *notice* the elements of life that would trigger Anger, or in some cases you may have learned to direct the anger into destructive patterns that are "passive-aggressions." Recovering your Anger may feel primitive or childish, but if you practice intentionally looking at the world through the lens of Anger, you can begin to address the aspects of your life that create suffering for yourself and others.

Getting Angry About *Being* Angry

I suppose you could say that the repressive Anger script I picked up in childhood was the opposite of the Attack-Other script Nathanson described as a defense against the Shame Affect. In the Attack-Other script, a person will habituate a way of experiencing Anger whenever their Shame is triggered. Mine was exactly the opposite. I felt Shame every time Anger was triggered.

When it comes to Anger, the opposite of a repressive script like mine would be those who feel angry about feeling angry. Just as we can feel shame about feeling shame or distressed about our distress, we can feel angry about our anger. In each of these cases, we fall victim to *emotional flooding* in which all of our thoughts are infected by imagery that amplifies our experience of the emotion.

These scripts can also wreak havoc on relationships. Imagine a partner who seemed to always be angry and who, when in the throes of this Affect, seemed to remember everything he had ever been angry about before. His thoughts flow with imagery, re-triggering and amplifying his Anger beyond any capacity for modulation.

To be sure, anger is a powerful emotion that can motivate us to make important changes. Anger can also blind us by our passion so we take things too seriously. Without cultivating an awareness of how past images of anger can magnify our angry experience of the moment, we can do a lot of damage.

If you have identified with any of the scripts I have described, then I suggest that you may benefit from doing some reflection using the exercises I have included in this book to help you learn more about your own experience of Anger. With greater awareness of your particular scripting, you can gain a great deal of choice in how you respond to Anger.

If you tend to be repressive of Anger, what can you do instead? If you tend to flood with Anger, consider more of the Yin – Yang image I suggested earlier. You may find much greater success in your relationships if you can learn to flip Anger over and see it from the creative side.

This alternative may not feel very satisfying for some people. The drama of righteous anger is addictive, and to deny ourselves this drama may feel repressive, especially if scorching the earth with our anger is our habit. It takes quite a bit of practice to learn how to flip your Anger over to look for its creative gifts. The questions we can learn to ask of our Anger are: "What is it that I really want?" and "What was it that I expected and didn't get?"

If you become aware of the "unfulfilled desire" or wish beneath the Anger, it is often more helpful to re-assert your desire than to complain and assign blame. To be direct and assertive in these moments, without the blaming and judgment, we can often open a more productive dialogue with everyone involved.

We tend to pick up our scripted experience of Affect and habituated imagery largely from our early experience of family, culture, and even the landscape of our early environment. Our emotional experiences are never ultimate truth, but they *are* our personal truth in that moment — a truth that is usually fleeting. I may be very angry that my friend forgot to pick me up from work and then find myself feeling deep empathy when he shares how he had been served divorce papers earlier in the day. Choosing to Evolve is about putting these emotional dynamics into their proper place.

We live in a time where strident voices often turn our airwaves shrill and critical. We need a new way to think and talk about the things that are important to us. That dialogue will require an evolved capacity for the kind of consciousness that can question its images, habituated patterns, and emotional motivations — all while speaking our momentary truth to others.

CHAPTER 10

Meet the Affects, Part 5: Surprise-Startle

Of all nine of the Affects that Tomkins classified, there was only one that Tomkins considered to be "neutral." This neutral Affect that Tomkins observed is Surprise – Startle. We experience Surprise-Startle to varying degrees — from mild to jolting — depending on the intensity of the stimulation and our body's particular sensitivity to the stimulus. Tomkins believed that Surprise-Startle is triggered by any dramatic rise in neural activity, *followed immediately* by its recession. What makes this Affect different from all the other Affects is that it serves as a sort of "reset button."

Think of it this way. Imagine suddenly hearing a car backfiring or a friend saying, "Boo!" Oftentimes, your body will jump without your even thinking about it. There are lots of other times when the sensory world provides us with a similar bump in stimulation, sufficient to trigger our Affect of Surprise-Startle. What's more, all babies make the same face — and experience this Affect as a disconnection or "reset" from whatever was engaging their attention previously. The stimulation required to trigger that reset is usually some sudden and brief event in the external environment. However, just as the abstract imagery in our consciousness can trigger other Affects, the same is true for this one.

Wait. Our own *thoughts* can startle us? Yes. You read that right. It *is* possible to be startled by your own thoughts. Have you ever had the experience of suddenly remembering you were late for something — or that you left the oven on? Even memories can be startling when they pop up, seemingly out of nowhere.

What interests me about this Affect even more is that there is also growing evidence that we do not all have the same sensitivity to stimuli from birth. The same stimulus that triggers a little bit of

Surprise (displayed as briefly widened eyes and open mouth) in one person could trigger the full-body jerk of all-out Startle in others.

How would it feel to live in a world where every honk of a distant horn or any mild but sudden change in our environment triggered not just a little bump of Surprise, but a full-fledged, jump-out-of-your-skin, Startle response? Over time, the repetitive nature of this kind of disruption to your life could begin to trigger Distress — or even Anger.

Do you get irritated when someone drums his fingers on the table, clicks her fingernails together, or taps a foot on the floor? You might be one of these folks who are sensitive to the Surprise-Startle Affect. And, in most cases the people you find to be irritatingly fidgety are *less* sensitive to external stimuli. However, being less sensitive to Surprise-Startle is not without its costs. For some people, being under-stimulated for a long enough period of time can trigger Distress. I have seen more than a few marital conflicts with this dynamic. Maybe online dating services should include this as a personality matching measurement! Stimulation-seeking people and stimulation-sensitive people should know about the predictable conflicts they are likely to experience in their relationship before they get married.

I have also found that some of us develop scripts that confuse the feelings of startle with feelings of fear. For instance, if I accidentally run into someone in a doorway and they say, "You scared me!" I like to reply, "No, I *startled* you. You *scared* yourself." (This is why I have no friends.)

All levity aside, this response can be a result of having past experiences in which we were startled — and then hurt. With enough of these kinds of repeated experiences, or sometimes even one significant experience of being surprised and hurt at the same time, a script can develop to immediately connect the experience of startle with Fear.

The same can be true for some of us who have systems that are particularly sensitive to stimuli. Over time, having perhaps been laughed at for over-reacting, we may develop a fear of Startle.

One additional side note about this Affect before we move on: There are people who use the Surprise-Startle Affect to control, manipulate or even abuse others. Sometimes this can be an effective tool for growth and change, but I mention it here as a way to help free you from unwanted emotional manipulation.

If the Startle Affect serves human consciousness as a sort of reset button that disconnects us from whatever we are engaged in and prepares us to respond to whatever is next, then we are biologically predisposed to having this response, whether we want to or not. At least one study has suggested that repetitive startling can be a warning sign for future spousal abuse. I hope that anyone who is in a relationship with someone who seems to enjoy "scaring" him or her will talk to someone about it. Yes, it may be all in good fun, but there *are* people who use the Startle Affect to control and abuse others.

For that matter, because of their biological roots, *any* of the Affects can be used to manipulate someone. And make no mistake; businesses and advertisers mine the capacity to trigger our Surprise-Startle Affect daily in hopes of influencing our behavior. Human motivation is innately emotional — and if they've done their homework, they know it.

Try this. The next time you are watching television, see if you notice how many times you feel startled. Now ask the question: Are you being manipulated? All this media psychology makes me wonder how much more powerful the medium will become when a Virtual Reality component immerses us more fully and with even more lifelike imagery. One thing seems clear, we are entering an age where humans will either evolve to a new awareness of their emotional dynamics or they will become even more manipulated by those who *do* have this awareness.

In 2010, Carl Paladino, a Buffalo, New York businessman, was hoping to be elected governor of New York. The New York Times reported that one of his campaign's tactics was to attack his competition by sending out a postcard that read, "Something really stinks in Albany."

What made this bit of propaganda different is that the postcard was coated with a substance designed to smell like rotting vegetables. The reporter who sampled the card, which was evidently folded, said that you could smell it before it was even opened, and after opening, the smell of the stinky card intensified — until it smelled exactly like a landfill.

Paladino did not win that election, but let's consider for a moment *why* this kind of tactic could have been effective — and why it wasn't. To illuminate this discussion more fully, I'll need to introduce you to two more Affects that Tomkins observed. Disgust and Dissmell are most often found on the faces of babies when they are offered food.

CHAPTER 11

Meet the Affects, Part 6: Dissmell and Disgust

As you may well know if you've spent any time at all with babies, sometimes a baby rejects food even before tasting it, and sometimes he rejects it *after* that first taste. You know the look I'm talking about, right? The wrinkled nose and pulling back of the head with pursed lips when a baby rejects a food even before allowing a morsel of it to cross his lips? This is the Dissmell Affect.

Tomkins found that Dissmell was a separate Affect from its cousin, Disgust, which involves the *rejection* of a food after tasting it, which triggers that familiar opening of the mouth, protrusion of the tongue, and a sincere effort to spit out whatever offensive thing has been taken in.

Discovering these two somewhat related responses among the nine innate Affects, Tomkins termed Dissmell as the Affect more associated with smell, and Disgust the Affect triggered more through taste. While today there has been little to no research that makes this distinction, I think it's important to review Tomkins' earlier research on what today appears to be a combination of the two under the heading of Disgust.

So why is this distinction so important? Well, for starters, it just makes sense. There is a big difference between the experiences of rejecting things prior to sampling and rejecting things after sampling. If you don't think this is true, then go ahead and drink some old milk. There is also a considerable amount of research that reveals rather startling evidence: our thoughts are impacted by these Affects whether we are aware of them or not. For instance, one study found that if you set off a foul odor in a polling place, people will vote more conservatively. Another found a correlation between political affiliation and the intensity of Disgust people registered from accidently taking a drink from another person's soda. Once again, this raises questions as to whether our political polarizations may have more to do with emotional scripting than pure ideology.

Tomkins believed that Dissmell evolved in humans to protect us from ingesting poisonous or spoiled/rotten food. Think of all the times you have opened a carton of milk and given it the sniff test. If the milk is bad, the smell is likely to trigger an automatic reaction on your face. (You are probably doing it now just thinking about it!) Dissmell is a powerful Affect.

Dissmell may have emerged very early in humans, and it is also highly contagious. If you walk into a room with the expression of Dissmell on your face, others will likely mimic it.

As we go through the early years of life, we pick up images like shells on a beach. And, as we have discussed, many of these images have an emotional charge attached to them, and calling that image to mind will elicit the emotion. So it comes as no surprise that we can learn to associate the Affect of Dissmell with just about anything. As we get older, we are programmed by our immediate environment to associate Dissmell with many things other than foods.

If you observe the faces of people you will find them expressing Dissmell about places, races of people, sports teams, or even particular ideas. You may even be reading this book with a predisposition for Dissmell that is triggered by anything that feels psychological or spiritual or just overly self-reflective. If so, I challenge you now to reflect on that predisposition. Where did it come from?

As we've already learned, Affects are both innate and unavoidable, and they direct and "flavor" our attention. Another piece of information essential to our understanding of Affect is that our experience of every single moment is defined by how we *were taught* to feel about things. Imagine that you were raised in an environment where you witnessed the expression of Dissmell every time your family members spoke of people who were of a different race than you. Without an evolved consciousness, any image or experience of that race would automatically trigger Dismell. In other words, the Dissmell Affect would be telling you to "reject without sampling."

Imagine for a moment that we are prehistoric humans hunting for food, and we suddenly come upon a dead animal. We are also starving, so you can imagine our excitement as we discover this immediate availability of food. So we get right to it — each of us pulling apart pieces of the animal. Now imagine that one of us recoils and makes the Dissmell face — that same face we make today when smelling sour milk. Because of the contagion of this Affect, we'll likely survive this rotten meat.

So as you can see, Dissmell and Disgust can be very important to the preservation of life. However, the scripts humans have developed around these two Affects have also had a hand in *destroying* life. As Sam Keen once told me in an interview, "We are taught by seven or eight to hate the people our relatives hate," I couldn't help but think of my own upbringing in Mississippi.

To be clearer about what I mean by that, *I* was never taught to feel Dissmell for black people. In fact, my grandmother quit the church and started volunteering at the hospital on Sundays after a dark-skinned missionary she had invited to speak to her Sunday school class was turned away at the church doors.

When I lived through desegregation as a sixth grader, I saw first-hand how people had been trained from their earliest years to hold prejudices — and these were more than just ideas. When we talk of prejudice, we can now recognize that it is not just a way of thinking that children are taught. Prejudice is something far more powerful than ideas, and it survives into our times today because of how children are *trained* to feel. Our scripts operate silently, behind the scenes of our thinking, quietly directing our attention.

Sometimes Dissmell becomes so generalized that it can become a permanent feature on the face of a person — and a go-to script in what must be a miserable existence. I have often found Dissmell on the faces of people who were required to go to a training that they did not want to attend. Teachers, for instance, who have been subjected to a "new program of the year," every year for 20 years, might find themselves already predisposed to Dissmell for any new training program.

If the role of Affect is to direct and flavor our attention, then how is that possible with Dissmell and Disgust? How do they direct our attention? The answer to that is a little bit complicated, but here it is in a nutshell. Direction includes both engagement and disengagement. Some Affects push us *toward* engagement while others pull us *away*. Some Affects actually direct our attention by modulating our other Affects.

Dissmell and Disgust operate in a way that disrupts or modifies our Interest or Enjoyment. In the case of Dissmell, interest in even "sampling" something is disrupted. Disgust, on the other hand, seems to protect us from *resampling* what has been previously experienced.

Even though Dissmell and Disgust provide us with important protections, they both may be more of a liability to us at this point in our evolution. Let's face it. Having corporations and political campaigns attempting to manipulate our natural emotional systems is nothing new. Who hasn't been emotionally manipulated through commercials or movies? (Propaganda has become an art form in our culture.) How we deal with this issue may determine much of our actual experience of freedom and choice.

The Affects of Dissmell and Disgust are powerful and extremely contagious. When accompanying a political argument directed at an opponent, these two Affects can insidiously lead people to reject without question and, at some level, feel that the opponent is worth-less or even toxic. I challenge you to watch a political speech where an opponent is being attacked and see if you don't witness at least some Dissmell on the face of the speaker.

Dissmell, Disgust, and the Evolving Consciousness

We may well need Dissmell and Disgust when it comes to sour milk and rotten food, but when it comes to people and ideas, this can be a toxic combination. If we're not careful — and aware — Dissmell can cut us off from a fresh experience, and Disgust can prescribe for us a sense of unwarranted contempt for a repeat performance.

I believe that if we want to stem the tide of shootings and stabbings in the world, it is essential to understand these components of consciousness. As I see it, some of the most dangerous people in the world are those who have been habituated to Dissmell or Disgust for others — and who also possess attack-other scripts for dealing with their Shame. These people are all around us. They are rich, they are poor, and they come from every ethnicity and religion.

For a person who has been socialized with the volatile combination of Dissmell, Disgust, and Attack-Other Shame scripts all that is needed to create a horrific outcome is for enough Shame to be triggered. What makes this person particularly dangerous is that very often he or she is also drawn to participate in groups that routinely express Dissmell or Disgust for other groups. And, although the leaders of these groups may "disown" them, saying that they have never preached violence, these leaders should no longer feel so innocent.

There are people right now with this combination of scripts who are participating within the ranks of hate groups. These folks often need to feel heroic as a way to overcome some feeling of shame or insecurity. In such cases they will be willing and motivated to do what others would not. Believing that he or she is being heroic, they take action by doing what others will only talk about behind closed doors. A person desperately caught up in these scripts is unaware that their "heroism" is fueled by a need for relief from their own negative Affects made all the more intense through the scripts they have accumulated.

If you are someone who feels bonded to friends and family over your mutual Dissmell of others, shedding these scripts is a lonely journey, and you will need support. When you choose to transform a racist Dissmell script, your friends may feel betrayed. It is no wonder that anyone in this growth process will have to deal with a lot of relational resistance.

Our knowledge of these Affects and of our own particular scripts provides the thread of awareness we need for change. In the case of Dissmell and Disgust, this thread makes a difference in our capacity to love and connect with all people. If we want to stop the violence perpetrated between tribes and ethnic groups, then we would do well to learn about our own scripts first.

Before we turn our attention to the ninth Affect, I offer the following suggestions that may help us avoid having our innate Affects of Dissmell and Disgust manipulated to someone else's agenda.

Suggestions for Safeguarding Your Dissmell and Disgust

Begin to watch the expression on the faces of the people who want your support.

Notice how much time your preacher, politician, or friend spends attacking others versus offering a positive solution.

Observe which people and what ideas others around you "reject without sampling."

Ask yourself if your preachers, politicians, and friends seem to be open to learning about their perspectives or are they frozen in their defensive preconceptions when they're making fun of or being dismissive of others.

Think back over the last few days. How much of your own thoughts, words, and actions express a feeling of Dissmell or Disgust?

Where did you learn who and what to associate with Dissmell or Disgust?

CHAPTER 12

Meet the Affects, Part 7: Fear-Terror

We have just one more Affect to explore. The last Affect Tomkins found on the faces of infants is the range he called Fear-Terror. I have saved this one for last because it can be such a problematic Affect for so many people. It also plays a big role in communities and movements.

Take a minute to think about your own experience of Fear. What are some of the images you associate with this Affect? How do you manage your feelings of fear? Do you like being scared on rollercoasters, scary movies, and haunted houses? Or do you tend to avoid situations that may trigger your Fear Affect?

Tomkins believed that the Fear Affect is triggered whenever our tide of neural firing and density rises more rapidly than the pattern of firing that triggers our Excitement Affect.

As we have discussed with the other Affects, for infants the triggering stimuli is the sensory experience itself. As we grow older, however, Fear is triggered just as easily by our internal stimuli — the images that reside in our memory and imagination. These internal stimuli can be either images we hold as a negative anticipation of the future *or* images of our past trauma. Either of these types of stimuli are sufficient catalysts for magnifying our current level of fear into a higher orbit.

What this means is that it's possible to panic, not because there is any significant threat at play in the moment, but because our minds have suddenly become awash in negative anticipation. And then, as with all Affects, we develop scripts for Fear based on our exposure to particular experiences, and these scripts then shape our automated responses and rituals.

Some of us manage our feelings of fear by staying clear of situations that might trigger our Fear Affect. We may withdraw at first from only a few particular settings where we have felt fear in the past, like public speaking or flying in an airplane. This withdrawal can become more problematic as it spreads to more facets or our lives.

Others manage feelings of fear by numbing themselves to experiences that might trigger the Affect of Fear. A good example of this would be a script of immersion into the scary experiences of your life. This script can toughen you, like callouses on fingertips from regularly playing a guitar. In this kind of script, however, the fear response is muted at best, and sometimes it becomes hardly noticed, even in danger.

Some of us have had the exact opposite experience with Fear. I have worked with many people who suffered from panic disorders, and I believe that the best way to describe many of their experiences is to say they developed a *fear* of Fear. Let me explain.

If for some reason you had an unexpected intense feeling of fear, it might seem overwhelming and disabling — as if you have lost control of your emotions. You feel defective in some way. Your mind races, looking for a solution: "What is wrong with me?" The source of this feeling of fear might seem totally unknown. For some people even taking cold medicine can trigger this out-of-control feeling.

The more your mind races, the more the fear is re-triggered, again and again. So now you've experienced what we know as a panic attack. It's really awful! But what is even worse is that now in your memory you have the image of this traumatic panic experience. What will happen the next time you feel fear begin to rise within you?

At this point, when any amount of Fear is triggered you are afraid of the feeling of fear, fearing that you will panic again. And ironically, that fear of your fear makes you panic again. The basic engine of your consciousness will call on the memory images from your previous panic episode to define what's going on. Remember, calling up our memory images is what this basic engine of consciousness does all the time.

Recalling past images associated with your Fear Affect is exactly the same as the process that recalls the image of where you left your phone. Unfortunately, when the image stored in your memory carries an intense level of Fear, that intensity adds more fuel to the Fear being triggered in the moment. This is how a one-time panic episode can predispose us to fear *any* Fear, and that feeling causes our escalation to panic, time after time.

I wish everyone who suffers from panic attacks could hear me when I say that I have seen major healing of this issue just by gaining awareness of this cycle. It is helpful not only to know that you are not alone, but also to learn why this cycle is happening and how to stop it. Ending panic attacks can sometimes be as simple as recognizing the things that I just shared and learning to welcome the feelings of fear rather than to automatically fear them. Yes, to find this healing means that you have to make friends with Fear and learn to replace those memory images of intense Fear with new images of productive responses to Fear.

One of the complicating factors of the Fear Affect for some folks is that they feel ashamed of their fear response, so for them, a panic episode is utterly humiliating. When we fear the Shame that would be triggered by having a panic episode in public, we bring *anticipatory imagery* into the mix. Now the images of possible future shame are triggering Fear, and the images of past panic are too. The mind is simply doing what it does, making meaning out of the moment with the images it has available for reference. It is easy to see how adding these can magnify even a small, passing fearful experience into a prolonged panic attack. Because of the way consciousness operates, most of this happens so automatically that we don't realize how our thoughts have been directed — so the first step in managing panic is to get out of our heads and focus on the senses.

The good news is that the work of healing these destructive dynamics is the very same work I have chosen to call Choosing to Evolve. When someone who has suffered from Panic Disorder learns to manage the Fear Affect differently, he or she is already learning to work with consciousness in a new way. These people can become amazing teachers for the rest of us.

Conflicting Fear Scripts

Since we all have unique scripts for experiencing and expressing Fear, it seems likely that these differences will be a source of conflict in our relationships and in our culture. Imagine a young man just out of the service who comes home to his wife and kids. Let's say he is one of the lucky ones to come home without issues like Post Traumatic Stress Disorder (PTSD).

But one day his wife is talking about her fears about global warming. As she expresses her concern about how the warming planet may impact their children, his eyes turn a little cold. He is dismissive, maybe even disgusted. She is sounding like a "frigging Green Peace tree hugger." Maybe he makes fun of her in even more sarcastic ways.

From there the conflict between them grows worse. This escalation is not just because they have different scripts around the acknowledgement of Fear, but also because the conflict *itself* has created a loss of empathy and emotional connection between them. Any conversation we have that turns into defending or attacking causes us to lose empathy for the other person's experience, making it very hard to build any real understanding.

Taking this same dynamic back to a more global perspective — from a more cultural/political vantage point — I think both progressives and conservatives have tried to motivate their followers with fear. But here's the thing. Sure, you can make a case for *all* of these fears. There *is* danger in the world, and Fear is there to keep us remembering that. However, neither denying fear nor living in a state of panic is helpful to anyone. In both cases we are missing important input to our choices.

Widening the scope a little bit more now, it becomes easier to see that when Fear is triggered by some threat to our ideological imagery, it can be very hard to work through. One of the keys to talking through our deepest differences is to first acknowledge the images *we* carry — and where we got them. Then, when we can acknowledge our Fear that is associated with any threat to those images, we can begin to have more productive dialogue with those whose ideological imagery is different from our own.

When FDR uttered his famous quote, "The only thing we have to fear is fear itself," I know he was trying to prevent widespread panic, so I really don't mean this critically; however, I do need to interject a bit of clarity here. The fear of Fear is Panic, and while repressing our Fear may be helpful at times, it can also put us in great danger of making choices that are not wise.

I don't want to board a flight and hear the pilot come over the speakers saying, "I wish we didn't have to fly today because the weather is really scary looking and I'm not sure I can do this." But I also don't want to board a flight where the pilot has become so numb to Fear that he or she might fly right into a storm to save time — or fly when he or she is exhausted or otherwise impaired.

It is important to mention that a big part of our culture finds relief from Fear in religious beliefs. Believing in life after death, the power of prayer, and the supernatural "miracle" acts of God offer us important images that empower courage in the face of danger. It is not my intention to challenge or undermine any of that. I must point out, however, that sometimes these beliefs can create a self-fulfilling prophecy.

Faith may provide great relief to our fears of death and provide a wisdom and courage for living our life. However, the less we fear the end of the world because of our faith in the salvation of God and our promised place in Heaven, the less we may listen to the Fear within us that would otherwise direct us to respond more actively to threats.

There are those whose faith seems to direct them toward a certainty that all manner of evil should just be expected and tolerated because "the end is coming soon." No action on our part required. Do you see any scripts here? I do! Scripts that serve to deny Fear, the very Affect that might otherwise motivate our rapid, productive response to global issues, are snuffing out our chance of making real changes in the world for the good of everyone.

How does your spiritual experience shape your Fear scripts? Have you ever used religion to numb your Fear? Do your beliefs create a way to rationalize a life that is fearless? Is it possible that this rationalization is creating a problem for you when it comes to feeling motivated to face real dangers and make positive changes in your life?

Fear is a part of our innate human consciousness for a reason. Perhaps it would be helpful for us to stop using our spiritual images to deny Fear and allow faith to play its most important role — providing us with the inspiration we need to confront the *sources* of our Fear.

The Evolving Consciousness and Fear

Imagine what would happen if the threat of global warming were to trigger the same level of Fear as the warring factions did during World War II? What kind of amazing mobilization might occur? Unfortunately, the gradual nature of this kind of threat does not provide the urgency that bombs and bullets do. Even the images we see of gradually rising seas are unlikely to serve as an adequate trigger for our collective Fear until it is too late to do anything about this problem. Perhaps it would be more effective in triggering our collective Fear to show more images of the *end result* of global warming instead.

Some threats don't trigger a Pearl Harbor moment. They just gradually impede our life experience until it is too late. We need Fear, not Panic. We need a consciousness capable of letting Fear crack open our denial and direct our attention to the breaking dam, telling us to. "Rise up out of your sleep — and bring a shovel!"

The consciousness that is evolving knows how to de-habituate its images and how to allow Affect and imagery to be transient, even the imagery we hold of ourselves. Similarly, the evolving consciousness knows how to choose when and where to allow emotional motivation and expression to flow freely (as in the flow of Excitement-Joy at the birth of a child), and when, in other circumstances, to place the emerging emotion under observation and questioning — to Move Alongside emotion to allow it to help us be Learners.

The new evolving consciousness is also awake to the limitations of scripting, making us more capable of both deeper intimacy and productive conflict. The more we know our own emotional story, the more we are able to enter conflict with balance, empathy, and flexibility. Without gaining this kind of understanding about the emotions that motivate us, we remain blind to our true experience — and vulnerable to being manipulated by those who do.

CHAPTER 13

Taking the Next Step

Now that you have a greater idea of the components of consciousness that we have explored, you will probably begin to notice things about yourself or others that you haven't observed before. Maybe you have begun to hear the voices in the media — and within your own house or head — with a new awareness. You notice the emotional dynamics attached to the imagery that has been habituated. Maybe you see Shame scripts playing their role in some conflicts and other issues you observe.

Knowledge is power, they say, but how we *wield* that power is the key question. It is important to Wake Up to the habituated nature of our limited imagery. But what does this mean? What to do with this new awareness? There is an old Buddhist saying, "Before enlightenment, chop wood, carry water. After enlightenment, chop wood, carry water." In some ways this is the core message of this chapter. More awareness doesn't mean you cease to do the same daily practices that sustain life for yourself and others. It does mean, however, that you approach those practices with a different awareness.

For example: Perhaps you have become aware that you have a defensive layer to your personality. Let's say it's an Avoidance script that has helped you manage your Shame for many years. Now the script is as habituated as the way you drive your car, and you are *really* good at driving your car. As you practice following the thread of your new awareness, you will begin to notice the Avoidance script as you go about your life. As you catch yourself doing the old script you will practice Moving Alongside the emotional evasion and observe the experience long enough to shift your attention to welcoming the emotion that you are avoiding. All of this happens in the midst of doing the same things you have done before, only now you are gaining the capacity to experience the world without Avoiding Shame.

There are some of us who have grown up in the information age who have been so continually bombarded with insights and ideas that we have not identified with any of them. One young man once asked me: "Why are you reading that book?" I responded by trying to describe what had drawn me to the contents and the author. "No, that's not what I mean," he said. "Why that book and not all the others you could be reading. My father would probably never read that book... There are so many books out there! How am I supposed to decide which ones are important?"

What this thoughtful young man was expressing is the distress I have heard many times from the Internet generations. It is a side effect of growing up in a world with so many images that it is difficult to personally identify with any of them. So for some of us, the challenge is to even begin the process of growing an identity. If this describes you, then your journey of evolving may need to begin with identification with something. What do you love? What makes you curious? What is life about for you? Sure, these things will change as you grow and learning leads to learning, but it is important to begin somewhere and fall in love with something.

The key to Choosing to Evolve is not just gaining awareness of our habituated patterns and learning to Move Alongside them. It is how and when we choose to do that. It is to honor both the capacities and the limitations that our habituation processes bring to our lives and to gain the ability to recognize when we need to flow with our habituation and when we need to move our attention to the level of awareness that can help us de-habituate.

So before we move on to look at how we may apply this awakening to various arenas of our lives, let's look at a few mistakes we could make in applying the knowledge we have explored so far.

Healthy Self-Doubt versus Self-Consciousness

Some of us come to this awakening with emotional scripts that already predispose us to being self-conscious about what we think, say, or do. In fact, people who don't have some degree of self-consciousness are less likely to pick up a book like this one.

Any number of scripts may play a part in what we call self-consciousness, but in general it seems to develop as a tentativeness about trusting your own perceptions and imagery. Now that, in and of itself, is not a bad thing. People who have learned to live with a certain amount of self-doubt would be among those we have called "the meek," right?

Here's the thing. There is a difference between having a capacity for questioning your images and perceptions and having an insecurity about owning those questions. This distinction is important, so let me give an example.

Imagine that you are in a conversation, and somewhere along the way it turns toward a political issue that you don't really know much about. Other people in the conversation seem to be opinionated and confident of their perspectives, but you feel unclear about what you think or feel about the issues being discussed. You have some ideas, but you don't feel as sure about them as the others seem to feel about theirs.

Self-awareness and self-confidence don't have to be at odds with one another. It is possible to confidently enter into dialogue as a Learner and to bring questions to the conversations that are helpful to everyone. Sometimes, however, we can't do that, due to scripts we have that trigger Shame. In this case, self-consciousness is a label we can give to what we feel when this Shame is triggered.

In that moment, if you stay silent or move out of the conversation, you may be Withdrawing to preempt the possibility of more Shame. You could also flip to an Attack-Self script and say something like, "I don't follow politics it's just too complicated!" Or perhaps you might attempt to change the subject to something you *are* knowledgeable about to Avoid the Shame. Depending on how much Shame is triggered in the conversation, you might even have Attack-Other scripts that have you thinking about the others as stupid, ignorant, or some other negative image.

Once we understand that self-consciousness is mostly just a label for how we experience these kinds of moments, we can return to the image we have explored about the path of meekness that can help minimize defensiveness. Remember, Shame need not be defended against. It is a normal part of our daily experience. It signals the opportunity to learn through embracing what is not known as opposed to escaping it. This can happen only when we are more identified with growing and learning than we are defending and controlling.

To Flow or to Observe

As we have suggested, Choosing to Evolve is about choosing when to flow with our habituated scripts and when to enter a process of Moving Alongside our feelings in order free ourselves from our limited images and stuck emotional scripts that are at the root of our suffering. The question is, how do we know when should we flow with our automated scripts and imagery and when we should Move Alongside?

It would not be possible to fully de-habituate our lives, nor should we try. Life is not likely to become discernably better if you forget how to talk or hold your sippy cup. But there are times when de-habituation is the only path to wellbeing. If we do not practice the art of Moving Alongside in some situations, we can get lost in the spirals of our own labyrinths — and sometimes in other people's as well.

At the same time, too much disruption to our habituated patterns can create a sense of life becoming more difficult. That is because the very nature of habituation leads to effortless automation that allows us to shift our attention to other things. Without that level of development you couldn't read and understand this book. This system is at the core of all of our abilities, and, oddly enough, it can actually help us to manage our habituation. In other words, with practice, we can habituate/automate our capacity to de-habituate! When we get there, we'll find Moving Alongside to be just as effortless as flowing with our habituated scripts and images.

So the key to Choosing to Evolve the way we participate in consciousness is in what I would call the playful practice of de-habituation. The more we practice this when the game is not on the line, the more we experience having the capacity to Move Alongside in the big moments when more is at stake. So as you participate in doing the exercises included in the previous chapters, try to have fun with them. It's not about trying to create perfection or Shame ourselves into higher consciousness. It is all about the beauty of life that can be found in the freedom of Waking Up.

Shaming the Shame Scripts

Perhaps the biggest mistake people tend to make as they learn about the defensive scripts we all tend to develop around Shame is to begin criticizing the people in their lives for using them. I repeat this now as a way to emphasize this issue because it can create more disturbance than it resolves.

Remember that defensive scripts are the coping mechanisms we employ when our positive self-imagery is threatened by intense Affect, and to take away or undermine that coping mechanism will tend to force us to confront what we needed to avoid. These forced confrontations are more likely to produce greater defensiveness than before unless they happen in a setting and relationship of unconditional positive regard.

Many of the intractable conflicts I have witnessed in couples therapy have centered around two people attacking each other's Shame scripts. This is a no-win situation. One person Withdraws and the other Attacks and the cycle goes round and round for years with each person feeling all the more righteous in their defensive scripts. In every case, the answer for the stuck cycle starts with accepting the necessity for the defenses. That is what opens the door for change and transforms the argument into a dialogue.

These are the precise moments when we need to find Ariadne's thread. These strands of insight we have been exploring can guide us through the layers of our defenses — the barriers we have built in our hearts. The more we have learned about our uniquely-scripted emotional world, the more that thread can help us see through scenes like this. We begin to see the argument for what it is — two people trying desperately and defensively to hold onto their own positive imagery and causing even more conflict in the process.

Following this thread looks like this: I pause in the flow of the argument in order to take hold of the thread. This lifeline is my connection to the aspects of my consciousness that are not caught up in the defensive script. Remembering the insights we have been exploring allows me to Move Alongside my emotion of the moment and the thoughts that these emotions are generating. I turn my focus to the sensations of my body and I become curious. I remember how these arguments never solve anything. I regain empathy for the plight of my partner who is struggling to hold on to a positive sense of self, just like I am. I recognize these Shame scripts as a trap that always ends up creating more conflict between us. The intensity of the feelings begins to pass, as the imagery of my thoughts no longer retrigger the emotional response.

At this point it may help to, first, remember the positive experiences that have been shared. Second, to postpone further conversation until we are not fixated on the issue at hand in such a way that all the positives of the relationship are ignored. And then, at that later moment, we can enter into a less defensive process of inquiry into what each person is experiencing of the issue. This inquiry must include both partners sharing their images and emotional attachment to those images openly while listening with empathy to the other.

This process is our best hope of having a real conversation and stopping the cycles of Shame scripts that destroy our relationships. The alternative is to escalate the conflict or escape it unless one person gains an upper hand and overpowers the other. In this case, he or she may well win the argument — but damage the relationship even more. You can win an argument and still be wrong.

It also must be said that there are times when Shame scripts can make someone unwilling or unable to do the work I have just described. Maybe they are just too insecure or traumatized to become vulnerable. Whatever the reason, sometimes we are just not capable of the kind of intimate relationship desired by our partner. It is easy to see how intense anger and even violence can erupt given the scripts we have explored. These insights can be important for determining whether or not a relationship is safe.

I highly recommend that you address your *own* defensive scripts in this same way. Begin by just noticing that everyone develops some process to defend against negative Affect. You are not fatally flawed and your defensive scripts are only a part of your experience. Go gently. Get curious. Be open to discovering something you never realized about your own imagery and scripts.

Shame scripts are often secondary to something else. When you begin to face and embody the Shame you avoided through your defensive scripts, you may remember the time when this particular Shame was first triggered. The scenes in which the Shame was first triggered are more important to awareness than the defensive scripts that followed.

Learning what dynamics led to the Shame in the first place is where our greatest growth may occur. However, uncovering the issues at the center of the defensive labyrinth will never happen when you or your partner are caught up in shaming your Shame scripts.

So there are two aspects to working through defensive scripts. First there is the process of looking back to understand the origin of the script. Sometimes this leads to new insights into the dynamics of our earlier experience that triggered Shame in the first place. There are many examples of this spread throughout the book, but these early dynamics often involve trauma that sets us spinning into defensive scripts as we attempt to manage the Shame. Over time, these defensive scripts become the cause of conflict or rejection in later relationships.

Recognizing these early dynamics and working through them is the first aspect of healing them. The second is the recognizing the defensive script itself. Even though we recognize and heal the trauma and dynamics that led to the need for defensive scripts, those scripts have likely become quite habituated over time. In fact, they may continue even after the healing of the deeper issues that birthed them. To learn how to stop running, withdrawing, drinking, escaping, showing off, or attacking others requires the practice of de-habituation that we will continue to explore in the coming chapters.

It Helps To Have a Map

As a child, your challenge is to fill your absorbent mind with the world. Exposure to images and habituation of activities will provide a great deal of capacity as you mature. There will come a time, however, when some of that habituation will begin to *limit* your capacity for growth and function. Then, in order to continue growing, you will need consciousness, creativity, and commitment.

The material we have just reviewed is a map to help us explore where we get stuck and why some habituation is resistant to change. If we know that the basic engine of consciousness is the habituation of imagery that allows us to move through life with a sense of knowing things, and that this imagery is attached to emotional scripts and Affects that direct our attention before we even know it, then we have a map that can provide creative possibilities for participating in the automated processes of our consciousness in a new way.

The reason we can Choose to Evolve is that once we gain knowledge of these inner workings of our minds we gain a new capacity to participate in our consciousness differently. The more that you build this awareness of your own images and scripts, the more you begin to realize when you might need to practice paying attention in a different way. We can find freedom through this combination of awareness and practice.

The awareness I'm referring to here comes from our loving acceptance and curiosity for self-reflection as we learn how our story has defined us. Where did you lose Affective plasticity as you were socialized to feel or not feel certain things? What are the images to which you were socialized?

The practice we must develop in order to find freedom involves the habituation of activities that will help us *de*-habituate when needed. Mindfulness, Moving Alongside, sensory-focused meditation, and learning to direct our attention to the immediacy of the moment are among these practices, and we will explore them as we move through the coming chapters.

Chop Wood, Carry Water

Mindfulness isn't about sitting on a mountaintop in a puddle of bliss. At least not in the context we're exploring here. The kind of mindfulness we're seeking in our Choosing to Evolve is more about training our mind to focus on our freedom to embrace what is, as it is, and to participate whole-heartedly, with total affective plasticity, and without fixations. Learning how to live with a sense of presence and without defensiveness is well worth the work it takes to heal our stuck patterns. This awakening can open us to a whole new world.

The practices we are exploring can transform your life — and even offer salvation. The meaning of the word, "salvation" as defined in Hebrew scriptures is one of wholeness and wellbeing, and it is not meant so much personally as it is communally. Salvation is for *us* — not just me.

Imagine sharing some of what you are learning with others and what practicing these insights together might do to change the very nature of our communities. In the coming chapters we will explore more arenas of life where Choosing to Evolve can address many of the issues that are at the heart of our human struggles.

Take a Knee Here and Let This Settle

Before you move on to SECTION III, I'd like to suggest you take a good long pause here to let this information "soak in" a little bit more deeply. Go back and actually do all those exercises (or do them again!) and allow yourself some time and space to really consider the life-changing impact this material could have if you can learn to apply it in your own life — starting in the most obvious places at first, and then expanding to all the other areas of your life as well.

My reasoning for suggesting this here is two-fold: First, now that you've learned some new things about how your consciousness works, this awareness alone will help open you up to receiving and applying this information on deeper and deeper levels. And, the more you actually begin to work with this information, the more ways you'll see to apply it. This knowledge is what makes it possible to even *notice* the scripts in your life. To do this, however, you have to do the quiet work now of getting still, turning this information over and over in your mind, and just looking around your life, particularly in areas where you see patterns that may not be serving you, and just get curious about what scripts may be there.

Second, taking some intentional time at this point in this book to really absorb all we've explored so far will help make this information more accessible and applicable to you going forward. By moving beyond an academic understanding of what I'm presenting here, you can only begin to integrate this information to attain real help in your life once you fully incorporate the exercises and suggestions I've provided into your awareness. With this increased awareness you will be well prepared to use the tools and practices in the coming pages to learn to manage and participate in your consciousness in a whole new way.

Remember, this is the gentle work of meekness. Don't force it. Some of what we are exploring is challenging to our habituated patterns, and these patterns offer stability even if they are destructive. I suggest that you spend some time playfully enjoying instability as you do this work. Play with *enjoying* not knowing — and not needing to know. Notice that the world doesn't come to an end when you actively embrace its mystery.

SECTION III

Waking Up:
A New Way to Participate in Your Life

Chapter 14

Fight or Flight — Freeze or Please

Now that we have explored human consciousness from both the memory/anticipation/habituation angle and the scripted emotion perspectives, there is one more aspect of habituated consciousness we need to explore before we begin to bring it all together. By now I think we can all agree that given all of the ways human beings develop emotional scripts, conflict is inevitable. This is true even when you grow up as a part of the same culture or family. Even differences in birth order can impact our self-imagery and how we learn to feel about things.

If you want to encounter some of the scripts you have developed in the course of growing up, then get involved in a long-term intimate relationship. I doubt that there is any arena of life that is more likely to become a mirror for your dominant scripts. In an intimate relationship you will be forced to face the uniqueness of your own habituated imagery and emotional scripts, but you may also be drawn to encounters that mimic the very forces that created those scripts in the first place.

I have yet to meet a couple that did not find this to be true. And, whether these scenarios become opportunities for personal growth and healing or lead to even greater scripted defenses depends largely upon how a couple learns to manage their conflicts.

So what do we do when conflict emerges? How can we manage conflict in a way that protects and enhances our important relationships? What would the meek do?

As I'm sure you can imagine by now, how we *deal* with a conflict is a concern at least equal to — if not more important than — the conflict itself. In fact, it is how we manage the conflict in our lives that determines much of our life experience. Personal growth, spiritual maturity, relational intimacy, parenting, and cultural health are all impacted by our ability to process and address our conflicts in a healthy way.

In the personal sphere, how we approach conflict will determine how open we are to others, how much we learn from one another, whether we can interact with others successfully, and so much more. How do you feel when you sense a conflict emerging? What Affect is most often triggered for you?

In our intimate relationships, we often have a tendency to confuse intimacy with harmony. Sure, harmonious interaction is great, but it's not always all that intimate. The more honest and open we are with another person, the more we reveal those aspects of ourselves that are different. As we have already discussed, human beings don't always deal very well with diversity, likely because of the ways in which we tend to cling to static images of ourselves, others, and the world as we have experienced it.

As parents, how we deal with conflict is probably the single most important skill we can learn. Our children don't just learn *what* we tell them, but *how* we tell them: *How* do we wield our influence over others? *How* do we gain control (or try to gain control) during a conflict? Our children's observations of our own conflict resolution skills in action will likely impact their development in this area as much — if not more — than the content of *what* we tell them about conflict.

Within the social/political world it is easy to see the dysfunctional way human beings tend to handle conflict. And, because the level of enlightenment in a country's political elite most often reflects the state of its people's inner awareness, learning to manage conflict well is up to us. In other words, if we want better government, then we must become masters of conflict.

Strategies in Conflict

World-renowned German Psychoanalyst Karen Horney theorized that there are three basic strategies we develop as children for managing conflict. We Move Toward the other, we Move Away from the other, or we Move Against the other. Further, she believed that *all* of her patients' neurotic experiences could be traced to the overuse or underuse of one or more of these strategies.

So when we Move Toward another in conflict, we set aside our own plans and needs, join with the other, and build bridges of understanding. In other words, we become "pleasers." When we Move Away from someone with whom we experience a conflict, we find a way to escape the current moment and find another time and place to get what we need. When we Move Against another during conflict, we "stand our ground" and "fight for our rights," perhaps because we grew up learning that we had to fight for what we wanted. Some of us learn all three of these strategies for managing conflict. Some of us learn only one. What's important to remember here is that none of these strategies is good or bad, and each of these three strategies has its upside and its downside. Horney believed that each of these strategies has its appropriate time and place in our lives.

Moving Toward

On the positive side, Moving Toward the other in conflict can bring about reconciliation and quick resolution to conflict. On the downside, overuse or exclusive use of this strategy tends to create a dynamic that looks more like codependency. As the old joke about codependency goes, "You know you are codependent when you are about to die and someone else's life flashes before your eyes." Always setting aside one's own dreams and desires to make things better for others may be noble, but this Moving Toward strategy often leads to resentment. I have worked with many people, mostly women, who seemed to have been trained from childhood to deny themselves so completely that at 35 or 40 they had very little idea what it was they truly wanted.

Moving Away

When we Move Away, we don't waste precious time in a conflict that has no hope of successful resolution. That's the upside of this strategy. And sometimes, it is good to know how to walk away. Think of all the times that your parent or spouse was so overwhelmed with other issues that to enter into a conflict with them about your own needs would only make things worse for both of you. In these cases, it's far better to "keep your powder dry" and wait for a better moment when communication might be more successful.

The downside (or overuse) of this strategy is that we are always running away from conflict, sabotaging all the possible learning and transformation that could come from our exposure to differences.

When we Move Away, we don't learn how to negotiate, discover our capacity for standing our ground, or discover the common ground of joining with the other. We find ourselves running away from one scene after another.

Moving Against

The upsides of Moving Against others in conflict is that we usually get what we want, people always know what we think, and we can most often be assertive about our hopes and dreams — not only for ourselves, but for others as well. Families that are good at these strategies are almost playful in their fighting; their conflict doesn't undermine their sense of attachment — it tends to deepen it!

The downside (that tends to come with overuse) of the Moving Against strategy is that we turn every conversation into a fight. And, if we are blind to our own pre-conceptions and resort to the vilification of others, even worse things can happen. In this case we may even develop a false sense of victimization: "Our way of life (or faith, or beliefs, or values, or traditions) are under attack," when actually the conflict we're experiencing is merely evidence that we live in a diverse society.

Your Strategy in Conflict

Horney's childhood strategy model has often yielded insights into relationship issues for the people with whom I've worked. Sometimes I can see these different strategies at play with a couple in our very first session together. For instance, consider what can happen for two people who are habituated to different strategies. What if you never Move Away, but you marry someone who always does? What if you both always Move Against, but neither of you has any experience in Moving Toward?

Consider the various combinations of these strategies and how they might be a part of the dynamics in your own relationships. Then see if you can notice these dynamics in the larger cultural dialogue about national and international issues.

You may also notice that these strategies seem to mimic the Compass of Shame. I believe it is likely that Horney and Nathanson were looking at some of the same scripts, but through different lenses. Horney, without the opportunity to be exposed to the work of Silvan Tomkins, could not have known that these strategies were automated scripts that developed over time from the triggering of Affect. Still, her insights can be helpful in understanding our responses.

Conflict is almost always an impediment to positive Affect and therefore usually a potent trigger for Shame. If we fail to notice this, we may be easily drawn into whatever script we have developed to manage our Shame, thereby short-circuiting any new awareness.

Let's pause here for a moment of reflection. What is *your* dominant strategy? Which of the three are your "go to" responses in most of your conflicts? Which of the three do you employ the least?

Simply developing this awareness can save you from a life spent imprisoned in a repetitive experience. Always joining, always running, or always fighting — or the opposites: never joining, never walking away, or never standing up for your truth — can be a source of great limitation and suffering. Understanding this simple system of sorting our responses to conflict can lead to a fair amount of enlightenment if you take the time to reflect on your own tendencies.

Awareness is not the only thing required for changing our habituated scripts. That kind of transformation also requires both creativity and commitment. Sometimes we need new images — and lots of practice. To dig into this idea a little more deeply, let's go back and examine conflict resolution from the perspective of meekness. Maybe by looking to those who have developed the capacity to let their own images be "in process" — and who can allow Shame to happen without defending against its threat to their self-imagery — we can discover a new model for managing conflict.

Which of Horney's three conflict strategies do the meek tend to embody? The answer may surprise you: All of them. I say this because each of these three strategies, when done with humility and non-defensiveness, can emulate meekness.

In times of conflict, meekness offers a path for retaining empathy for the other. Meekness is all about knowing when to step back from a conflict to help another person recover his or her positive sense of self. It is also about knowing the difference between assertively speaking your truth and desires versus aggressively demanding your own way. I must add, however, that I believe there is yet another strategy for managing conflict that the meek also employ that is none of the above. As presumptuous as it may seem, I believe Horney missed a fourth childhood defense strategy: Moving Alongside.

Moving Alongside

When we are able to Move Alongside someone during conflict, we are not joining, fleeing, *or* fighting. We are letting the moment of conflict simply exist on its own for a while. We are stretching time and allowing for an opening to happen for empathy on both sides to help create an unforeseen solution. What's funny is that I see this response/strategy in young children more than older ones — and almost never in teenagers and adults.

You see, young children are quick to recognize that there are many things that are beyond their understanding. Because much of verbal communication requires years of exposure, children are able to just "go along," and continue to relate to others who are clearly doing and saying things that the children do not understand. In situations of conflicting desires, sometimes a young child may inquire about a point of conversation or tell us about how they are making sense of the world, but they are not really joining, leaving *or* fighting. They are Moving Alongside until they can comprehend what is going on.

The good news is that while children seem to come by this strategy naturally, in certain situations adults do, too. Though they may hardly even notice it when they are Moving Alongside, we see this strategy happening in adults during conflict when they are able to pause in order to become mindful of what is emerging in themselves or in the conversation. This pause gives them a chance to reflect non-defensively on the issue at hand and see things with greater empathy.

In his book, *Dialogue, the art of thinking together*, William Isaacs presents the Core Choice Diagram that seems to illustrate what I am calling Moving Alongside. Isaacs suggests that when conflict or deliberation emerges in a conversation, we make a fundamental choice whether to suspend judgment or become defensive. It is this "suspending of judgment" that I am referring to as Moving Alongside.

Suspending judgment, or Moving Alongside, allows my image of the moment, of myself, of the other, and of the world to be "in process" and not yet finished. By also suspending my need to *defend* those images, I gain the capacity for real conversation in which all sides in conflict can reflect on the images they carry, where they got them, and what meaning they are attributing to them. In an outward way, we are literally taking a walk together — moving down the road a piece without running away, appeasing, or fighting.

This image, of "moving down the road together", reminds me of my childhood when my brother and I would fight. My parents would often tell us to go run around the block — in opposite directions. (I'm thinking now that they didn't really care what happened on the other side of the block, as long as it didn't happen in the house!) More often than not, we had let off steam by the time we passed each other on the other side, and I suppose we would have been embarrassed to be fighting in some stranger's front yard.

While I think my parents were onto something (whether or not they realized why), I wonder what would have been different if they had said, "Let's go for a walk," and then, as we walked together, reminded us of what good friends we were to each other most of the time. What if then they had given each of us a chance to express what we wanted to say in a way that wasn't defensive or blaming? Maybe that would have worked better — and maybe this image will help you the next time you find yourself embroiled in conflict with someone you care deeply about.

Moving Alongside those with whom we encounter conflict is a way to deepen the sense of connection we need to build understanding. Without that deeper connection, you may win the arguments, but what you lose in the process is the trust and care in that relationship. Many a marriage has been demolished as a result of the wounds created when empathy and trust dissolved in a defensive argument that somebody "won."

And, taking this concept inside ourselves, Moving Alongside is precisely what must happen for someone to be able to reflect on his or her own images and emotions without Shame or blame. In this scenario, we allow ourselves to become aware of a feeling while holding it with a sort of curiosity, rather than judgment. This capacity is the cornerstone of our consciousness evolution *and* the empowering quality of meekness.

The In-tension-al Life

As we become more aware of the limitations of our imagery and of how our emotions can be scripted in defensive ways, we can learn to Move Alongside those responses — and sometimes to transform them. This process of Moving Alongside points to the opportunity for the evolutionary leap the entire human race now faces. Human consciousness could evolve through simply habituating more and more images, along with fine motor skills, and it is likely that this evolution will happen in some way whether we Choose to Evolve or not.

As I see it, the only real choice we have in our evolution comes when we gain the capacity to Moving Alongside our habituated processes and learn the skills required to live with greater intentionality. At the heart of this work is the capacity to retain enough stability in our self-imagery that in the midst of conflict we are not so threatened that we automatically employ our defensive scripts. It is also helpful if we are able to adopt such a sense of wonder at our own human journey that we embrace being Learners. With this image at the core of our identity, we can embrace the ambiguity of not knowing — without needing our defensive scripts. Ambiguity — letting there be a time where we are not judging or deciding but merely exploring — is the key to Moving Alongside.

That is not to say that we can't let go and roll with our images and emotions to appreciate the joy and beauty of life. It only means that we now have the capacity for more choices, particularly in those inevitable moments when the diversity we encounter offers us an opportunity for productive conflict.

As the world becomes smaller, the greatest threats may be not so much in the conflicts that emerge from diversity, but rather from how we deal with these conflicts. One of the challenges in our digital, socially networked world is that conflicting perspectives are often treated as more important than relationships. And what's worse, the ability to anonymously eviscerate someone online has brought out the worst in us as human beings.

When we have no commitment to each other and no agreements about how to work through issues together, we usually become defensive. When we become defensive, the tone and intensity of the conflict then escalates. Eventually, when this spiral of conflict proves useless at producing anything positive, the result is that both sides withdraw from one another. At this point, a married couple may stay legally married, but they are emotionally divorced. And, on a grander scale, you could say the same for much of the important public discourse today. Lacking the skills we need for productive conflict and having limited commitment to one another as fellow citizens, we retreat to the bunkers of our well-defended positions, hiding from any possibility of a doubt or question that might create a moment of ambiguity.

Some people, however, are taking a new path, evolving into a greater acceptance of ambiguity. By becoming more at home with not having to have all the answers, is it possible that we as a people could one day find our sense of security in our capacity to learn, rather than in clinging to our certainties? Could we then someday evolve into a people who celebrate the mystery of not knowing?

"Life is not a problem to be solved, but a mystery to be lived."
— Sam Keen

"Out beyond ideas of wrong doing and right doing, there is a field, I'll meet you there. When the soul lies down in that grass, the world is too full to talk about. Ideas and language, even the phrase, each other, doesn't make any sense."
— Rumi

A Risky Business

Because each person is different, shaped by life experiences, and chock full of images and emotional scripts gathered through the years like shells that washed up on our beach, we experience every single moment in time differently from one another in ways that are hard to imagine. The same is true for our words, including this communication we are having right now as you read my words on this page.

Every word I have written here likely triggers something different for every reader. For example, if I write, "I think allot of the books people read are simply bullshit," one reader may feel a certain friendly companionship with me — while another is quite offended at my choice of the word, "bullshit."

Depending on how you feel about the last book you read, whether you ever read at all, how you were taught to feel about books, and whether you studied language enough to know that I used the wrong spelling for "a lot," your unique response to that sentence will be all your own.

To have a conversation about anything important is to engage in a history lesson between its players. True conversation is like spelunking in the caves of the heart to discover that the ancient paintings on the walls are unique to every soul. This eternal truth is just one reason why my use of the word, "meek," is a bit risky.

Imagine a former slave reading this book. How could someone whose life has been consumed by years of powerlessness be drawn to the idea that meekness could save the planet? The impulse within that person would likely be a desire to dominate the dominators. On the other hand, those who have suffered the most from another's domination and abuse of power may hunger and thirst the most for a new vision of how power and authority are shared.

Granted, it is hard to imagine the kind of personal strength it would take for a former slave to Moving Alongside a former slave owner. Meekness often requires *exactly* this kind of courage, and we must acknowledge that it is not always possible. The meek are able to see that *all* people are acting, feeling, and perceiving through the patterns to which their consciousness has been programmed by their previous experiences. Sometimes Moving Against the destructive dynamics of another person *really is* the best option. In these situations, however, the meek never lose sight of the humanity of the other, and they always remember that their differences are as much a matter of chance as choice.

Many people struggle with some particular dynamic, often due to traumatic memories that create extreme sensitivity to particular images. Even the slightest hint of one of their traumatic images can trigger a flood of emotion — and then trigger scripted defenses against that flood. Moving Alongside can be impossible when we're locked in the throes of such a tsunami of emotion.

Imagine a woman who was sexually assaulted as a child. Now try to imagine that same woman as an innocent, trusting, six-year-old girl being manipulated by an adult. What might that have been like for her? How would this experience impact your images of your self — and of others or the world? How might it create carefulness, a hyper-vigilance for certain situations, tones of voice, or interactions with others?

It may be easy to see the way a trauma of this kind might brand itself into someone's consciousness. What is harder to see is that something like this happens to *all of us* in one way or another.

We are all shaped by the life experiences that predispose us to pay attention to some things and not others. We enter every moment with certain sensitivities — or lack thereof. These inclinations act like filters for our day-to-day encounters with the world around us. How conscious are you of these tendencies? Have you ever paused to notice them? How might an exploration of your emotional scripts reveal your own unique filters?

When you were young, did you ever play on a merry-go-round? When I was a kid, this piece of vintage playground equipment was my favorite part of going to the park. You don't see them much anymore; I would imagine that playground safety standards nixed them a long time ago — and probably for good reason.

I'll always remember how the older kids would get caught up in the excitement of spinning the thing around. I can remember barely being able to hold on at times as the centrifugal force pulled me toward what I assumed would be certain death. I also remember trying to stare at something as I went around in hopes of slowing down my dizziness in this whirling world. If you have ever had this merry-go-round experience, then you may recall learning that if you can stare at one particular spot as it goes by — and then quickly find another as the first one disappears from sight — it's a fairly effective way to stop the overwhelming rush of stimuli.

One way to consider this prime metaphor of old consciousness is to view it through this lens of fixation. Each of us, in some dizzying moment of life, became fixated on images of ourselves, of others, and of the world. These images then became the fixed points on our inner map, and we continued to fixate on them even when the stimuli were not as overwhelming. Sometimes fixation helps, but it can also rob you of your sense of flow. Let me take a moment here to demonstrate how you can observe this process physically.

I love to practice *not* fixating while riding in a car. The next time you are a passenger, try staring at the road in front of you right before it disappears under the hood of the car. As the asphalt flies by beneath you, notice the tendency you have to try to fixate on something stable. Try practicing *not* doing that. See if you can just flow with the car. After a few minutes look up and continue to not fixate. You may be amazed at how different everything feels. In the same way, when we learn to Moving Alongside our images and emotions — and even the fixations of our senses — we can get a visceral sense of flowing with life and what emotional freedom feels like.

Here is another exercise to illustrate how we can learn to disrupt our fixations: Lie down or sit in a place where you won't be interrupted for at least 10-15 minutes. Close your eyes and notice your breathing. Notice the sensations of the body. Then try placing your right hand on your heart and your left hand on your forehead. Just feel the warm pressure of the hand against your chest and the hand against your forehead.

Breathe into the hand on your chest and alternate that with breathing into the hand on your forehead. Don't think. Just give attention to the sensation for a few minutes. Now, practice "breathing into" both hands at the same time. Feel both of your hands equally, without giving more attention to one than the other. Now, try switching the positioning of your hands and continue the same practice.

Over time, you will find that this practice can help you disrupt some of the sensory fixations that tend to accompany your emotional scripts. These and other "de-habituation" exercises are just part of how we can gain some skills to modulate our more intense Affects. This kind of mindful de-habituation can help us learn how to return to our conflicts without defending — and with more capacity for suspending, or Moving Alongside.

I know that for some of you, all of this may seem way too far out of reach. The idea of practicing mindfulness or meditation techniques can be daunting — or even scary. If we stop our inward spinning, and if we stop fixating on whatever we have latched onto, what is there to stop us from sliding off of this mental merry-go-round and into the oblivion of confronting all that is wrong and bad and shameful within us?

I hope you can believe and understand that there is no judgment in this place of stillness. No judgment for your past mistakes or for your most shameful memories. No judgment for even your most unattractive traits, either. Don't be afraid of getting still. Don't fear your failings. Remember that it is our *brokenness* that opens us up to a bigger life. Often, what may seem like mistakes are just the results of images and emotional scripts set into motion long before we had the capacity for any real choice.

Our Conflict with Conscious Evolution

When you think about it, any *real* conversation we have allows for the exploration of our preconceptions. That kind of conversation may go something like this: "Where did each of us get our predispositions and sensitivities to [insert the subject at hand]? If you'll share your images with me, I'll share mine with you. Then we can explore what seems to be most important about each of them."

It's important to realize that dialogue of this kind is impossible when we are defensive, but it is our only pathway to true communication. Without dialogue that helps us identify and explore the preconceptions on our inner map in this way, we are doomed to a continuous cycle of one side winning an argument but leaving the other side feeling victimized and disenfranchised.

The hard work of *real* dialogue will unearth some of the fixations within us that have kept us stuck. And, once you taste the flow of life without fixation you will look forward to having those fixations broken again and again through compassionate dialogue.

Sometimes this can get complicated. The images we carry of ourselves, others, and the world can be intimately entangled in how we have learned to manage negative Affects. For instance, if my image of "heaven" plays a role in how I manage my Fear of death or my feelings of grief, then an experience of conflict over that image may threaten the role my imagery plays in regulating my emotions. So my belief in a heaven is not just a matter of faith — it is the only thing that is holding my uncomfortable feelings at bay.

When these kinds of issues emerge in our deepest conversations, it can be difficult to understand what's happening. Sometimes it may feel kind of like hitting a wall, but don't give up. Continue to Moving Alongside your own feelings and those of the other person. Just being present with one another — not running and not fighting — will provide the opportunity to hold the tension of the moment to become a Learner.

Remember my little analogy of the guitar string? Which is more free – the string on the guitar or the one in my hand? True dialogue is about revealing the tension and limits to which our images are strung. Learning and expansion can happen when we are in that awareness.

The practice of Moving Alongside is mostly about giving our attention to this new level of consciousness rather than to the habituated images that make up our map of our inner world, which is the actual territory of this momentary experience. Or, as German Semantics Scholar Alfred Korzybski famously said, "The map is not the territory."

The strategy of Moving Alongside may well be the key to moving *beyond* the stalemates of our conflicts. With practice, we can learn how to then shift our attention to the experience of the moment without fixating on one thing or another. In the process, we learn to take in "what is" with acceptance and silence.

The Silent Level of Consciousness

Though we may have a library of images and scripts that keep us moving through life with a sense of stability, providing the necessary illusion that we know things (and people, etc.), we must acknowledge another aspect to our experience. The practice of Moving Alongside is actually about moving our attention *away* from our images and *toward* our body's physical sensations. Even in the midst of conflict, moving our attention to the immediate body sensations of our momentary experience is a powerful practice for moving beyond the defenses and limitations of our habituated images.

Gary David, PhD, is a talented jazz musician who apprenticed with J. Samuel Bois in the 60s and 70s. He is certainly among the most knowledgeable people on the planet with regard to the works of Bois, Korzybski, and Tomkins. Gary calls this primary experience of life un-interpreted, without words, the Silent Level of experience. Before you try to make sense of, label, classify, or describe an experience, the Silent Level is its undefined flow.

Most of us don't give much attention to this level of experience, but it is always present. And, when we practice shifting our awareness to this Silent Level of experience, we can gain a greater capacity to move beyond our scripted responses. The Silent Level is our least scripted experience of life, even though it is still just a sip from the fire hose of all that is going on within each moment.

It's also important to realize here that even our most immediate experience of "what's going on" is directed by Affect, even before we become truly aware of it. So even our most "raw" experiences have already been filtered by whichever Affect is directing our attention in that moment. Still, this is the closest we'll get to our unfiltered life, something Alfred Korzybski called "First Order Experience."

The practices we are exploring as de-habituation, or Moving Alongside, will help us learn how to move our attention to this First Order Experience level of awareness. The Silent Level of our consciousness is more sensory than intellectual. Or, as Gary David puts it, "Acceptance is the key, and acceptance in this sense is more felt than thought — it's a releasing in the body."

When we are motivated to move our awareness to the Silent Level, we find that the world is, as always, gushing forth in its ecstatic dance. In my experience, a regular practice of bringing awareness to this level is the domain of mystics. It feels like all of creation steps forward to welcome us home again, to the place where we belong, where ideals, "oughts and shoulds" are poor substitutes for the poetry of the now. But here's the exciting news. This Silent Level of awareness is no longer just for mystics; it can be where we all actually live. As Matthew Fox once wrote, "All children are natural mystics. To be a mystic is the opposite of taking things for granted."

Draining the Swamp

In the 2016 presidential campaign in the United States, there was much talk about "Draining the Swamp." This rhetoric reminded me of how Robert Blye used the same language in his book, *Iron John*. In that story, the kingdom is in peril. No one who goes into the woods ever comes back. But one day a hero arrives and offers to go into the woods.

In many ways this story is also similar to the Greek myth, "Theseus and the Minotaur," that I shared earlier, but in the *Iron John* tale, the hero travels into the forest with his dog companion.

As they are passing a swamp, a big hairy arm comes out of the water and drags the dog under. The task of the hero then becomes to get a bucket and bail out the swamp to capture the wild man named Iron John. The rest of the story involves a boy who eventually sets Iron John free and in the process, enters his own journey of discovery and transformation.

Looking to the metaphorical meanings of this story, we can see Iron John as the primitive and uncultured inner self that is free from societal pressures to conform. The "swamp" is the consciousness backwaters where this powerful being hides. The journey of a boy becoming a man is a careful dance of directing these wild energies into productive service.

From the vantage point of an evolving consciousness, one could say that the journey of wellbeing involves "draining the swamp" of the defensive scripts that hide in our unedited experience. We greatly enhance our wellbeing when we recover this authentic energy and integrate it into our lives. The practice we need most for this work, both inwardly and outwardly, is Moving Alongside. Otherwise, the swamp of our scripts is just too murky.

To drain our cultural swamps of failing images in education, relationships, racial conflict, political polarization, and every other arena of life, we need to get smarter about how human consciousness actually works. All of these issues are connected, and whether we realize it or not, all of these struggles reflect the same problematic dynamics. Until we are ready to Choose to Evolve — and make the next evolutionary leap of human consciousness together — these dynamics are likely to continue.

By Moving Alongside our own images and emotions, and in Moving Alongside the images and emotions of others, even in the midst of conflict, we can learn to be Learners. And even when we can find no common ground, we will have gained a richer understanding of ourselves and retained the empathy that equips us to keep talking.

The alternative is to continue our defending and attacking, our demonizing and dehumanizing — with the cycle of winners dominating and losers feeling misunderstood and disenfranchised. It may seem easier to stay with that false sense of security found in communities that have circled their ideological wagons, but we should know better by now.

Let's face it. The deep bonds so often forged between peers who share a mutual image of "the enemy" can feel pretty comfortable, but in the long run this is a false sense of security that leads to relational stagnation and personal fixation as the merry-go-round just keeps on twirling.

Are you ready to give Moving Alongside a try? Here are a few steps that can help you learn this life-changing practice:

Take a moment to think of something that feels important to you right now. Make sure it is something with some urgency to it. Whatever it is, immerse yourself in this feeling.

Begin to bring your attention to your sensations. Notice the sounds around you. Notice your breathing and posture. Don't change anything — just wait.

As you attune to this sensory experience, be fully present. Accept what is and welcome it. Welcome the thoughts and feelings that sometimes emerge and distract you from your sensations. Observe without judgment.

Notice — and resist — any urge to move toward a goal or ideal state. Instead, engage with what is present in your moment with silent acceptance. If you try to speak at this point, you have already moved away from the Silent Level and are back in your habituated images.

Accepting your experience is all about being in it and swimming through it, whatever that may be.

Carl Jung once wrote, "We do not become enlightened by imagining figures of light, but by calling the darkness into consciousness." Try just being present in the unknown, the undefined, and the unspeakable. When you do, it can be a magical journey to rediscovering territory that never made its way onto your inner map.

Chapter 15

The Problem with Enlightenment

Whether we realize it or not, from the moment of our birth we are all more or less automatically shaped by the worldview we're born into. Were you born in the US? North or South? Urban or rural? Were you born on another continent? What are the dominant ideological images of your culture? What is the religion or ethnicity of your family? What education and exposure to the world did those who influenced your early experience offer as you were first forming images of your self, others, and the world around you?

Here's the thing. It really doesn't matter what images you received from your culture and family. The real questions are, "Can you question these images?" Have you done the work of noticing the limits to which your guitar string is strung? Do you have the freedom and courage to expand those limits, even if it means you will have to live in a way that is at odds with how you were raised?

I once had the opportunity to interview Sam Keen, the American philosopher, professor, and author who co-produced the award-winning PBS documentary, "Faces of the Enemy." In our interview, Keen quoted the German-Swiss psychiatrist and philosopher, Karl Jaspers:

"The problem with enlightenment is at first it's all bad news... I've been brainwashed..."

Let that thought linger in your mind for a moment. How does it feel to consider that from the moment of your birth you've been inducted into a tribal mentality? Regardless of where you were born and to whom, you were taught how to think (and more importantly, how to feel) about everything in your existence, even before you developed your own capacity to choose.

And now, wherever you happen to be in your life, how certain do you feel of your own beliefs, perspectives, and worldview? Would you feel as certain of these things if you had been born into a radically different place or people? Would you cling to those images as tightly as you cling to the images you have now?

I think it's important to recognize that everyone is similarly "brainwashed" by the random chance of his or her birth. Although the term, "brainwashed," is usually associated with a lot of scary history (and plenty of icky moments on the silver screen), I find it to be an appropriate term when we are talking about the socialization and manipulation of our deepest thoughts and feelings. Some of that "brainwashing" is helpful — and some of it can be incredibly destructive.

The new model of consciousness that we have been exploring here together demonstrates that all "brainwashing" (or "thought reform," as it is sometimes called), is a combination of imagery *and* emotion. If you choose the path that Jaspers calls "enlightenment," then the deprogramming of your "brainwashing" will have to include more than just the images and beliefs you were taught to take for granted. It will also require a review of all the scripted emotional dynamics you absorbed in your life up until now. The emotional scripts we are given play the biggest role in our "brainwashing" because emotional scripts direct and flavor our attention in a pre-conscious way. Cultivating our awareness of the emotional scripting we have absorbed throughout our life can offer us a powerful new way to understand the issues we face in our world today.

For instance, if you really want to understand why racism and tribalism are so resistant to change within a culture, take a look at the emotional scripts that sustain them. Racism doesn't persist just because someone told someone that someone was a lower form of human. It persists because someone showed someone Dissmell about someone. And because the Dissmell Affect became scripted to be associated with that someone, Dissmell continues to do what Affects always do — it directs and flavors any attention given to that someone before any conscious choice is made.

Our experience of race may even be at odds with beliefs we develop over time. It is possible to speak the words, "all men are created equal" while at the same time feeling Dissmell at the very mention or vision of someone of another race. Without knowing why, we immediately feel contempt and a desire to "reject without sampling." We experience the "other" like we do spoiled food.

Have you ever questioned how you were *socialized* to feel about others? Until we become aware of our preconceptions, our initial programming will continue to define our lives. Making new choices requires first shining the light of awareness on our own "brainwashing."

In the process of writing my master's thesis on the subject of thought reform ("brainwashing"), I came across a paper that broke down the process of the original form of brainwashing — or at least what we came to *know* as "brainwashing" — during the Korean War. This original system of brainwashing that the Chinese had learned from the Russians was developed under Yeshov, the Commissar of Internal Affairs under Stalin.

It works something like this. When an enemy combatant was captured or a dissident was incarcerated, they were put into total isolation and deprived of comfort, food, water, and sleep. Sometimes this experience also involved torture of some sort as well.

At some point there would be a meeting with an authority figure who would accuse them of crimes against the state. This accusation of guilt might be a complete fabrication. For instance, a journalist or a dissident might be accused of being a spy.

In order to receive relief from his or her suffering, the prisoner would then be required to make a confession, acknowledging their part in this alternative story. After enough torture or deprivation, the prisoner would usually get to a point where he or she would "repent" and make the desired confession. Now here's the important and most interesting part of this process. The confession is not accepted the first time.

The prisoner would be told that his or her confession lacked sincerity or that he or she was only making the confession to end his or her suffering. The prisoner would then be sent back into confinement, now with the intensified suffering imposed by the requirement that he or she feel sincere about this confession. Eventually the prisoner, exhausted and moving in and out of dissociation, would "break."

Now think about this for a moment. Once a person goes through all this and finally gets to the breaking point, making the difficult decision to concede in order to gain relief, can you imagine how disorienting it must be to then find that relief is not granted? Do you see how the Yeshov Method employs two powerful human Affects, Fear and Shame?

Are you also now asking, "What in the heck does this have to do with you and me today?" A lot, actually. As scary as this classic wartime brainwashing process may seem, it is not all that different from the ways many institutions and cultural forces are involved in our own "thought reform." In fact, the only difference may well be the intensity of our suffering.

Think about it. The Yeshov Method is more about transforming Affect scripts than beliefs. To make this possible, it actually calls on the same two emotions most often used to socialize children to manage their feelings. We embarrass children for crying, getting overly excited, being fearful, or becoming angry. Sometimes we may also threaten them with punishment: "You'd better stop crying or I'll give you something to cry about!"

Shame and Fear are not only the Affects used in the socialization of how we express feelings; they are also a part of how groups of people maintain their homogeneity. In fact I would submit to you that if you were to decide to leave the herd of your own peers by questioning an image that the group holds dear, you would be subjected to a great deal of criticism (Shame) and the spoken or unspoken threat of banishment (Fear).

That is why anyone undertaking the process of real growth through questioning his or her habituated images and emotional scripts is probably in for some major resistance in his or her social group. It helps to develop a clear awareness of how threatening your questioning will be to those who are clinging to those images. In fact, the more we acknowledge that we, too, have had the same need to cling to our images, the more we become open to the reality that there is no one image that is perfect. We are all just taking our own small sips from the fire hose of life.

It's also important to understand that if you take this journey of questioning the images of your clan and culture, you will need to solidify an image of yourself as a Learner. By grounding your security in the image of being a Learner, you can find the guidance you need to deal with any rejection or criticism you may face.

Knowing from the outset that your critics, as well as anyone else who thinks you are abandoning him or her, will trigger your Fear and Shame Affects, it will be much easier to find the capacity to Moving Alongside your critics — and your own feelings — with a non-defensive curiosity for truth. Let's take a look at some of the ways we may experience pressures to conform that mimic the Yeshov Method.

Conscious Evolution: Resisting Emotional Manipulation

Perhaps you have noticed that the Yeshov Method bears some similarities to processes you are familiar with from other areas of your life. I can certainly draw parallels to my experience of Christianity in the Bible belt. I bet you can also see bits and pieces of this process within the educational system, medical school, law school, and the military, just to name a few.

> Here are the steps of the Yeshov Method again:
> Accusation of guilt
> Promise of relief from suffering if one confesses
> Requirement to conform emotionally as well as intellectually
> Conversion
> Acceptance

A person doesn't have to suffer torture to be manipulated by this kind of process. What's interesting here is that the more empathy you have, the more vulnerable you are to this emotional manipulation. In fact, compassionate people are often the ones most easily manipulated because they are the ones most prone to feeling what others feel.

I have to admit that once, a long time ago, I tried out being a "distributor" in a multi-level marketing venture. I only stayed with it for less than a year, but during that time I got a pretty good glimpse at the MLM's inner workings. I found it particularly interesting that they would hold "sales rallies" for the sole purpose of "pumping up" the distributors. It reminded me of the religious revivals I attended as a teenager.

All the same pieces were there. The same zeal, the same emotional contagion, and, as I now realize, the same dynamics of Fear and Shame with the promise of relief from suffering. In the case of the MLM, this relief would come with almost certain financial success. However, in order to achieve this relief you couldn't just *sell* the product. You had to *believe* in the product, be excited about it, and entice others to get whipped up into the same level of excitement.

You can see these same dynamics in almost every high school, peer group, professional association, and even behind bars. For any teenage girl who is a part of a group of friends, there is a required conformity to express certain emotional dynamics about certain things. If she seems to go along, but does not express the emotional components at or near an equal intensity level to the leader of the group, she will probably be questioned about it. Then she will be accused of not believing in the cause, subtly threatened with excommunication and social stigma, and then pressured to convert to the group norm.

But what happens if the group leader, the one who sets the emotional tone for others to follow, is caught in a Shame spiral that results in an Attack-Other script? This happens all the time for both men and women. In this case, the contagion of Affect and the demand of group conformity can lead to groups of people doing destructive acts that are far beyond what they would ever even think of doing as individuals.

What happens when others who wish to control us, dominate us, or keep us docile and obedient begin to manipulate our emotions? The reality is, other people very often influence our Affects, whether we — or even they — know it.

The commercialized world we live in provides us with a daily barrage of advertisements designed to trigger just the right emotional motivation in us. Manipulation or control of others through emotional means isn't very hard to do. Simply matching someone else's emotional expression is often enough to establish trust. And, as it turns out, any clear expression of *one* of the nine affects is likely to find resonance in some people.

That is just one reason that showing happy, smiling people drinking beer on TV sells. Knowing where the beer comes from isn't going to motivate the masses, but viewing the expressions of Excitement, Joy, and Pleasure on the faces of people consuming the product will. It will also not surprise you to know that fast-moving images and loud music can also stimulate us enough to trigger our Excitement Affect. This will predictably grab young people's attention — at least until they become habituated to that level of stimulation and find themselves numbed to it. This is probably why television commercials are often so much louder than the shows they interrupt.

The Affect system is designed to be collaborative. Tomkins called this phenomenon the "contagion" of Affect. Studies in the neurobiology of emotion confirm that our feelings *do* rub off on others around us. And now we may be discovering that this "Affect contagion" can happen even more efficiently through the use of technology.

We know that smiles and laughter are more infectious than a cold bug — and that fearful screams can spread panic through a crowd in the blink of an eye. But what if that crowd is millions of people watching a "viral" video? We are beginning to learn more about the risks posed to humanity by the way propaganda can manipulate masses of people through technology when the ones using it have become "wise" to the power of emotion.

As adults, we often develop scripts that limit how much we are moved by other people's expressions. Nathanson called this development the "empathic wall." The good news is that as we gain the capacity to create an empathic wall, we also become a little more immune to manipulation. The bad news is that these scripts can become a problem when they lose their flexibility.

Blessed are those who are somehow able to both raise and lower their empathic walls. There is a time for dropping the wall and letting ourselves flow with the feelings of others. There is also a time for us to raise that wall to limit our empathic experience so that we are less manipulated. Raising our empathic wall does not mean that we have to lose our compassion. It is quite possible to distance ourselves from the emotions of another person and still care for them. Parents do it all the time.

Explore Your Own Brainwashing

"Fake news" and campaigns by political agents that seek to manipulate our emotions is now a major issue in the media and in the common vernacular. However, the truth is that these manipulative efforts have been a part of corporate advertising for decades. The intentions are the same; only the delivery vehicle has changed. It is also highly unlikely that this type of manipulative effort will ever cease unless enough people Choose to Evolve beyond the reach of its effectiveness.

What I am suggesting here is that when we feel "moved" by the presentation of a speaker or the images of a viral video, we can develop the skill of Moving Alongside. We can turn our attention to the Silent Level and tune in to what is happening in our bodies. From there we have a much greater capacity to be aware of the emotional dynamics of the moment.

The evolution of consciousness I am describing is precisely the awareness we need to resist this kind of emotional manipulation. If we want to have a democracy that is resistant to mass manipulation, we seem to have two choices. We can shut down the mass media, or we can Evolve in a way that can mindfully notice the kind of images and the emotional dynamics that are being presented.

And yes, our freedom *does* actually depend on this. When mainstream media is forced by the nature of their business to cover every tweet of a politician or celebrity, the whole culture experiences a barrage of daily messages. If those tweets are delivered consistently over time to trigger a particular set of emotional responses, then we begin to see habituation. In this case, the more the politician or celebrity tweets, the more entrenched our response becomes — even if the tweets are ridiculous or misguided.

Can you imagine what might happen if every adolescent and adult in this country were to learn what we have explored so far in this book? Can you see yourself and everyone you know becoming capable of Moving Alongside the images presented through various media — and then taking a breath to be mindful of which emotions and images are being played upon in order to trigger the desired response?

If you can picture this Evolved reality, then you may have as much optimism for humanity as I do. We can't change the fact that some people are always going to be born into environments and dynamics that brainwash them into becoming master manipulators to serve powerful interests. I believe that, with the right information, we can all Choose to Evolve as a people. Once we understand how human consciousness works and how easily it can be manipulated, we can Evolve our capacity for making better choices.

I am also optimistic that this information will help us continue to transform both parenting and early education. If we have learned anything from these insights, it is that our most important scripts are habituated early in life. But how many parents attend any kind of parenting education?

I wish every parent and preschool teacher could spend some time with some of the adolescents and adults with whom I have worked. If they could hear these people talk about their early traumas and the emotional dynamics of their families and teachers that set them up for a lifetime of challenges, they would understand as I do the power of this information we are exploring together.

Your initial brainwashing and the emotional scripts modeled for you can be transcended, but surpassing our emotional upbringing will take consciousness, creativity, and commitment. If you have made it this far in this book, you are already on this path and gaining some general awareness of the issues at hand. And, while general knowledge is great — and it is where we all must begin — it is only with *applied* knowledge that the evolution of consciousness I am suggesting truly begins.

Exploring your own "brainwashing" can begin with a review of your images, remembering where you got them, and analyzing how they operate in your life right now. It can also begin by practicing what we have called Moving Alongside in our moment-to-moment experience of life. This is a creative process that takes commitment to daily practice over time. After a while, it does get easier and becomes more "second nature."

Start the Deprogramming

The practices that follow can be quite powerful in gaining an applied understanding of the ideas we have shared thus far. It is important to mention here that just knowing what you now know is enough to make a big difference in the evolution of your own consciousness. The next step is to take that knowledge into your day-to-day experience. The following nine-day practice can help get you started.

Affect Journaling

One of the most enlightening things you can do is to explore your history with each of the nine Affects. I suggest you take a day for each of the following topics:

Day 1: Excitement
Day 2: Shame
Day 3: Distress
Day 4: Anger
Day 5: Fear
Day 6: Startle
Day 7: Dissmell/Disgust

Day 8: Enjoyment
Day 9: Shame Scripts

Begin each day by writing about your history with one of the nine Affects. The object here is not to re-traumatize yourself by recalling hurts and disappointments from your past. And, if you find yourself struggling with a memory, it may help you to write something about that down and take it with you to a therapist or trusted friend.

Here are a few questions to prime your reflections:

What are your memories of feeling this Affect?

Who in your family expressed this Affect most freely?

Who did not?

Who are you more like?

How did you feel about others expressing this Affect at these times?

How do you feel about others who are expressing this Affect now?

When was your most profound experience of this Affect?

How well did you tolerate the feelings associated with this experience?

What happens when you experience this Affect now?

Do you tend to dam it up? Do your emotions tend to flood?

Make a Date With an Affect

Once you have written about each particular Affect, try making a date with it. Deliberately seek out an experience of the Affect and its associated feelings as an experiment in self-awareness. Now let's be clear. I am not suggesting you do anything drastic — like having an affair or hurting someone. What I *am* suggesting is that you deliberately trigger each Affect in a small but specific way (Get on a roller coaster, ask someone to dance, tell someone about something you are embarrassed about, smell something bad, take a spoonful of food you hate, express your anger just to feel it, write a letter to someone you love, get a massage).

Choose one experience each day to help grow your awareness of each Affect as you experience it. Notice how you *feel* each Affect in your body. Where do you feel it most? Does it have a color or a shape? Pay attention to the way each Affect impacts your thoughts, and then see if you can practice Moving Alongside those thoughts without believing everything you think.

Now, as you take a whole day (or more!) to study each Affect:

Set an Alarm

Set your watch or phone to alarm once an hour. When the alarm goes off notice whether you have experienced or expressed this Affect in the past hour.

Observe the Media

As you interact with media, watch for this Affect on other people's faces and listen for it in their voices. Notice how contagious this Affect is to your own emotional experience.

Faces in the Mirror

End each day by looking in the mirror and giving yourself permission to form the facial expression of this Affect. Try making a sound to go with this Affect when it's on your face. Close your eyes and feel the sensation of your facial muscles expressing this Affect, and then open your eyes and just observe what you experience. Notice any judgments you tend to want to make about what you see and feel around this Affect. Where did you get these judgments?

Shame Scripts

On the final day of this nine-day series of exercises, once you've given your full and separate attention to each Affect, reflect on the Shame Scripts in your life and relationships in just the same way. Try evoking them on purpose. See if you can notice at least one situation in which you *used* a Shame script. Consider inviting your embarrassment over this to come and sit with you for a while. If you can, acknowledge this embarrassment to someone you trust.

Remember, exploring our Shame scripts is how we learn and grow. Defensive scripts around Shame are major stumbling blocks to our Evolution, but they can be overcome. Can you take this bold step toward living your truth as the occasionally foolish, still in process, Learner that you are?

Conflict Strategy Exercise

In addition to the previous Affect exercises, I suggest you also explore your relationship with the following conflict strategies on *three* days of your nine-day practice:

Move Toward Seek peace, appease, give in, let other's win by tuning into what they need

Move Away Practice keeping your own opinion or desires to yourself, but make a plan to express them elsewhere

Move Against Stay assertive about what you want or what you think

Move Alongside Stay connected and curious — don't give in, don't judge, and don't immediately accept or react to criticism. Instead, consider it, reflect on the differences you discover, and explore together how you each came to where you are on the subject.

Developing an awareness of our tendencies to use these strategies in our conflicts is yet another way to open up new avenues for growth and learning. To deepen your understanding of each strategy, I suggest that you set up experiences in which you can play with each one of these strategies. For this exercise, you will need to enlist a friend to help you. Pick a topic or an issue over which the two of you can at least pretend to have conflict. Try out each one of the **first three** conflict strategies on the same issue for about five minutes each. It's important that you only use *one* strategy for each five-minute time period; don't resort to a second or bounce between them. After each full five-minute time period, take a few minutes to discuss with your friend how he or she felt about being on the receiving end of that particular strategy before you repeat the exercise with a different strategy.

After completing and discussing each strategy in its dedicated five-minute exercise, try shifting to the Move Alongside strategy. Remember that the object of this strategy of conflict I'm suggesting is to just stay connected and curious and follow these ground rules: Suspend, don't defend. Don't correct, just connect. See how long you can stay curious and non-defensive. Try to dis-identify with your own images and try on the other person's. Don't accept any outcome where anyone has to win or lose.

> Do you both come out of this final conversation having learned more than you would have when using the other three strategies?

> Does this new knowledge open up possibilities that will make the old conflict no longer as important — and perhaps allow new insights or questions to arise?

This work is not easy at first. The way we interact with each other has long ago become second nature to us. We defend against any conflict or criticism without any thought that this interaction could be different. There is always another choice; see if you can see it. See if you can feel the difference it makes.

> What if the first thing that comes out of your mouth when a conflict appears is a question?

> What if this question conveys your sincere curiosity and empathy for what the other person is experiencing?

> What if it even communicates your openness to appearing foolish?

The reality is that truly transformative dialogue can best take place when we suspend our need to defend *or* decide — and we choose, at least for a while, to Move Alongside.

The Practice of Presence

We have discussed how habituated imagery once helped humans climb to the top of the food chain. We have explored how the habituation and abstraction processes can also limit us and rob us of fresh experiences. So during your nine-day practice, I suggest that you also add daily experiences to help you learn to push back against your own habituated images and abstraction processes. Here is a brief list of some additional practices to insert into your days:

Yoga and Meditation both offer the opportunity to tune into the body and quiet the inner dialogue. You may find it helpful to have a teacher or participate in a class where you are guided in what to do. Choose a class that is appropriate to your physical abilities. If you can't do yoga due to your physical limitations, just try some gentle stretching followed by meditation.

Sensory Focused Meditation: One of the best ways to learn to quiet our inner dialogue is by giving concentrated attention to our senses. Try sitting or lying down with your eyes closed and look at the backs of your eyelids. Try shifting your gaze left, and then right, as you breathe and relax. Then, resting the eyes, give your complete attention to your hearing. Listen to all the sounds around you. Don't label the sounds or assign them meaning; just take in the resonance as energy that is flowing around you. Breathe. Enter the flow of the moment without resisting or seeking to hold onto any of it.

Releasing Sensory Fixation: Take a walk and look at the ground as it goes by beneath your feet. Try to just let your eyes flow over it without focusing on individual elements. Gradually raise your vision to see more of the world around you. Try to retain the same sense of flow as you continue walking; keep your focus wide-open to everything.

Caress the Detail: Annie Dillard found the mystical experience of life in what she called "caressing the detail." Find something or someone you take for granted and practice taking a more detailed look at all that is there. Hug a tree, memorizing the patterns and scars in its bark. Have a conversation with the neighbor you barely ever talk with and see what there is to learn that you didn't know. There are a million things in your life for which you have habituated images. Pick a few of them and see what you have missed about them.

Lose Your Language: There are several ways to explore this experience, and here are just a few. Go to a fast food restaurant and use sounds and your face — no words — to order food. Get together with a few friends and see if you can have a conversation without using words, only sounds and facial expressions. Try this same experiment while hosting a dinner party. (You might want to clue your guests in beforehand to what you're doing!) Have fun discovering who you are without your usual language.

You will find even more suggestions and resources on the Choosing to Evolve website: www.choosingtoevolve.com. Whether you use these exercises or make up some on your own, the value of these insights is in applying them. We Choose to Evolve our consciousness through insights and practices that help us to gain the new capacity for observing and participating with the components of our consciousness. There is a big difference between *thinking* about evolving how we participate in consciousness and actually *accomplishing* a new experience of it.

Chapter 16

Education, Justice and Accountability

M any of us are concerned about the educational system and how to foster positive values, teach empathy, and reduce apathy in today's students. We are concerned about school violence, bullying, dropout rates, and drug abuse. The very same dynamics of habituated images and emotional scripts we've been discussing throughout this book are playing a dominant role in all of these issues. Schools and justice systems — even government systems — can Choose to Evolve by gaining a deeper understanding of human consciousness. In this chapter I'll be sharing practices we have put into place that have brought about dramatic positive changes in schools.

Accountability

One core issue for our evolving consciousness as applied to education, parenting, and justice systems is how we approach accountability. Knowing what we know now, we can no longer ignore how early childhood trauma and the habituation of dysfunctional and disabling emotional scripts impact the behavior of humans. In the older notion of "rugged individualism," where willpower and personal responsibility were most highly valued, there wasn't much room for the nuanced understanding of human motivation we have been exploring.

So how *do* we hold people accountable for the choices they make — and in some cases the harm they do — when we understand that they have been shaped by life events that were beyond their control? If we look closely enough in some of these cases, we can often see the influences that formed the memory images, self-imagery, and images of the world that ended up sending a person to prison. It is hard to grapple with this understanding in a system based on the premise of personal responsibility. If you do the crime you do the time.

What makes matters worse is that there are plenty of people whose life experiences, habituated images, and emotional scripting have led to their development of manipulative patterns to try to "game the system." These people tend to make cynics out of even the most well intentioned teachers, lawyers, and judges who are continually exposed to them. Anyone who has worked in the justice or educational arenas has a story or two of how they lost their innocent naiveté and optimism after giving a second and sometimes third chance to someone, only to end up feeling duped.

However, most of those who work on the front lines of educational and justice systems also have plenty of stories of those kids who never had a chance at all. They remember the kid who was always in trouble, failed by a system that never understood the challenges — and the defensive scripts — that had turned his or her life upside down.

No child starts out in life looking to become a thief, a bully, or a killer. In all the years I have spent training teachers, counselors, and principals, I have always begun those trainings with a central premise: *All disciplinary issues are actually emotional regulation issues.*

I will not spend the extensive space required to fully introduce my program for helping schools to take this premise into their DNA to create *restorative learning communities*. There are many books and trainers now available on the subject of social emotional learning in the classroom and restorative approaches to discipline, and you will find a few of my own recommendations in the back of this book. For now, however, let's just hit some of the basic ways we can Choose to Evolve in the world of education, parenting, and justice.

Restorative Discipline and Accountability

Part of the challenge to this new consciousness involves how we hold people accountable. It's important to realize that the habituated images and emotional scripts we have accumulated are our window on the world. The truth is we have *all* been brainwashed by the experiences that fill our memory banks. So if I had those same images and emotional dynamics that you have, I might do exactly what you are doing! In that light, it is easy to see that punishing someone for his or her bad choices is really just punishing him or her for being born to a particular place and time, and this punishment will most likely just cause the creation of new defensive scripts.

I know. This premise makes *many* people uneasy. If all of us are simply the sum of our experiences, our habituated images, and our emotional scripts, then what about free will? How in the world do we hold people accountable for harm they cause to others? If we take all this to heart, won't that make for a more complicated, lax, and strange system of justice?

These are all reasonable questions. Anyone working in the fields of education or justice knows this conundrum all too well. However, whether we like or agree with it or not, these are the realities of human consciousness. If we want to create a more just and peaceful world, we must learn to embrace these ambiguities.

It helps to know that there are many people in these fields who have already made this Leap. In fact, systems of accountability built with this new understanding in mind already exist — and they do work. What's exciting to me is that they *actually* work far better than our previous systems that are based in our more punitive paradigms.

Over the past 20 years, an approach to managing conflict and harm between people — and for holding people accountable — has been spreading across the globe. Whether it's called Restorative Justice, Restorative Practices or Restorative Discipline, success stories around the world now illustrate what happens when we begin to operate a school or a justice system in a way that honors the dynamics of human consciousness that we are considering in this book. In my own work with schools in Texas, we have found that disciplinary issues can be reduced by as much as 80% in a single year.

What is Restorative?

In our current models for discipline and justice, an external authority imposes a penalty that is supposed to create resolution. The primary differences in the restorative approach are that the resolution is found in dialogue between the parties involved, and everyone gets to express his or her emotional experience in the presence of the others.

Peta Blood, a constable in New Zealand, first observed this idea in action by studying the justice system practiced by the Maori, the indigenous Polynesian people of New Zealand. Though these practices have spread and evolved to include a wide variety of settings and disciplines, they continue to hold in common a basic thread: keeping the resolution of conflict in the hands of those most affected.

Restorative Practices (RP) can include both formal and informal approaches. A trained teacher gathering students in a daily sharing circle is an example of informal practice. Formal practices include victim-offender conferences where those who have caused harm are involved in reflective dialogue with those who were most affected by their actions.

In these victim-offender conferences, those who have been harmed have an opportunity to say how they experienced that harm and eventually take part in deciding what needs to happen in order for the matter to be resolved and good relations restored. With the proper support, those harmed by others find this process much more satisfying than traditional forms of punishment. They often report on surveys that they feel less traumatized, sleep better, and think of the incident less often after participating in a restorative conference.

Justice for All

In most traditional approaches to justice, the emotional dynamics involved in accountability are not important. In fact, in our current system, the more consideration given to any mitigating life circumstances of the offender, the less those who were impacted feel satisfied, regardless of the punishment imposed. RP, on the other hand, creates a dialogue that encourages the emotional expression of all parties. It makes sense that if the motivation behind the actions that caused suffering is always emotional, and if the role these emotions play is to actually direct and filter our attention, then it will take an emotional process to change the perpetrator's scripts. We don't need statistics here. We need poetry.

In most cases where traditional punitive models of behavior management are practiced, the offender never has to truly face those impacted by his or her actions. And even when these offenders *do* face their victims, this encounter happens in a courtroom setting where any real dialogue is impossible. And then, when the outside authority figure delivers the punishment, it tends to only perpetuate the Avoidance and Attack-Other scripts that were a part of the perpetrator's emotional motivation in the first place.

Given what we have learned about defensive scripts, and Shame scripts in particular, it is easy to see why the current authority-based punitive processes so often fail to bring about the sort of changes they seek. Rather than learning from the incident, gaining a greater sense of empathy for the impact of harmful actions, or learning how to manage emotions differently, offenders simply develop more deeply held defenses.

So how can our newly-evolved understanding of human consciousness help to transform education, parenting, and justice systems? I hope that by now you have begun to see that an effective means for managing harm can be carried out without denying the reality of the challenges some people face in how they were shaped to think and feel. A restorative dialogue may result in an agreement that the perpetrator should spend some time in jail or in therapy, but the opportunity to explore what *led* to the behavior offers a much-needed opportunity for learning and growth. If we want to better address the issues in our families and schools that often lead to incarceration, we would do well to consider how the self-imagery, the hero images, and the emotional scripting of a child can set them up for failure.

Scripts Colliding in the Classroom

Imagine what it must be like to attend a structured classroom with an authoritarian teacher if you have an emotional script to feel disgust for any image of authority? When classroom experiences trigger intense Shame, Anger, or Distress, what are the scripts that students have learned to manage these?

One thing is clear. Children will Evolve when parents and teachers Evolve. Children who never witness an adult acknowledging Shame and productively processing that Affect without using defensive scripts have no model for processing their own Shame. Once we recognize that children are most likely to use whatever defensive scripts have been modeled for them, it's easy to see why children raised in settings with limited emotional freedom or poor containment and regulation are not actually *choosing* to be apathetic, disruptive, or disrespectful. They have been programmed to act in these ways.

And what's more, punishment won't change these behaviors for many of these children. Instead, it will reinforce their defensive scripts — and sometimes spawn new ones. We now have a better way: the restorative paradigm.

Before we leave the subject of accountability, it is important to note that there has been promising work in schools that are now teaching mindfulness as an alternative to suspension/detention. In these programs, rather than being sent to the principal's office, a disruptive student is sent to a room where they are supported with yoga and meditative practices.

Given what we have explored about human consciousness so far, it should be easy to see why these practices are already showing better results than traditional, punitive ones. By giving a student an opportunity to reset and reflect, we support them in developing the capacity to Move Alongside the emotional dynamics that triggered their problematic behavior. I believe these practices can be enhanced through the information we have explored. Mindfulness practices that are particularly focused on the somatic and "first order" experiences can make these interventions even more successful.

This is a huge development in education. When we begin to recognize that to simply punish children into compliance is dysfunctional and at cross-purposes with best ultimate outcomes, we see how our *own* emotional scripts come into play. Real change can happen only when we take seriously the scripted nature of defenses against Shame in both the student *and* the teacher/administrator. Supporting our children in changing those scripts takes a commitment to unconditional positive regard and an environment that offers alternatives that don't reinforce the defensive scripts that will keep them stuck.

Evolving our Understanding of Learning

Beyond the issue of accountability, we would do well to apply what we now understand about human consciousness to our approach to learning in general. This is already happening through a multitude of programs around the world. Programs that introduce social-emotional learning to students are showing great promise; however, it would be helpful to the evolutionary process if more of these programs were connected to a more robust understanding of the workings of human consciousness. When it comes to this kind of work, precision is helpful, and unfortunately, Tomkins' work is too often overlooked.

In general it seems clear that efforts to enable children to better understand the emotional dynamics of their lives will be of great benefit to them — and to society as a whole as they grow into adulthood with this knowledge. While relational intelligence has often been ignored in the past, it's becoming clearer and clearer that it is very often the key to success — and the issue behind failure. With schools and families who understand restorative dialogue, we'll be able to better fulfill a basic need for forming healthy human communities.

We have much to learn about the way the Shame Affect undermines the learning process. As I mentioned earlier, David Boulton describes a number of learning issues in his work, *Children of the Code*. The key issue is the way in which Shame dynamics impact the learning of language. Boulton coined the term, "Mind Shame" to describe what happens when a student is unable for some reason to match the pace of his or her peers in learning to read and write. "Mind Shame," most often begins somewhere around the third grade, when children begin to make the shift from *learning to read* to *reading to learn*.

In this debilitating experience, students begin to perceive that their minds are defective. They feel shame about their own minds, and as a result they often then resort to one of the scripts Nathanson described as part of the Compass of Shame: Withdrawal, Attack-Self, Avoidance, or Attack-Other. For many of these young students, this experience will initiate a lifetime layered with defensive scripts, each one to cover another. In my work with many young adult clients, the withdrawal scripts undermining their success began in just this way.

Awareness of "Mind Shame" can help sensitize us to the challenges our children face in the very important task of learning how to participate in the world. We can help them learn how to manage Shame in ways that do not exacerbate the original problem but instead create positive solutions.

Finally, it is important to note that when it comes to parenting, education, and justice, we can Choose to Evolve by simply acknowledging the role our emotions play in our motivation. Remember, it is our Affects that direct our attention and our emotions that respond. If that doesn't make sense by now, try imagining yourself sitting in a classroom, trying to pay attention to the lesson while feeling the urgency of diarrhea. How much Interest would have to be triggered by the teacher or the subject matter in order for you to ignore that physical urgency?

One of my life's most embarrassing moments came in the first grade. It was time for music class, and I loved music class so much that I ignored my body's signals — and the Distress triggered by them —

until it was too late. I wet my pants. These kinds of moments in life are usually punishing enough all on their own. There is simply no need for authorities to pile on with additional "punishment."

I wonder what a difference it might have made for me if, rather than being sent to sit on the floor in the bathroom in my wet britches while being laughed at by my peers, I had been protected from the feelings of shame by an adult who whisked me out of harm's way with unconditional positive regard. I can hear that imaginary angel now, saying, "Charles, you must love music so much that you didn't notice you needed to go to the restroom. I know it's embarrassing, but I also know that you will learn to stay in touch better with taking care of these things. And with your love of music, I bet you will grow up to be a musician yourself one day! Will you sing me a song while I get you some dry pants? What is your favorite song?"

The Inner World of Images

There are so many stimuli that constantly compete to trigger the Affect-directed attention of a child. I was a daydreamer, and mostly I imagined building things. Quite often there was *way* more stimulation available in my imagination than in the classroom. If imagery can trigger Affect, and Affects direct our attention, then you can imagine why my attention generally flowed elsewhere. I hope parents and teachers can recognize that this is not in itself a bad thing. Instead of punishing our daydreamers we should be helping them learn to channel the fascinating imaginings of their minds.

Giving children time to dream should be a priority for us as we continue to Evolve. As we recognize more and more the value of the arts and imagination, we are finally beginning to realize, as one neuroscientist put it, "The arts are not the icing on the cake, they are the baking soda."

For this reason, I encourage teachers and parents to stop asking children what they *know* as much as asking them what they *don't know*, because there is a magical difference between these two questions. If you ask a child what he or she *knows,* you set up a scenario of success or failure — and possible Shame. However, when you begin a class by asking a child what they *don't* know, you set the stage for curiosity that triggers Interest — and *that* is where learning happens.

Gary David, says that true learning is about extending one's presence into the world. What better place to start than to acknowledge the unknown?

A Few Additional Suggestions

Digital media has presented us with the issue of constant overstimulation. The perpetual triggering of our Interest-Excitement Affect through novel visual stimulation is creating a generation that is bored with the pace of the natural world. That is to say nothing of the banal images and gratuitous violence some video games offer — and to which our young people are becoming habituated.

If you have ever worked with someone recovering from addiction to meth or heroine, it is hard to miss the similarity to the way a 14-year-old acts when deprived of media. As one addict told me, "when I'm high, even cleaning house is exciting." And without the drug, *nothing* was.

The ubiquitous nature of digital media is what is making this overstimulation and habituated imagery a major public health concern. We have no idea where this grand experiment will lead us, but I think we are beginning to get hints from the headlines.

Think of it this way. Anything that stimulates our positive Affects has the capacity to become something we depend upon to escape our negative Affects. The more we escape our Shame, Distress, Fear, and Anger through our electronic devices, the less likely we are to develop skills at managing the associated feelings without them — and the more likely we are to avoid addressing the issues that trigger our negative Affects. Who cares about global warming when they are binge watching a new series on Netflix? Why worry about failing my science test when I can escape both Shame *and* Fear with a 3-D video game?

Unfortunately, most of the ways we tend to address these addictive issues with children involve criticism and punishment, which only reinforces the idea that digital media is some kind of reward for being good. As adults, we need to get creative in how we monitor and limit the use of digital devices when we see them taking a role of this magnitude.

Rummy with Mother

From the time I was young, my family played cards. We played all kinds of card games, but mostly we played Rummy. Now, these games are far more than they seem, teaching children plenty of lessons about participation and interaction. We often laughed and talked as we played.

Now that my mother is in her 80s and confined to a wheelchair, playing Rummy is one of our favorite things to do to pass the time together when I visit. On a visit just after I started working on this book, I mentioned to her that I was writing a book about human consciousness. We talked during that game of Rummy about habituation and fixation, and she was quick to see some key similarities to the game we were playing.

In Rummy, as in most card games, you never know what cards will come up next. You may put together a hand and then wait for the right card to complete it until it is too late and someone else completes his or her hand first. One of the most important tricks to winning at Rummy is to quickly create as many options as possible. And then, it is equally important to not fixate on one option and miss taking advantage of others. Games like Rummy demonstrate for us the delicate balance between making a plan and going with the flow of opportunity. Note that one is proactive and the other is reactive. How do we teach both of these skills? Do the video games our children play train their minds to this balance? Are video games helping our children learn to be proactive — or simply reactive?

Expanding Consciousness

How many times can you remember making a leap in your experience of life? Did it happen in school? I have to say that was not true for me. School was most often the place where I proved I had a working memory and was exposed to things about the world. For me, school was seldom, if ever, a place where I sensed any expansion of my consciousness.

To "extend your being into the world" is a very different process than memorizing periodic tables — unless, of course, that bit of knowledge begins with a real sense of curiosity and engagement.

Being exposed to more and more labels and categories of the human condition may provide us with a rich matrix of language for life, but these labels and categories won't provide us with any expansion of our being. That is a journey calling for the practices we're now exploring in these pages: Self-awareness, Affective plasticity and freedom, and the capacity to Move Alongside.

Chapter 17

Faith and the Evolving Image of God

I suppose it could be argued that raising human consciousness is a central theme to the religious arena of human experience. In fact, throughout the ages, individuals and communities in a variety of traditions have sought to practice a higher consciousness. In many cases, it has been people of faith who spoke up for the underprivileged and stood in the gaps of social justice.

It can also be said that religion has been used to "brainwash" large groups of people to live and act in ways that are detrimental to humanity as a whole and to the individuals who fall under its spell. Throughout human history there has been so much violence in the name of God that many of us have issues with the more legalistic and tribal expressions of religion. I believe the antidote to all this "religion gone wrong" are the prophetic voices calling us to new revelations about our lives, much as the voices of those who have influenced this work have truly been for me.

Perhaps the contents of this book can help "vaccinate" young people (and older ones as well!) against the emotional manipulation used by some spiritual leaders who seek power and influence. Yes, there are those who prey upon us in our most vulnerable moments, and since the 1980s some of the manipulation has been for political purposes. I continue to believe, however, that most religious leaders operate from the highest of intentions, and I have seen how exploring the ideas we are discussing here has helped many a pastor gain a greater understanding of the importance of their role in people's lives. When religious leaders create a safe, relational space in which to wrestle with the dynamics of our scripts and the meaning of our images, they truly offer salvation.

A faith community is still a *human* community that tends to run into the same challenges as any other. Though we tend to want to believe those challenges won't happen within our house of worship, they are often even more likely to emerge there.

Flavil R. Yeakley, Jr., PhD, is a passionately positive critic of faith in America. His book, *The Discipleship Dilemma*, describes a study undertaken in the 1980s in which Yeakley used the Myers Briggs Type Indicator (MBTI) to look for personality shifts in converts to various religious groups.

Yeakley's protocol was to first have a sample of the group's members, in one case over 800 people, take the MBTI three times. The first test was to be answered as participants believed they would have answered prior to joining the church, or five years previous. The second was answered as they perceived themselves in the present, and the third was answered as they believed they would answer in five years.

The results of the study revealed radical shifts in personality types within groups that had been widely identified as "cults." It is likely that these shifts were made possible through small cell group processes, sometimes called "shepherding," which provided a vehicle for emulation and conformity to a particular type. Individuals in these systems begin to copy others' personalities as well as their beliefs rather than to expand their own unique experiences.

More than 50% were moving toward the same *one* of the 16 possible types. Would it surprise you to learn that this happened to be the pastor's personality type?

Yeakley's study, to which I have certainly done a disservice in this brief mention, had one more dynamic I find interesting. "There was a clear pattern of changing from introversion to extraversion, from intuition to sensing, from thinking to feeling, and from perceiving to judging…" It is as if "conversion" involved shifting everyone to being an ESFJ! The majority of church members saw a shift toward a high value of Extroversion (be a good ambassador for the faith). They also experienced a shift toward Sensing, which tends to focus on faith as facts, not ideas. A shift toward Feeling created a focus on personal/emotional connections to beliefs – not logic. Shifts toward judging put the focus on order, with less interest in flexibility.

For an ESFJ (Extraverted Sensing Feeling Judging) type identified by the Myers Briggs Type Indicator, the most dominant mental function would be what Myers-Briggs called the Feeling mental function. This is the personality you would want to foster in order to encourage personal devotion.

Now, don't get me wrong here, I'm not saying that being an ESFJ is a bad thing. Quite the contrary, I love my passionate ESFJ friends! The issue to consider here is not the personality type, but how someone can subtly be coerced into changing his or her personality by a system that seems to thrive on creating more "passionate soldiers." We have to wonder what becomes of the Introvert, Intuitive, Thinker, and Perceiver in such a place. Are they automatically rebuffed?

For people who find themselves in chaos, faith groups offer the imagery they need to bring a new sense of order to their lives — and a community to reinforce those images. But what if all that imagery and emotional catharsis causes more psychological problems than it heals? Jung believed that when we are somehow coerced to conform to a personality type that is different from our own, then this conformity becomes a likely source of mental disturbance. He called this "falsification of type."

Gathering and conforming has its upside. Communities of conformity feel safe and easy, harmonious and pleasing. Not unlike that movie Pleasantville before the kids discover their true passions and their real questions. But diversity must be kept to a minimum and exposure to new ideas must be strictly controlled. If you are living in this kind of bubble I highly recommend you stick a pin in it. Life, faith and God are bigger than that.

When we get passionately attached to the images we are given, any new experience we have will be categorized and defined through the *lens* of those images. Such is the power of our high-order images of faith. What you believe about the big questions of life can come to direct *all* the questions of life

Doubt and Faith

In his study of multiple faith traditions, James Fowler, PhD, former Professor of Theology and Human Development at Emory University, wondered if there were observable stages to the experience of faith. In other words, do people experience changes to their faith over time? Fowler found that beyond the initial experience of a religious indoctrination, there were later stages that developed. He named these stages "Doubting Faith" and "Owned Faith."

Those of us who delve more deeply into the faith will often encounter questioning and doubt. While many people never question the images provided by their religious institution and its authorities, there was an observable, distinct stage of faith growth in the various religious groups that Fowler studied.

The impetus for questioning the images of a faith can begin with our growing awareness of differences of opinion among believers and the authorities of the religious institution. Sometimes these "deeper divers" encountered some aspect of the faith that did not seem moral or true to them.

At this point, Fowler found that these people would then tend to move into a phase of doubting, and that phase most often led them away from the comfort of the congregation as they began to think and speak of things that were disquieting to the others in that faith community. Those who continue to experience faith at the indoctrination level will tend to feel threatened by anyone who challenges the security of the images and authorities to which they have become attached. But Fowler found that moving through this stage of questioning was a part of a maturing faith. He found that only those who encountered doubt would move on to the deeper experience he called "Owned Faith."

Drawing from Fowler's observations, it seems important to recognize here that a willingness to question always involves a shift in the "locus of authority," or the centralized place where authority is found. To doubt something we have been told requires a sense of our *own* authority as opposed to our continued subjugation to another's. So when this shift occurs, the community in which the "doubter" has participated will then most often reject him or her for their "heresy." (Who are *you* to question the authority of the pastor?)

On a larger scale, this shift away from relying on external authority to relying on one's own awareness is an aspect of maturity in all areas of life. In fact, it is the journey of all humans as they move from dependency in childhood to greater independence — and then interdependence — in our maturity.

Some religious groups provide imagery combined with an emotion-driven sense that they are the *only* path toward God — and away from chaos and suffering. In these communities all truth is to be found in the continuing revelations of a prophetic leader. In such a closed system it is easy to feel harmonious and secure. Unfortunately, such systems create an ever-increasing distance between the images of our inner map of habituated images and the "unfiltered life" territory Korzybski described.

With this closed-loop dynamic in a community, and the security of "black or white" thinking about the imagery of the faith, we often find that a type of hero worship will develop around a charismatic religious authority figure, as if he or she were God's mouthpiece. All of this adulation serves the need for certainty and security among the followers, and the more perfect the authority seems to them, the more secure they feel in the imagery they have received. It's no secret that this self-serving system, taken to the extreme, can produce a great temptation for narcissism in religious leaders.

Let me pause here in my examination of the images and scripts involved in our experience of spirituality and religion for a couple of important announcements.

First, let me say that the dynamic of religious fanaticism I just explored is a source of great suffering and intense conflict in our world today. The violence we experience is the result of our inability to consider or meekly accept the limitations and incompleteness of our images and visions.

When religious leaders, enjoying the power and prestige of their positions, play upon the emotional dynamics of their followers, the result can be disastrous. But these leaders are not the real problem, either.

The real issue is our desperate need for stable images of a God to cling to. Maybe the time is coming for a global movement of people of faith to move away from this insecure clinging to our limited images. When that day comes, we will be less easily manipulated by those who want us to be soldiers in their self-serving causes, and we will create a more peaceful world.

Sure, we *all* need stability at times. We want a rock-solid foundation on which to build our lives. Questioning any tenet of the faith to which we have been indoctrinated can feel like yanking the ground from beneath our feet. However, it is actually our *lack* of questioning and doubting that does the most damage to our maturing faith. A God that cannot withstand doubt and questioning is far too frail to inspire us — and far too anthropocentric to feel real. Can you imagine what would have happened if the prophets of the past had not been open to new movements of inspiration because they needed the stability of the images they had already acquired?

My second announcement regarding imagery, scripts, religion, and spirituality is this: When it comes to moving through the doubting stages of our experience of faith, and we begin to question the images we've been given in order to enable our transformation and growth, we often encounter a hitch. That hitch is social. In many cases, to question or doubt our religious imagery means we can become isolated from deep, caring friendships — and sometimes even family relationships. Here's the thing to be aware of: Every shift of consciousness we make will affect our entire web of relationships — and how these relationships then change or fail is something that is beyond our control. This truth can be an evolutionary sticking point, especially if you are not aware of it until it arrives on your doorstep.

Fowler's "Owned Faith," is a stage of faith maturity in which we may continue to question, but we have made the turn toward affirming what we find to be true for ourselves, rather than just what we *don't* find to be true about the others.

In his book, *A Different Drum*, renowned author and psychiatrist Scott Peck, MD, explores and renames Fowler's stages in a way that I think is especially useful to our purposes as Learners. Peck's term for Fowler's later stage of faith development is the "Mystic – Universal" stage. Arriving at this stage, and having moved through earlier stages of Skepticism and Doubt, we find ourselves in a place of attaching to the *essence* of our faith as opposed to the *form* of it, and we are then able to define our faith through personal experience rather than the creeds and belief systems created by others.

There is a big difference between attachment to imagery and engagement in the *experience* of spiritual practice. This evolution of our consciousness involves both. As we come meekly to hold our habituated images more lightly, we know that even our most cherished imagery is incomplete. With this awareness we can then become open to new visions that emerge from the territory of life rather than continuing to rehearse the limited images that already make up our inner maps. We feel awake to the ambiguity of the present and mysteries of spiritual experience — and life.

In his PBS series of interviews with Bill Moyer entitled *The Power of Myth*, Joseph Campbell, American mythologist, writer, and lecturer, makes an important distinction between the historic roles of shamans and priests. I would express Campbell's distinction in this way: Shamans commune with burning bushes and bring the fire of illumination down from the mountain. As one Guatemalan shaman once told me, a shaman is just someone who has fallen in love with the sacred. Priests, on the other hand, play a more functional role in blessing our culturally acceptable norms, rites, and rituals. In the Judeo-Christian tradition, you can see these differences in much the same way as the characters of Moses and Jesus compared with Aaron and Paul. I think it's important to differentiate between these experiences because they mirror our own experience.

Here's what I mean by that. Within each of us there is both a Moses and an Aaron, and both a Jesus and a Paul. One seeks the transcendental while the other creates order out of that experience, conducts services of remembrance, and tries to put these mysteries into words.

As Carl Jung once said, "Religion is the best defense against a religious experience." I don't hear these words as an attack on faith, but rather as a clarification. Putting this into my own words, religious belief is not the same as a spiritual experience. Beliefs are images to which we have become habituated. These images are always incomplete abstractions of the lived experience, just like a picture will never capture the *experience* of the Grand Canyon.

Like so many people I know, there came a point when I found my own faith to feel unfinished. Prior to that time, I had plenty of habituated images to answer all my questions, as if the jigsaw puzzle of life had already been completed for me. And then I somehow came to realize that many of those pieces didn't really fit. I came face-to-face with the reality that there was a whole box full of pieces I had omitted without realizing it.

In many cultures, religious traditions are good at the indoctrination of their followers into religious imagery, but not so good at supporting our *spiritual practice*. However, there are spiritual practices found in almost all religious traditions that are very similar to the practices I have presented for how to transcend our habituated images. I would imagine that these practices are not often taught in faith communities where questioning our images is not valued.

There are many spiritual traditions with a rich history of sharing the same basic spiritual practices: prayer, meditation, contemplation, mindfulness, and the ecstatic practice of dance/movement. While the images of God held by these traditions may vary according to the culture, landscape, language, and history of its people, spiritual practice itself is remarkably similar across the landscape of religious traditions.

I believe that these common spiritual practices have a great role to play in the evolution of our human consciousness. Whether this role will be developed and embraced as we move forward in our general and inevitable evolution is yet to be seen; however, it's pretty easy to see that a number of spiritual practices across many religious traditions have already contributed to our current state of consciousness. Or, as Matthew Fox once wrote, "If Christianity can't recover its mystical tradition — and teach it — it should simply close down and go out of business."

What does all this mean to you and me in our experience of faith and spirituality? As we have explored previously, we all experience faith through our human consciousness; the families and cultures we are born into provide us with religious answers and cosmological imagery infused with emotion. As we grow up drinking from that fountain, we habituate these images and probably take them for granted as undeniable truth.

From our analysis of the basics of human consciousness so far, we now know that what we call "faith" is in fact a powerful set of images and emotional scripts. Although these scripts are somewhat different for each of us, there is a great deal of commonality that tends to connect us around the same imagery, emotion, and scripts. For this reason, we don't just *think* our religious beliefs. We *feel* them. In a nutshell, we experience our religious faith in a way that fits our emotional scripts.

Here's an example that might help bring this home for you. Imagine that you grow up in a culture or family that represses both Excitement and Enjoyment. This is not too far from what we know as "the Puritanical work ethic," named for a religious sect that came to America for religious freedom in the early 18th century. It is likely that people were drawn to become Puritans because of their own pre-existing emotional scripts. As the Puritans lived these scripts, their religious practices reinforced those scripts. There is a blissful resonance in this self-perpetuating cycle.

I would suggest here that whatever your own religious experience has been up until now, it has always been filtered through the images and emotional scripts you've acquired thus far. As these images, tied to their emotional scripting, are habituated, they become like colored glasses we don't even know we're wearing.

Why does a person choose one form of worship over another? Why does every religious service in your town have its own unique envelope of emotional expression? If I have emotional scripts that trigger Shame whenever I get excited, I am not likely to attend a service where people jump up and down, wave their arms in the air, and shout, "Hallelujah!" When it comes to a religious experience, what makes something moving or meaningful to us depends on our own images and the emotional dynamics imprinted upon them.

With this understanding in mind, it's pretty easy to see that beyond providing images of God, religion incorporates all of our own imagery, including our images of self and of others. Perhaps that is why questioning any religious tenet to which we have become indoctrinated can be so difficult. It is not just the images of our faith we're questioning; it's also the images of our self we're exposing and testing. This makes it all very, very personal. As German theologian, philosopher, and mystic Meister Eckhart once wrote, "if the only prayer you ever pray is 'thank you,' it is enough… If I could just study a caterpillar long enough, I would never need to read another verse of scripture, so full of the Word of God is one caterpillar."

If you find yourself resonating deeply with the idea that spirituality is as important — if not more important — to our evolution of consciousness than religion, maybe Eckhart's words will be helpful to you. I don't believe that spirituality has to be complex — or that it should necessarily replace religious tradition. But I do believe that embracing our spirituality is a necessary part of Choosing to Evolve in the area of faith. In fact, I think it is impossible to ignore.

The Big Picture

As human beings, we have no choice but to develop images of the big picture. As we grow from the concrete thinking of our childhood into the more complex mental processes of adulthood, we relate to everything in our world through abstract imagery. It's our thing! Every kind of cup you pick up to drink from has already become an image. What this means in a practical sense is that without even thinking about it, your image of that cup tells you the amount of effort you need to use to grip it (Styrofoam vs. glass). In exactly the same way, without really thinking about them, our images of the world around us tell us whether we are safe, whether we are being good or bad, how to relate to nature, how much attention to give to a stranger, how to respond to death, how much to value life, what is a miracle, and much, much more.

These high-order abstractions help us to guide our lives. We each have our own images of the world — and of our place in it. And, even if those images don't include a God, we still have them. In fact, even if we have come to a place of not adopting any religious belief at all, we still have an image of what faith is, what a house of worship looks like, and how we acquired our emotionally charged perspective on faith and religion.

If, as Theologian Paul Tillich wrote, faith is our "ultimate concern," it begs the questions: What is *your* ultimate concern? How does faith shape and direct your life? Whatever your answers to these questions, I suggest that what we call "faith" is much more than religious belief. It includes a big-picture image of life, who we are, and who we are meant to be in the world.

What we experience in life may be most profoundly impacted by the abstract images we hold about God, life, and death. While these images may provide us with stability in the gushing immediacy of living, the *lens* these images present is always going to be imperfect — or, as St. Paul put it, "Now we see through a mirror dimly."

I want to suggest that there is a shaman within you who is seeking truth, spiritual experience, and communion with life. And there is also a priest, trying to form a system that will manage and interpret all you have experienced. The shaman/mystic part of you is the part that is open to experiencing everything in its raw, unfiltered essence. The priest in you prefers stability to the mystical, structure to the ephemeral, and control to the ecstasy. Our current balance between our coexisting needs for security and adventure/exploration may well be found in how we have habituated our Affects of Interest-Excitement and Fear-Terror.

I think the reality is that we need both the shaman *and* the priest in our spiritual life. For example, my United Methodist upbringing offered beautiful and inspiring images that formed my early experience of faith, but I did not find my personal spiritual experience until I began exploring Native American spirituality. That is when I learned how different it was to pray in a sweat lodge and the way a drum dance could create a container to encounter my own visions. Today, while my inner priest is consulting the lectionary for this week's scripture, my inner shaman is on a vision quest in the desert.

Every center for religious learning will encounter the tension between our human need for stability and our conflicting need for growth and inspiration. There are few places in the world where human beings submit more willingly to authority in hopes of learning who they are, what their lives mean, and what a good life looks like. I think it's very important to realize that *no* authority or leader is perfect — we humans are *all* operating from limited experience and awareness. Perhaps the greatest gift a spiritual teacher may posses is meekness.

The imagery we communicate and receive can define a big part of our life. Images provide us with place to start, a launching pad for our life. But when these images become too fixed and concretized, they end up limiting our growth. In this scenario, we reject new inspiration — or simply codify it into the former system — rather than cracking open and transforming our fixed imagery. Perhaps that is why at one point in his life Meister Eckhart prayed, "that God would rid me of God."

Some might read this statement from Eckhart and consider him a religious "backslider." I think it might be better to understand him as one who has delved deeply into his own imagery and found it to be more like the false idols all of our images of God tend to become.

To undertake such a journey into our own imagery is to meekly recall the limited nature of our images. In this case this also involves the ability to Move Alongside the religious images we have received. When we see our religious imagery anew through the lens of meekness, it can be a beautiful awakening — and it can also feel a little scary. The images that have served to protect us from our fears are particularly hard to question. However, when we learn to Move Alongside those feelings as well, we move into the immediacy of our being to gain more capacity to choose how we attend to Fear.

To be sure, there are plenty of scary things in the world. Faith can offer a general sense of safety that goes beyond the evidence at hand. For most people, it takes only a basic religious belief to keep those fears at bay. These basic beliefs often take the shape of reassurance and comfort. Sometimes they offer a promise that if certain religious practices are kept, then good fortune will be ours.

Our religious imagery often provides us with a vehicle for managing our fear and frustration, so to question *anything* is to risk opening the door to those feelings. That is part of the reason I always work with people on managing their emotional world first. Once we have gained the capacity to tolerate and release high levels of these Affects, suddenly we don't need to cling to images that have outlived their capacity to inspire or heal us.

A Bigger God

To sum this up, our human consciousness operates through imagery, habituates that imagery, takes it all for granted, and then moves on to the next experience. The reason why our high-order abstractions work for us is that they allow us to wake up in the morning and not worry about why we are here, whether the world is safe, what will happen if we die, and so many other crucial questions. Free from these existential concerns, we are then able to go about our work of living our life.

However, if you can set aside these images, even for a moment, you may discover that life is bigger than you ever thought it could be. You may also find that God may be bigger than you imagined, and with these new realizations you may find yourself entering the arena of spiritual experience. The tools for such a journey can be found everywhere, from the contemplative and mystical traditions of Christianity, to yoga and meditation from the ancient Sutras, to the ecstatic love religion of the Sufis and more. These basic tools for spiritual discovery are in many ways similar to some of the exercises we have explored earlier in this book. And, while you may or may not find them in the place of worship you attend, I hope you now have the encouragement you need to pursue your own unique, mystical, shamanic journey of faith.

In this exploration I have pointed to some of the key differences between religious abstract imagery and spiritual practice. I see this as the essential distinction between religious habituation/fixation and a fresh, unfiltered experience of the moment.

I think the good news for all of us is that most of the spiritual experiences we find among the various faith traditions seem to operate as vehicles of de-habituation. In a way you could say that it is not religious belief that is the problem in our world. It is rather that the deep spiritual practices found within them are so often ignored. I believe that these spiritual practices are at the very heart of our human evolution of consciousness. By gaining greater capacity to choose when to flow with the automatic habituation machine of the mind — and when to slow things down through practices that help us de-habituate — we can learn how to be present in the mystery of the moment.

Chapter 18

Institutionalized Imagery and Relinquishing Defenses

We could spend hours talking about the nine Affects and how our individual scripted experience of each Affect can define our lives. For now, though, let's start with a look at a few defensive scripts that may easily become institutionalized and reinforced through the rituals and practices of a community. When we become aware of the scripted nature of our emotions — and particularly the defensive scripts we have developed — it is hard to ignore how some institutions are operating with the same scripts.

Earlier in this book we explored how the Affect of Shame-Humiliation is triggered when we are faced with an impediment to good feelings, often leading us to engage defensive scripts that tend to get habituated over time. Even though all learning involves some experience of humiliation, defending against Shame-Humiliation is one of the most efficient ways I know of to undermine any new illumination or enlightenment.

Think of it this way. If a close friend pulls you aside at a party and tells you that you're talking too much, what do you feel? Shame, in the form of embarrassment, would probably be the first Affect triggered, right? So then what? You may automatically avoid the Shame with any of the four scripts we explored earlier in our discussion of the Compass of Shame (Avoidance, Withdrawal, Attack-Other, Attack-Self). We have already seen how each of those scripts will cut us off from wellbeing and growth, often sending our emotions into a downward and destructive spiral.

Here's the good news. The *experience* of Shame-Humiliation doesn't *have* to be so overwhelming. Once we have cultivated some degree of meekness, we can accept critique and feedback from others, and then learn from it rather than defend against it. You see, all learning is a dialogue with Shame-Humiliation, and the same is true for our images of institutions including those created around faith and spirituality.

Religious groups often call upon defensive scripts to varying degrees as they seek to hold on to good feelings and ignore their own failings and incompleteness. That is not to say that some religious groups don't provide the very thing we need. Some of them may offer practices that enable individuals to review their personal experiences of Shame, confess their wrongdoings, address the source of Shame, and seek to make positive changes.

But at other times, religious institutions may play a significant role in the perpetuation — and institutionalization — of the defenses Nathanson describes as Compass of Shame scripts. Let's take a look back at each of these four defensive scripts, now in their institutional and religious context, to see what we might learn.

Withdrawal Scripts

It has been remarkable to see how insulated many institutions and faith-based groups choose to become over time. I am not just speaking of those who move off to remote locations and behind fortress-like walls. I think it is safe to say that even mainstream institutional and religious groups tend to form social dynamics that limit exposure to conflicting perspectives that would challenge the dominant images of their group.

It's easy to see how this "circle the wagons" mentality can be seen as Withdrawing from the possibility of exposure to Shame. In the context of religion, the Withdrawal script usually begins with religious leaders who prefer to retain their own images no matter how limited or ill informed they are. Still, they have to contend with anyone within the group who raises questions.

There are hundreds of ways to undermine the credibility of an alternative voice in any institution, from whispered innuendos to outspoken movements that demonize or threaten that voice. In some instances, we see anti-intellectualism and a distrust of any skeptical analysis. Or, as one minister told me, "Never doubt. Doubt is of the Devil!"

Here's the crux of it. When the images we have received from a teacher or an institution are so fragile that they must never be questioned, when they are so certain that to question them means we must be exiled from the "faithful," then we are in trouble. It is only through the destruction of our idolized images that there can be any new movement of our spirit.

Learning and growing always involve the *breaking* of former images, and that breaking will likely trigger Shame-Humiliation. And of course, defending against feelings of shame in the spiritual context is actually the *opposite* of faith. Father Wes Seeliger, Episcopal priest, author, and founder of the Foundation for Contemporary Theology, used to tell the story of his childhood love of playing with cars. He would say something like this:

When I was a kid I loved to play with little cars and my favorite way of playing with them was to go over to my grandmother's side of the house where she kept the drapes drawn so the furniture wouldn't fade. In that dark room I would arrange my cars all around me in a neat little circle and I would sit and admire my cars.

Then one day, completely unannounced, my cousin Susan came for a visit and she came rushing in and started kicking my cars all over the place until there was nothing left of my circle. My grandmother told me later that I cried for two hours without stopping. It was like my whole world had been destroyed.

Later, after Susan was gone, I went back in and began finding my cars. I was able to reassemble the circle and everything was all right — until I found out that Susan was coming for another visit! So I decided I had better try to meet her outside and negotiate. That's what I did.

Then a strange thing happened. Susan convinced me that it might be more fun to take my cars outside to play with them. I had never thought of that! It was amazing! We put real dirt in the dump truck and we ran cars up and down the walks. Susan even convinced me to crash a couple of them. I never dreamed you could have so much fun with cars!

The lesson I learned from Susan was more than anything I learned in school — even in seminary — and it is this: We all have a tendency to want to surround ourselves with the things we love and to keep all of our security systems in place. Life has a way of coming into those well-ordered scenes and disrupting our sense of security and familiarity, leaving us feeling utterly devastated. But God has a way of coming in the midst of that chaos and inviting us to a life of faith. Faith is the willingness to risk the things you love most in the great outdoors.

I have always loved this image of faith that I learned from Wes by way of Rev. Bert Scott. Bert and I traveled the back roads of Louisiana in the 70s, leading workshops on the weekends during my college years. I listened to Bert tell this story a dozen times, and I think it helped me to take a big leap of faith as I was beginning to face the limitations of my own adolescent imagery. I had arrived at college with all the right answers — and none of the right questions. This story is a good counterbalance to the all-too-human tendency to develop defensive scripts, even in the journey of faith.

Attack-Self Scripts

It probably won't surprise you to know that there is also a long history of religious groups using the Attack-Self script to defend against the experience of Shame-Humiliation. You may remember from our earlier exploration that the basic process of defensive scripting involves immersion into the expression of Shame in a way that actually lessens the experience (If I attack myself, others are less likely to humiliate me) and may instead offer relief.

There are probably extreme examples of Attack-Self scripts in many religious traditions — those who submit to suffering as a sign of their devotion. However, it's pretty easy to find lesser expressions of Attack-Self scripts in various traditions when you examine some of the language in various prayers that seem to carry this flavor: "We are not worthy so much as to gather the crumbs from under thy table…"

When the image of self must be perfect, any action or thought that is not ideal will trigger Shame. Through attacking the "self" responsible for the less-than-ideal thought or action, we can dis-iden-tify with that "self" and shift our identification to the ideal. Problem solved, right? No more cognitive dissonance between the Ideal Self and the Actual Self. This is one way to see the process involved in the "Attack-Self" script.

Unfortunately, however, the scripted images and emotions that led to the triggering of Shame in the first place are unlikely to be trans-formed by this process, and a repetitive cycle of similarly unacceptable thoughts and/or behaviors — with the required repentance — begins again. Lather, rinse, repeat. After a while, this particular Attack-Self script simply becomes a tool our psyche uses to retain a positive self-image in the midst of mounting evidence to the contrary.

In is interesting to consider that institutions and religious groups that encourage this kind of Attack-Self scripting to relieve Shame may be more toxic to the world than we think. How many religious leaders have abused the vulnerable in their parishes while justifying their ongoing bad behavior through confession and pardon?

In my years of counseling I have run into more than a few individuals who were deeply traumatized by religious leaders. Sometimes these were ritualized instances of abuse that used religious themes to suggest that the abuse was somehow essential to the victim's salvation. Although it is hard for most of us to imagine the level of self-deception required for a religious leader to sink to such evil, it may be that their well-established defensive scripts for defeating Shame-Humiliation plays a part in these dynamics. The dissociation of Shame can become so automatic to a personality that he or she loses all capacity to call thoughts and behavior into question. Thinking is subservient to feeling — and you can't think what you can't feel.

When we start examining the dynamics of Shame scripts, we must also consider the large-scale subjugation of cultures. When Karl Marx described religion as "the opium of the people," he probably had no idea how much the scripted response to Shame plays a part in this numbing. Some religious teachings are often interpreted to mean that we should not challenge our lot in life or strive for justice here on earth; we should serve our masters and wait for our reward in Heaven. This, of course, is completely at odds with our new understanding of what it means to be meek.

Once you start looking for it, you may find that there is a subtle Attack-Self script at work in many places of worship. There is an important difference between the healthy reflection and repentance of one's own actions and an Attack-Self script. This difference is mostly evident in how we acknowledge Shame in the body and in the moment. The actual feeling of shame *can* motivate us to explore how our good feelings are being impeded and to address the *source* of those feelings. Unfortunately, in many cases religious settings do not offer the confidentiality or the consciousness needed to hold the thread of connection required for this healing process to occur.

Jungian Analyst and Episcopal Priest John Sanford suggested that if the easy forgiveness offered by his Christian tradition was all people needed, then why were those he counseled still haunted by dreams of their feelings of shame and guilt, long after their prayers of confession? This question heralds an evolutionary journey for religious/spiritual leaders. As we begin to learn about our own consciousness, as well as how the habituated and emotionally charged imagery makes human consciousness work, we can begin to care more effectively for the needs of those we serve. It takes knowledge and boldness to enter into another person's story and hold that thread when they are at their most vulnerable.

The strength of religious traditions lies in both their intent and their rituals. I believe that humans have a longing for a sense of community in which they can join with others to create rituals that help them reflect upon their experiences, process their feelings, express their intentions, and then align those intentions with the way they live. We, in fact, need *more* of that and *less* repetition of stale rhetoric and dogmatic conformity to images that are worshipped like idols. While these societies of certainty can be seductive to those in need of stability, they often create a prison for the growing consciousness of individuals.

Avoidance Scripts

You may recall that while at first blush Avoidance scripts seem similar, they are actually quite different from Withdrawal scripts. Rather than removing oneself from the scene in which Shame is triggered as we do in a Withdrawal script, the Avoidance script is more about *distracting ourselves* from the feeling of shame itself. There are few arenas in the human experience more rife with this defensive scripting than religion. In fact, it is even possible to see the entire experience of a particular faith as one big Avoidance script.

Now don't run away hollering, "Heretic!" Let me explain what I mean. Imagine that we are living 5,000 years ago, and we have grown up hearing tales of a great eruption of the nearby volcano that wiped out many of our people. There is great fear of this happening again, and everyone around us lives with this anxiety. And, over time, our people came to believe that the volcano God could be appeased — and our safety ensured — by an annual sacrifice. Now we have a way to avoid Fear and get on with life, as long as we keep serving the volcano God with our required sacrifice.

For this imaginary "us," this was an evolutionary leap. Rather than to live in constant Fear, we developed an Avoidance script. Of course the actual "threat" remains the same, but we now have more of a sense of control, and that relieves our experience of the threat. In much the same way, people sometimes use the images of religion to avoid Fear, particularly their fear of death. The scripted defenses they tend to adopt against Fear feels much better than being overwhelmed by it. If Fear were to dominate our lives, it would displace all other emotions that we might otherwise feel. A life stuck in Fear is the worst of human existence.

However, the evolutionary leap of habituating the Avoidance script as a way to escape Fear comes with a price. The very institutionalization of any system of denial of Fear will eventually just *perpetuate* the Fear we're trying to avoid, creating yet more Fear — and more need for denial. The Avoidance script as a way to mitigate Fear also allows us to continue living in a place or manner that is not in our best interests. We develop elaborate systems to keep the Fear or Shame away, requiring continual effort. Eventually, these efforts gradually creep into other areas of life, seeking to erase all ambiguity and fragility from our experience.

As these "sacrifices" to our Fear become institutionalized, there comes a need for some sort of "priestly class" to manage and direct this system. Unfortunately, as these are other human beings, they may have other agendas as well. They may even take advantage of our system of Fear and Avoidance scripting for their personal gain. They may also compete with one another for followers — and even pit one group against another: the true believers vs. the infidels.

Of course, I am not making a case here against *all* religious experiences. I am merely trying to paint a consistent picture of how our old evolution of consciousness that once served us very well can also create new problems. Today it is not just Fear we avoid through our clinging to religious images; it is Shame as well. Even *speaking* the words I have just written aloud will demonstrate my point.

Here's what I mean. Try reading this section to someone and watch what happens. Many of us recoil at the idea that our religious images can be questioned and to have someone suggest such will likely trigger one of the Shame scripts. We will likely first run to the defense of the images we have received, and then we will shift the conversation toward the scripted rationalizations we have accepted — and habituated — for those images. We will probably then try to show off some knowledge about these images and where they come from to avoid the issue that might otherwise undermine the way we have come to avoid Shame-Humiliation.

This is all very understandable. When we lean on an Avoidance script to manage our Fear and Shame, any discussion that questions the images we carry of that script are much more than intellectual beliefs — they are the cornerstones of our emotional stability. To remove our Avoidance scripts is to seemingly return us back to the world of fearing the volcano God's wrath. But there is another path.

The new consciousness we're exploring here is all about being able to *choose*. Choosing to Evolve is an evolution in self-awareness. When we choose this new awareness, we don't need to appease the volcano God *or* live in Fear. We become masters of our own images and emotions by learning how to Move Alongside them.

When we Move Alongside our images and the emotions that have become attached to them, we open ourselves to *listening* to our Fear without becoming overwhelmed by it. We gain the capacity to *face* our Fear courageously rather than to deny it or to allow it to dominate our lives. The truth is, we *need* Fear. Fear tells us, "Look out!" "Don't go there!" or "This is a dangerous!" In other words, God save us from the fearlessness made possible through our image of God!

Following Ancient Maps

We should also touch briefly on the institutionalization of an Avoidance script for managing Shame-Humiliation. Imagine that you are trying to find your way around your city, but all you have is a map from the third century. Think about that for a moment. According to the map you are holding in your hands, the earth is flat, and there is little information about the people who are living beyond your neighboring region. And of course, the sum of their beliefs and cultures is a complete mystery.

Now imagine that your parents and community leaders are telling you that this is the only true map and it will never, ever change. All other maps are evil and wrong. You look at the map and see that it is quite beautiful, filled with many inspiring insights.

Then one day, a stranger comes to town from the other side of the world, talking about the wonders she has seen. You sit down for a cup of coffee with her at a local diner, and you pull out your map.

"Show me where you come from on this map," you say.

"It's not on your map," she replies without even looking at the map. She then goes on to tell you that before your map was drawn, there *were* no maps; there were only verbal directions. People would just *tell* people about the things they had seen and how they had seen them. "The problem with maps is that once you draw them they can't change," she says. "It was better in the old days because whenever someone learned something new, they would just change the directions. The map you have can't change." Then she asks sweetly, "Have you ever heard of the Internet?"

Now you are faced with a choice. Your first option is the easiest. Just don't travel. Stay where you are and you won't even *need* a map. This choice, by the way, would be a Withdrawal script. Your second option is to defend the map: "I think you must not be looking at this map," you'd tell her. "Just *look* at the fine detail and the pretty scrollwork on the edges! Hey do you want some pie? They have great pie here. Oh, you know what? I need to go, I've got to meet a friend to do something *really* important."

With this choice you'd be serving up an Avoidance script (with Withdrawal for dessert). If you're really worked up and emotionally invested in that map, however, there is another response you might choose: "You are crazy. This is the map! The only map! You must be an alien, and I think you'd better get out of town before you get thrown out!" That response would illustrate your move from an Avoidance script to an Attack-Other script.

Attack-Other Scripts

As Nathanson describes it, the Attack-Other script seeks to defend against the experience of Shame-Humiliation by turning the tables on those whose very presence can trigger the Affect. For example, if you are failing in Chemistry class, you may find yourself making fun of the geeks who seem to learn things so easily.

In religious circles the Attack-Other script often shows up in situations where, rather than face a moment that calls our images of ourselves and the world into question, we turn on anyone who represents alternatives. Their questions are perceived — and often decried — as threats to the "true faith." To respond to this questioning in any other way would be to allow doubt to creep in and undermine the images we cling to as essential to our faith.

For those whose positive self-image is most fragile, even the tiniest bit of questioning feels like removing the bottom block from a Jenga game. When you understand this dynamic, it becomes easier to see why some religious groups seem to institutionalize and continually reinforce the idea that they are "under attack" and that the threats come from absolute evil. In the process of reinforcing this perspective, they become blinded to the humanity, positive intent, and wider exposure that could otherwise offer them an even more complete expression of the very faith they have claimed.

For this reason, the emerging evolution of consciousness we're examining here will continue to be a thorn in the side of any religious group that seeks to maintain an exclusive claim to the Truth of their images. And, for those who have adopted the kinds of scripts we have illustrated in these pages, this Evolution will be particularly difficult.

So what's the alternative? How can our experience of religion and spirituality Evolve as we see through the layers of defensive emotional scripting that have been a part of all human experience and institutionalized in all arenas of our lives? I believe that the path is narrow. Choosing to Evolve requires Consciousness, Creativity, and Commitment. All of the work we have discussed as a part of an individual evolution is also required of institutional ones. Find a faith community that is defined by non-defensive and authentic meekness. Find one that holds images lightly and values diversity. And if you can't find one, start one.

This idea is not new. In fact, it calls to mind a passage from the Hebrew scriptures: "If my people, who are called by my name, will humble themselves and pray and seek my face and turn from their wicked ways, then I will hear from heaven, and I will forgive their sin and will heal their land." Unfortunately, however, this theological perspective makes God responsible for our suffering. In this theology we suffer for our sin, but if we repent and choose righteousness, then God will heal us.

Some Christian scholars note that it was this theology/worldview that led John the Baptizer into his ascetic and prophetic role, calling his countrymen to repentance in response to the Roman occupation of Israel 2000 years ago. He believed that if enough people were to renounce their "wicked" ways, God would save them. It is also important to note that John's ritual cleansing of the people was tied to his renouncement of physical comforts and possessions. Christianity was born in this context.

Jon Dominic Crossan's book, *God and Empire*, describes that context in great detail. Jesus of Nazareth, baptized by John, gathered followers along the Sea of Galilee. Why there? Why these fishermen? The lake was about to be commercialized by the Romans and all fishing would be taxed. Religious beliefs aside, there have always been movements in spiritual/religious traditions in response to the domination of people and the planet. Unfortunately, those same religious traditions can be equally complicit in their silent ascent to the powerful forces that enslave and dominate, at times even providing the imagery to support them.

Let me offer a new interpretation of that ancient text: "God says, what you are perceiving of me is just imagery *you* have created. Some of it is cool, but don't make an idol of it. I'm way more than any image of me you're clinging to. I'm way more than *anything* you can imagine. Be meek in your approach to your perceptions of life. Your perceptions must always remain nimble and able to change and grow as you learn. I know that when people lose compassion and meekness, everybody suffers. It's unavoidable. Holding grudges, needing to feel powerful — all of these are paths to suffering, as are making yourself safe, wealthy, and powerful at the expense of others.

So how do we make all this better? First, you have to notice how you defend against the feelings of shame and fear. Acknowledge your Shame and your Fear and your grief with somebody, even if it's just one person. Then you can start finding your way to the healing path — and others will join you."

Ethics and Morality

The evolution of our consciousness we are now exploring here will, by definition, be accompanied by an evolution of our sense of ethics and morality. Everything we learn about the scripted nature of our consciousness will, over time, help us to generate new sources for compassion and empathy that will redefine our understanding of what is truly ethical and moral in this new light.

Here are some examples of the kinds of questions this shift may evoke. What does it mean to "live a moral life" if all the images we have inherited as people of faith tell us that we should have no compassion for those who live outside of our tribe? Does simply following the dictates of our religious leader make us moral or ethical? Is it possible that "morality" actually requires a capacity for questioning our indoctrination and subsequent attachment to a specific set of emotionally charged images?

In this light it seems that across the world we have millions of people acting in ways that they *perceive* to be both moral and ethical — while showing no compassion at all for those they abuse, the less fortunate, and the enslaved. The moral questions of our times are the same ones that have existed throughout human history; however, now the inequities are greater and the powers are more dangerous.

Heroes of industry have brought about prosperity in many ways to many parts of the globe. At the same time, however, this very prosperity we celebrate is also deepening our enslavement to material things and our economic dependency and conspicuous consumption of ever more limited resources. If he could, John the Baptizer would once again be standing out by a river in the wilderness calling upon us to repent. Buddha would once again find his way outside the palace walls and denounce his participation in the domination systems of his culture. Where are these heroes among the religious groups of our time?

We can never expect all people everywhere to gain the capacity to question the images they have received that dehumanize and dominate others. What *is* possible, however, is to create dialogue about the *sources* of those images that support domination and inequity. Religion seems to be one of the most important areas to examine.

The answer to the world's terrible ills is not likely to emerge from any institution. The people who are Choosing to Evolve from a consciousness that defends its narrow window of "reality" to a consciousness of transformation and learning hold the answer that can help heal our world. Jesus once said, "If you want to see the realm of God you must first become like a child." It is a good way to begin describing the journey. If we seek to create community that is more loving, whole, and beautiful, it helps to shed some of the images that blind us to what is.

Now, I realize that some who read these observations will see them as a rejection of all religious systems or an indictment of religion in general. My intent, however, is quite the contrary. I see the goal of achieving religious understanding as among the *highest* of human aspirations. Religious groups often teach compassion and can bring out the very best in what it is to be human.

We are most often much better off with some of the images we receive from our faiths, because our human consciousness tends to construct these images with or without the help of organized religion. That we have and hold ideological images is not the problem. The problem is our *resistance* to allowing those images to be questioned, broken, or replaced as we learn and grow.

I hope that what I have presented here will spark some new dialogue around the need for people in all parts of the world to step back from the propaganda and rhetoric in institutional, religious, and political positioning. Take a breath. Ask yourself which of these images are doing more good — or more harm. When you identify one of these images, stop and ask yourself, "Where does this image come from?" "When did I get it?" "What does it mean to me?" Notice that at this level we are all the same. We are all Learners in the classroom of life. How could it be any other way?

The Death of Compassion

Perhaps the greatest truth that faiths have celebrated across all times is that of compassion and unity — the oneness behind all things. Christians sing, "We are one in the spirit." The term, "Yoga," actually means "union." Bob Marley and U2 both sing of "One Love." But sometimes the emotional scripting and our attachment to images in our faiths actually work to *destroy* that compassionate connection.

If you think about it, you will quickly see the direct correlation between how defensive a faith group becomes and how little compassion they can experience for others. Whenever we become defensive, the first thing that happens is we lose our empathy for the perspectives, emotions, and experiences of others. Whether we are talking about the conflict in an intimate relationship or the emotional dynamics of a faith group, this is a big issue in our times. Faith groups may be one of the great hopes for humanity if they can recover and teach compassion, contemplation, and the skills of the meek.

As we've discussed before — and now can examine in a fuller light, the evolution of consciousness we are now facing as human beings will happen whether we like it or not. There will be no going back to a world where diversity is kept on foreign shores across insulating oceans. In our newly evolved consciousness, every encounter with diverse opinions and perspectives will create enormous opportunity to expose the flaws in old systems to reveal new truths and deeper understandings.

It seems important now to close this chapter with a sense of how the new consciousness can feel, rather than a continued critique of the old. Life is not a formula. It is poetry. So let's close this chapter with some of mine.

Revolution of the Meek
Let's go up to that mountain
Where the lands are not divided
Where lions sleep with lambs
And the wars have all subsided
Where peace is made of justice
and not of domination
The power of the meek is in
Their non-participation
Go bravely to your critics
Though their words may set you burning
In your humble openness
You can learn to keep on learning
Flow freely with your feelings
Your truth within this minute
But know that truth is only yours
For the moment that you're in it
To find this place it only takes
Two hearts to give permission
To speak their momentary truth
Defending no position
Right and wrong don't enter when

The goal is understanding
No need to plan ahead for what
The other side is planning
We celebrate our differences
Not seeking resolution
End the domination game
With a meekness revolution
Where strength is found in empathy
Not certainty or pride
And freedom's found through facing down
Defensiveness inside
On this daily precipice
The vulnerable remaining
Make heroes out of those who speak
Without a hint of blaming
And play in fields of freedom
Only meekness can reveal
And celebrate the holy state
Of being what is real

those who have ears...
who were you before
all the voices
and faces taught you
what to think and feel
about wild things like you?
their delight or disgust
like guiding lights
to the guaranteed path
of eternal reward
or eternal damnation
not everyone can see
their own brainwashing
but you saw it
and once you did
there was no turning back
until you saw exactly

how you were fed
from the tree
of the knowledge
of good and evil
how you left the wild garden
of your innocent self behind
for the expectations of others
the limits of their learning
and the slavery of pleasing
now the defining question is
have you questioned
have you tested teachers
and found their limitations?
can you do that still?
or are you finished with life
nothing left to learn
all the pieces put together
ignoring all the funny shapes
still inside the box

my story
everything led to this
subtle nudges to surgeries
a million moments
in an ongoing conversation
with existence
finding ideas like river rocks
gradually learning how
to throw some of them back
but always looking
for gold underfoot
like the poetry in the songs
and words I could feel
but had not yet spoken
feeling less lonely
in the world
looking for salvation

"liberation from ignorance
preservation from destruction
deliverance from danger
so says Webster
some beliefs were fickle
never saved me
from anything
but the ambiguity
that was my birthright
now it's all poetry
salvation is for the hungry
not the comfortable
who sit in safety
repeating circular thoughts
until life gets small
enough to manage
all the gods that we have
made in our own image
no longer receive our sacrifices
they don't require them
they never did
but don't throw out
the baby with the bath
baptize yourself
in what makes you love
not what makes you hate
maybe along the way
when you least expect it
when you are most vulnerable
you may catch a glimpse
of something moving
and you may sense
that out beyond
the things you once imagined
there is something more grand
calling your name

44th and 7th Reunion
She carried a bundle
Of wrinkled papers
The kind that litters every big city street
Pressed to her poncho
In reverent respect
For a savior she'd never meet
He was a honky-tonk singer
On a New York street corner
Shouting songs into the night
Returning the stares of the
Three-piece suit pairs
As they strolled in and out of the light
He sang baby take me back
To a place that I remember
Baby take me back to where the nights were warm
And we'll ride, beyond the danger
And we'll hide from all the pain
We'll ride the City down to Memphis
And let it rain
It was there on the corner
Of 44th and 7th
She wandered by his empty case
a meeting of chance
of a girl in a dance
and a lost boy
who just saw her face
And her eyes in that moment
Broke all his defenses
All the lies he was telling to himself
Just a moment of seeing
One innocent being
It's a mystery that no one can tell
He sang baby take me back
To a place that I remember
Baby take me back to where the nights were warm
And we'll ride, beyond the danger
And we'll hide from all the pain

We'll take the City down to Memphis
And let it rain

Trains of Thought

how long will you ride
on a train you didn't choose
get off!
go play your songs to the traffic
add your voice to the noise
face your fear of rejection
that keeps you bound
to pleasing and pretending
meet the angels who can teach
how to be free
you can't value conversation
until you have been alone
long enough that a stranger
can touch the core of your being
in a glance
trains don't really care
if you want to get off or on
they only demand decision
the doors will not bounce back
waiting for you to choose
i saw a tourist try
to jam his luggage in the door
and we waived goodbye
as his bag and I
headed down the tracks
if you want to try this train
then get on
leave the baggage if you must
just do it
before the doors close
or perhaps you need to walk
and walk for awhile
until your feet are dusty

and your mouth is dry again
and you feel your thirst
salvation is not
an intellectual exercise
it is not even a set of prayers
it is finding water
in the middle of the desert
what is best for you
is not my place to say
so if i offend
i hope you'll treat me as a foreigner
unfamiliar with your customs
every time we meet it is like this
we begin again
the gradual journey
discovering the landscape and
the places where the rivers converge
i know that you have your own way
your path is different from mine
even if we shared the same family
what you are seeing and feeling
is not for me to judge
i can't say what train
is right or wrong for you
even if we were best of friends
it wouldn't be my place
to say such things
in my own journey
i see hunger and thirsting
for truth
can turn any path
into a pilgrimage
with enough hunger
you may find the prophetic
on the margins
and the face of a stranger
offering resurrection

SECTION IV

Meet the Players of Team You

Chapter 19

Consciousness — a Team Sport

In this chapter we are going to explore your identity and apply an analogy of consciousness as a team sport. Who you think you are can be complicated. Most of us hate answering questions about our identity because there are no answers that will fully capture who we are. Bruce Cockburn's song, "Pacing the Cage" expresses this feeling well: "I've proven who I am so many times the magnetic strip's worn thin . . ."

There are probably no images more central to our lives than those that form an identity. Though we pick up these images like we do all the others in our memories, these images feel personal — we identify with them. That makes them all the more important in the scripting of our emotions and the way we talk to ourselves.

Before we dive in let's take a moment to get a clear intention about the work we are doing. It's important that you not use the information in this book to criticize yourself. Some of us do that so much already that any exploration of consciousness like this one only serves as yet another invitation to attack ourselves with criticism.

In this chapter you will learn some things that will help you understand how and why our efforts to apply what we are learning here can get derailed. In these cases, rather than actually *evolving* our consciousness we can easily find ourselves repeating the same scripts with new labels. Be gentle with your self. You can't really *make* yourself Evolve; learning to work with your imagery and emotions is more like *participating* in your evolution than forcing yourself to change.

I once worked with a middle-aged man we'll call Clyde who had struggled for many years with patterns that seemed resistant to any intervention and any number of antidepressants. After months of exploring the various scripts that had been destructive to his career and relationships, we seemed to be making little progress. It was apparent that Clyde recognized that he was still repeating the same scripted responses, even with his new knowledge of them. I began to wonder about the approach we were taking. It was clear that Clyde was dissatisfied with his life, his career, his relationships, and his own lack of discipline.

Eventually, Clyde began to see that this dissatisfaction was a dominant emotional script — and that the way he was approaching therapy was simply a repeat of that same old script. How could it not be? Even after all of the insights revealed to him in therapy, he had seen *all* of them through the lens of his dissatisfaction. Everything always began and ended there, and therapy had only served to make him feel more dissatisfied. As he became aware of this new dynamic of his old script, the challenge he faced was how to approach his constant dissatisfaction. His natural response, of course, would be to simply become dissatisfied with his dissatisfaction script. Instead, Clyde had to begin learning how to be *satisfied*. This was a goal that would require many shifts in his emotional scripts and images.

Life for Clyde had been full of conflicts and drama, which had become both familiar and second nature. To feel satisfied with himself was simply not in Clyde's wheelhouse. As I have shared in previous chapters, learning to manage our negative Affects will not automatically enhance your positive Affects. If your emotional scripts make Excitement feel dangerous, then you may not have had enough practice at expressing that Affect, and learning to *manage* your fear will not suddenly make you feel free to express it. Similarly, if you have a script that directs you to feel Shame every time you're relaxing and enjoying yourself, then it will be hard for you to *ever* feel satisfied, no matter what you accomplish.

The critical thoughts that seemed to automatically appear in Clyde's mind as he interacted with others — and were reflected in his actions — lacked both grace *and* gratitude. Because it's hard to be grateful when you don't feel good, and also hard to feel good when you don't feel grateful, what Clyde needed was *not* just more critique of his struggle with always feeling dissatisfied. He needed to learn and practice some ways of feeling satisfied. He needed to practice letting what *is* be enough — and beyond "enough," a *gift*.

Self-Help Shame

I share this story because I see this issue so often. We are inundated with all kinds of advice and self-help blogs and books. (There is even a great deal of data about "a better way to be" that we can access instantly from a smart phone!) In many cases, however, these insights only tend to make us more aware of our issues and dysfunctions. When we are struggling, these "fixes" can feel more like having someone describe the water in which we are drowning. Or even worse, it can be like discovering that the only way we know how to tread water is somehow wrong or unacceptable.

In some cases, however, it *can* be productive for a therapist to "name the Shame" and define the system, thereby making it more conscious. Albert Adler, the famous Neo-Freudian, coined the phrase, "Spitting in the client's soup," to describe a therapeutic intervention that makes it more difficult for someone to continue participating in a dysfunctional system. This is also the case for much of the "self-help" approach, offering up strategies and practices designed to make it harder to keep to our old, dysfunctional script. The problem with these "fixes" for our "problems" is that our consciousness may not yet have acquired the resources needed to do things any differently or better. If you disrupt someone's Shame script, they will often simply shift to another more problematic defensive script.

These Shame scripts are slippery! Shaming ourselves into facing them is not an option. To change a Shame script requires more acceptance than judgment. Why would I embrace another Shame experience when I already need a script to manage the Shame I have? Most self-help approaches underestimate this reality just as they overestimate our capacity to sustain new scripts without the hard work of building awareness of the scripts we already have.

Being able to recognize and address this distinction is what makes having an experienced therapist so helpful. The journey of evolving consciousness is one that all of us are traveling. We can choose to participate in each other's journeys and learn a great deal from one another, but it also helps to have someone we trust to be our Ariadne. A close friend could play that role for you, but it would have to be someone to whom you can tell anything and everything. Radical honesty is rare due to our scripts around Shame. It also helps if that friend is well acquainted with the material in this book. (That is why we train coaches to support others on this journey.)

Think about it this way. Sometimes your own inner Coach is a part of the problem, and you need to add to your coaching team. That was certainly the case for Clyde. It wasn't just the scripting of his Affects that were causing his suffering; it was *the way he talked to himself.* His inner Coach was scripted in ways that made even his own reflections and planning a part of the problem. Getting support from an external source who will hold a thread of unconditional positive regard — or at least hold you accountable on your commitment to learn — can help you move from absorbing these ideas to actually transforming your life.

Sometimes It's the Team – Sometimes It's the Coach

Many people often wonder about the source of their suffering — and there are about a million voices around us and within us ready to give us the answer. Let's take a breath here and answer that question through the lens we have just explored. Remember, the path to discovery is opened by loving acceptance. Without that kind of acceptance, any reflection will likely be tinted by the need to hide things from view.

In my experience as a therapist, I would have to say that sometimes the source of our suffering involves some sort of maladaptive glitch with one of our Affects. At other times, our suffering originates in how we are *reflecting* on our experience. To figure out where someone's suffering is originating, I sometimes imagine the Affects as "The Team" and the process of self-reflection as The Coach.

With the team analogy we can better understand some of the particular dynamics that are most helpful in *e*volving our conscious-ness rather than simply *re*volving through the same old scripts. Even though I feel a little bit conflicted about using this football analogy as our model (Football is a popular sport in the US, but it may be unfamiliar to many people around the world), for now it provides a complex enough analogy to serve our purpose of learning. So even if you have to learn a bit before you can apply it, and whether you like professional football or hate it, I think you may find that this analogy works fairly well as a map to explore what we have been discussing. Let's begin by examining the parts of the team we will use in our analogy.

The Center (the one who begins the play by hiking the ball) represents all of the somatic (body) signals including: pain, pleasure, urges, drives, tension, sensation, etc.

The Players include all nine Affects, including the full body responses they initiate when triggered — and the scripts they become over time.

The Coaches represent the processes of reflection/analysis (instant replay) and anticipation/projection (the playbook). Some of this reflection is habituated and hardly conscious (like the decision to change lanes on a highway while carrying on a conversation) and some is more consciously deliberated, as in, "What should I do with my life?"

The Owners are your guiding images, which you experience as your identity. These images feel very personal and valuable.

The more we can characterize these different components of our consciousness in a way that is simple to understand, the more able we are to home in on the sources of our challenges and begin to experience consciousness in a new way. Let's begin by distinguishing between what I am calling Players and Coaches.

When someone jumps out from behind a bush, without a moment of thought we probably experience the Surprise-Startle Affect, which is what makes us jump without thinking about it. As you may remember, this is the Affect that works like a reset button to disconnect us from whatever we were thinking or feeling before. The Startle Affect then points our attention in the direction of the stimulus. In this experience there is no time to think; our reaction is purely sensory/Affective, almost like a reflex.

And then, a split second later, we begin evaluating and comparing this experience with our memory images. Is this person friend or foe? Are they playful or threatening? Some of these instantaneous, rapid-fire reflections are already quite habituated and happen outside of our attention. Sometimes, however, our conscious attention is drawn to the process of more deeply analyzing the past and then projecting a future image. Or, in the words of our football analogy, creating a "play."

This reflection and anticipation is an aspect of consciousness that I am calling "the Coach." What we will soon understand is that this process of reflection is not objective. Let me say that again. Even how we *think* about our experiences is habituated and/or emotionally scripted. Recognizing this is one of the most important things we can discover in our process of expanding our consciousness.

Now, going back to our example of feeling startled. Imagine what might happen if, in the moment Startle was triggered, you had an overwhelming habituated response. Maybe you threw whatever you were holding up into the air as you jumped. Then, a few seconds later, you began to wonder if that response was appropriate — or just plain goofy. *This* moment of reflection is a little bit like the "instant replay" of a televised football game. You can review the whole experience in your mind's eye and then evaluate it against the other images you carry of previous experiences of (or witnessing) Startle.

As this same process unfolds within us every day around a variety of Affects, we tend to believe that The Coach is presenting purely rational and objective reflections on our responses, but this is far from the truth. The Coach, you see, is motivated by Affect, too! So, during all your reflections on your "instant replay," your attention on that replay is being directed by something. What do you think it is that directs our Coach's attention? Can I get an A? Can I get an F? Can I get another F? Can I get an E? Can I get a C? Can I get a T? What's that spell? AFFECT! What? AFFECT! Sorry for that foray into brief, lame and somewhat dated cheerleading. (It seemed appropriate, given our football metaphor — and for my role as the cheerleader for your Team)

We have each made our way through life by trusting the perceptions of our inner Coach. Without that trust we would be lost. However, the very processes of our reflection and anticipation are skewed by the memory images of our past experiences, as well as the emotional scripts we have developed. These reflections of our inner Coach are always defined by both the limitations of our available imagery (you don't know what you don't know) and by our emotional scripts that tint our perceptions like colored glasses.

When the attention of our inner Coach is being directed by a stuck emotional script or a particularly limited set of images, the play on the field is likely to get pretty messy. Sometimes when this happens we need to hire a whole new coaching staff! So, sensing a problem, we thumb through promising self-help books and attend meditation and mindfulness trainings, but even these well-intentioned efforts will likely only yield new editions of a the same old emotional scripting. The seminars and books we find attractive are only those that fit the map we already have. Real change almost always feels weird, strange, and awkward.

Mindfulness in this context is really about learning how to intentionally shift our *Coach's* Affect toward Interest in the heat of the moment. Interest, you'll remember, is almost always the Affect we need to call on to deepen our awareness and to develop new responses. We can begin making this shift by identifying and practicing ways to become curious *and* connected — both at the same time. Can you get interested in your reflections in a way that suspends your usual judgments and patterns of response?

Without developing this skill — and applying the elbow grease of intentional practice — it won't matter how many mindfulness trainings you attend. The habituated emotional scripts that have been driving your inner Coach in the past will still pull you toward those same old scripted responses in all the most conflicted and threatening scenes of your life. However, once we understand that it is not so much the cognitive, but the *emotional* dynamics that are involved in directing our attention, we can begin to see how these scripts are limiting our perceptions *and* our reflections. Then mindfulness can take on a whole new meaning — and mindfulness *practices* can bring about even better results.

The Silent Level of Now

Going back to the Silent Level of Awareness we explored together in Chapter 13, we can now begin to consciously apply this information to our intentional practice of shifting our Coach's reflections to the Silent Level of Awareness.

Interest Affect and sensory focus are the keys to making this shift. The more we learn to slow down and become curious about what is going on within us, and the more we practice giving attention to the sensations of the body rather than the imagery in our minds, the better chance we'll have at opening ourselves to new possibilities and transcending our habituated patterns.

When all this happens, our good old habituation system can begin to work for *us* instead of us working for *it*. The more we practice this shift, the more it will become second nature to Move Alongside our triggered emotion, even in the way we reflect. With this new practice in place, the Coach will be freed to make a conscious decision whether to continue flowing with that old, habituated emotional experience or to become open to all the other options now visible that might bring greater success and satisfaction.

Let me try to make this even clearer. When you seek to evaluate the stuck emotional tone of your reflections (the Inner Coach), you are reflecting on the way you are reflecting. This is essentially like putting a mirror to a mirror — and all mirrors are imperfect. What Clyde was doing in therapy was essentially this: He began to reflect critically on his self-criticism. Nothing new was happening, even though at times he felt inspired by his insights. The dominant script under which Clyde was suffering was really all about his critical inner Coach.

The reasons change can be so difficult is that emotional scripts direct our attention whether we notice them or not. It may seem too simplistic to think that the way to work with this trick of human consciousness is to become curious and to turn attention to the body and its sensations, but how else could we move our reflections beyond our habituated images and emotional scripts than to remove our attention from this mental imagery altogether?

So, if creating positive change in our consciousness is that simple, why aren't we already doing it? The most obvious answers to that question are our lack of awareness and habituation. Now that you know more about imagery, habituation, and emotional scripts, perhaps it will make more sense to try this approach.

While the approach does have its limitations, the basic practice of Moving Alongside can help us with all of the other interventions we may need to practice. Let's explore some of these a little bit further as we take a closer look at Team You.

Back to the Huddle

With this new role for the Coach in mind, let's take another look at the Team. Sometimes the issues we struggle with in our lives have to do with the Center (body sensation) or "The Players" (Affects) and how they are interacting. Sometimes one or more of our nine innate Affects may experience some kind of glitch in its functioning; sometimes there may be a biological issue happening with other body systems. The reality is that these glitches in our Affects can be biological, psychological — or both.

Let me explain. Every human body has its own unique sensitivity to stimuli. For one person, a sudden loud noise may trigger only a low-level-response, while for another it triggers a jump-out-of-the-skin Startle. Yes, both of these people have the same nine Affects, but the stimulation required to trigger each Affect can be very different from one person to another.

Going back to our earlier example of Surprise-Startle, if your body has a really high sensory sensitivity, it can create a very hyperactive Startle response. That's because Affects are a bodily system triggered from birth by sensory signals. Not long after birth, our imagery will also begin to trigger Affect as well, but we never lose that link between sensation (The Center) and the Affects (The Players).

In this case of extreme Startle sensitivity, we may need to apply therapy to The Center (the sensory body). Awareness of the dynamics of our system can help, but they won't change our sensitivity — or the resulting intensity of our Affective response. Fortunately for us, however, there are now multiple techniques for managing Sensory stimuli. There are even some that are not pharmacological. Neurofeedback, which is a type of biofeedback that uses electroencephalography (EEG) technology to provide real-time displays of brain activity to teach self-regulation of brain function is just one of these promising treatments. The goal of therapy for "the Center" in this case would be to help retrain our body's sensitivity to sudden intense stimuli.

On the other hand, our suffering may not come from the Center (body) but rather from a *scripted* response of the Player known as Startle. The particular way an Affect is scripted can make any moment automatically take on a particular meaning to you. What if you tend to feel *personally* attacked every time your Startle Affect is triggered? This is the kind of script we might develop if we grew up in a life situation where someone was always startling us on purpose and laughing at our response. Such is the fate of many a person born particularly sensitive to stimuli. Over time, even something like turbulence on an airplane would automatically signal, "the pilot is trying to scare me!" So if our spouse accidentally drops a dish on the floor, we just "know" that he or she "did it to be mean!"

This scripted response can become so automatic that it seems impossible to change. You see, the issue is not just our body's sensitivity to the stimulus that triggers our Startle Affect. Now we have attached *meaning* to the activation of that Affect (Player) and when we reflect (Coach) on the experience, even our reflections interpret any Startle as an attack.

And, if angry words have come out of our mouth by this point, it is likely that we now also have Shame associated with our hyperactive response. This is not true for everyone. Some of us with hyper-Startle may not feel any shame at all about it, but given enough embarrassing moments with peers in grade school, Startle can lead to all kinds of Shame scripts. So let's explore this as an opportunity to consider how scripts can lead to other scripts to form our labyrinths of defenses.

Assuming that our hyper-Startle response eventually triggered Shame, when our Inner Coach then reflects on this whole experience to realize that our response was "over the top," it will trigger Shame again. Is it possible for us to just feel the embarrassment and move on? Or will we feel a need to defend against it happening again? If our usual defensive script for Shame is Withdrawal, as we reflect on the embarrassing intensity of our Startle response we immediately bypass the feeling of embarrassment to become anxiously attentive for any future risk of feeling that feeling again. So the Play our inner Coach now calls for is to *Withdraw* from any people, places, and events that might lead to our feeling startled. Over time, this hyper-vigilance will become all the more automatic/habituated. Though the defensive script promises relief from Shame, it actually puts us at risk for experiencing *more* Shame, and still more layers in our labyrinth of defensive scripts will accumulate.

One Thing Leads to Another

As we discussed earlier, Withdrawal scripts allow us to avoid Shame by helping us to escape the scenes where Shame could be triggered. However, Withdrawal scripts also tend to create even more Shame as we find ourselves Withdrawing from more and more arenas of life.

In most cases the source of our struggle involves both "The Team" and "The Coach." In this example, where we are supposing being born with a high level of sensory sensitivity, we are susceptible to an intense Startle response. That sensitivity, in and of itself can create Shame, whether or not we actually have a memory of someone making fun of us — or startling us purely for amusement. Our experience of this Affect could easily feel very punitive. So at one level, it is the Center/Player that needs support and attention in order to relieve the suffering, but without that support we will find some way to cope.

So what do we do? For one thing, we may develop multiple layers of scripts in order to cope. First, of course, there is the Withdrawal, our hyper-vigilance to avoid Startle being triggered. And then, as Withdrawal starts to make our life smaller and smaller, we feel defective (Shame) and pretty soon another defensive layer is born — and this time maybe it's Avoidance

As you may remember from our previous discussion, Avoidance can take many forms including anything that serves to distract from what feels embarrassing and exposed. In this case let's say our Avoidance of Shame appears as hyper-functioning in other areas of life to protect our positive sense of self and keep the spotlight of attention off of whatever is likely to produce Shame. In this case, we begin to perform in an almost superhuman way. Unfortunately, this hyper-functioning will probably lead to burnout, and the *effect* of this hypersensitivity on our body will continue without regard to whatever script we choose to address it.

So here comes yet another layer of scripting: Attack-Self. As our defensive labyrinth of scripts expands into Attack-Self, we now find ourselves constantly telling others about our flaws, and we feel drawn to others who are likewise always acknowledging their own flaws.

Why does this happen? What is directing our attention in these reflections? You guessed it. It's The Coach, and these reflections are not in the least bit objective. The Attack-Self emotional script drives our attention toward acknowledging our Shame in a way that is characterized by helplessness.

Connecting with someone over this mutual vulnerability is both endearing and bonding. We are doing the best we can to "be real" and to "own our issue" in every way we know how. And of course, the issue just continues and we become angry with ourselves, secretly hoping that someone will relieve our self-deprecation with positive regard.

Eventually anyone we encounter who seems to believe they are OK and not flawed, anyone who is not Withdrawing, Avoiding, or Attacking-Self will be a threat. As we look at them through the lens of our critical inner Coach, another layer of our labyrinth will form: the Attack-Other script.

Now our inner Coach is wearing her bitch glasses. And yes, we all have a pair. When we put them on we become shamelessly critical and are always looking for the flaws in others. This does not make us feel any better, mind you. We just feel less odd if we have company in being messed up. Eventually this script can fill us with resentment as others succeed.

How can these dynamics ever change? Here you are, a person born into a body with high sensory sensitivity that you didn't choose. Your adaptive responses have evolved to manage something you don't even understand. To say that you are now *choosing* these scripts would be an overstatement of your capacity for awareness. Remember now the words of Tomkins: "Life is a dream we learn to have from a script we did not write."

What I have just presented here is a simplistic example using the Startle Affect and very high sensory sensitivity to illustrate how our responses become scripted over time. I will leave it to you to imagine other scripts that can arise from the many different kinds of interactions between each of the Nine Affects, the variety of sensory dynamics involved, and so on. To catalogue all of these would be far beyond the scope of this book.

I have added my contribution to the work of many others by sharing how I see layers of scripts and how they build upon one another. I believe that every person has his or her own labyrinth, and every labyrinth has many layers and connections. Every minute of every day we encounter these layers of scripts in ourselves — and in the people around us. With the insights we have explored, these encounters can become your keys to greater freedom. In fact, every encounter we have can become another opportunity for us to Choose to Evolve.

Why This Script and Not That One?

Not all Avoidance scripts are created equal. For example, how could you avoid Shame in other ways besides the hyper-functioning described in our example? Could you just as easily find escape through sexual adventures or a drug? There are a million ways to avoid emotion, but they all serve the same function of creating an Avoidance script. There's not even any real choice or debate involved in determining the kind of Avoidance script we develop. We are *all* shaped by other experiences to move in a particular way.

For instance, imagine that you had a Shame experience when you were younger in which your grandmother tripped over something you left on the floor, broke her hip, and then died of pneumonia. Avoiding Shame through hyper-functioning as a caregiver seems to be a likely response in that context. Though Shame scripts are common to all of us, how they emerge depends upon many, very individualized factors;

however, our memories and the powerful imagery with which we identify will always play a big part in determining the direction and shape of our Avoidance scripts.

Choosing to Evolve is about learning to recognize our personal labyrinth of defensive scripts — and to realize that these scripts are also present in the perceptions of our inner Coach. This process of learning to analyze and question our scripts is not easy. Healing at this level is easier with knowledge and understanding of how consciousness works — along with a new capacity to question our inner Coach. This is true for all of us, individually and collectively. What we do to Evolve as individual people is the same work we can learn to do within all of our institutions and communities.

The good news is that the Ariadnes among us will come whenever we are ready and willing to walk those dark halls to find our way into the light. She will introduce herself through kind and perceptive eyes that don't look away from our "flaws." Instead, she will hold the thread of human connection, saying, "It's not your fault, but it *is* up to you now to Wake Up."

Some of my clients have found success through a combination of therapies. At times, medications can be helpful when the body is simply wired to over-react to a stimulated Affect. But medications are seldom the answer without therapy for The Coach.

There are numerous biological issues that can impact the intensity of a Player (Affect). Sometimes it has to do with a person just being on the upper end of sensitivity. Sometimes the issue is due to some substance that has been introduced into his or her body. In most of the clients with whom I have worked, however, high sensitivity was not the primary issue. For most of us, our Players (Affects) are just doing what they are hard-wired to do. The problem resides in the scripted emotional/imagery of our Coach and our tendency to believe that the Coach's reflections are rational/objective.

Here's the key. Evolving our Coach is actually the specific reflective process that will give us the capacity to Move Alongside. This process of Evolving our Coach takes both training and practice. Moving Alongside also requires stability of our positive sense of self. If we can train ourselves to identify as a Learner, we can become more practiced at curiosity and genuine interest in our unique momentary experiences. Rather than allowing our inner Coach to constantly define the past and anticipate the future through our usual tinted glasses as my previous example of Clyde reveals, we are better able to notice the limitations and scripting of the inner Coach's reflections. Without practicing this new curiosity about our inner archaeology, we are likely to keep repeating our same old emotional dynamics in new costumes.

The Driving Imagery of the Owner

Now I'd like to introduce one more component of this football metaphor, "The Owner." The Owner is a tricky part of the analogy. Unlike the actual owners of professional football teams, the role The Owner plays in our consciousness is much more flexible and powerful. I use the term "Owner" to denote a sense of identification and identity. We don't just own our cars and our clothing; we own our scenes and the stories that identify us . . . as us!

Consider all the images you have inside of you, the sum total of all the minutiae of life that you have experienced, habituated, and take for granted — like cups and toothbrushes. Some of that imagery is inconsequential, so if it changes you aren't likely to experience much discomfort. However, there are some experiences that are much more personal, and we identify strongly with these images. In fact, we see ourselves as them — and them as us. In other words, our identity is composed of that with which we most deeply identify.

The Owner, then, has a very personal identification with images that "ring true." What will "ring true" will mostly be the stuff that fits well with the images we have already been given. Sometimes we are fortunate enough to receive a moment of grace where we are exposed to a better picture of ourselves and of our lives. These are moments when we truly expand and evolve.

One of the most powerful elements of your evolutionary leap will come as you consider how you came to identify with specific places, people, roles, etc. Have you ever seen one of your favorite places change beyond recognition? Isn't it funny how this experience feels like a loss of self as much as a loss of place? Identification works just like that.

It's important to realize here that our identifications are the guiding images of our Coaches. They make up our core sense of drive and purpose. They play a powerful and defining role in our choices, and we basically just picked them all up by chance or grace depending on what we have been exposed to since birth.

Going back and broadening our previous example of the grandmother who tripped over the floor clutter, we can now become curious as to how the child's response may have influenced her identity. After having felt Shame for what was perceived as responsibility for a loved one's death, this child began to identify with images of heroes and heroines coming to the aid of the underdog — especially the frail and the fragile. As this identity matures, the adult version of this child really can't — or won't — tend to relate to people who don't seem to want to give all they can to help others.

Because of this particular labyrinth of scripts, this is a person who identifies with deep caring, authentic sharing, and a childlike connection to those for whom they care. He or she also identifies most with intelligence and being knowledgeable about the tools needed for caring for others. For this person, the image of healing others isn't just a thought. His or her pursuit of knowledge is completely motivated by this identity.

And, going back to our earlier example of the Withdrawal script developed to manage the Shame brought about by hypersensitivity to the Startle Affect, the more this Withdrawal script develops, the more likely this person will be to identify with images of independence. As someone who strongly identifies with being independent and self-reliant, this person may then become isolated from other people, thereby reinforcing the cycle of his or her Shame scripts.

Though much of this identification was put into motion through the layers of defensive scripts we have already described, it's important to realize that there are always gifts to be found within the layers of our scripts. Even in the midst of our brokenness, our scripts may have caused us to make a positive difference in the life of someone else — and maybe for many people. Even in the script of professional hyper-functioning (a classic Avoidance script) we may discover many different kinds of gifts.

As you can probably see, to question the identity and identification forged by our scripts — or to criticize it — seems entirely wrongheaded. What we need is not more *judgment* (Shame) but *discernment* brought about by questioning. We don't need to cut *out* these identities in order to heal, but rather, to learn to Move Alongside them. It is possible to learn to accept — and even appreciate — the scenes from our past that once wounded us, because they likely came with a gift that, if we'll take the time to look deeply enough, has made a difference in our life or in the lives of others around us. This gift, however, always comes with a price, and when you become tired of paying that price, you will feel a deep longing to Evolve — perhaps finding more balance in self-care.

The Owner in this analogy is always standing next to the Coach, pushing his or her emotional buttons, whispering advice, playing armchair quarterback. The work involved in Choosing to Evolve requires the capacity to *choose* whether to listen to the Coach or not. To gain that capacity requires a new awareness, born of reflection first, and then followed by practice in the art of Moving Alongside. In this practice we deliberately direct our attention to our momentary sensations, stop thinking, and dis-identify with the images. To dis-identify is what I mean by Moving Alongside, and we gain the most when we learn how to do this, even with what we think of as "us." Moving Alongside is the source of true freedom.

The End Zone

Football is the only analogy I have found that seems close enough to be helpful in imagining these components of consciousness. I have probably spent far too much time thinking about it. You could go much further (especially if you like football), considering defensive and offensive players, referees, the replay screen (memory imagery), announcers and even the images from a blimp (Our big picture abstractions). Of course every analogy is imperfect, and the further we go the more we stumble (or fumble?) with it. However, because so many of my clients have found this analogy helpful, I offer it to you now. Let's sum up the analogy, and then I'll give you a few ways to explore your own team:

The body (The Center) hikes the ball to an Affect (Player) from birth. But as we gain more imagery, The Coach begins to evolve through both memory and anticipatory images.

The strength and nature of the sensory signal (The Center) impacts which Affect (Player) is triggered and the intensity of that Affect (Player)

The intensity of the Affect in our imagery (both memory and anticipatory) can be just as motivating as those triggered by the body (the Center)

As we gain more imagery, we evolve more capacity for reflection and anticipation; however, we also gain more scripted/habituated responses (Plays)

The Coach (our reflective/projective processes) is not objective

Scripted dynamics exist even in our most thoughtful reflections

Identification (The Owner) with certain stories, places, people, and scenes create a special set of memory images that are personal, defining, and directing

Challenging this identity (the Owner) is necessary to the process of Moving Alongside

To Move Alongside, we must dis-identify with our special set of memory images

As we do this, we can reflect on our reflections and then choose our response with greater freedom than before.

One key to practicing this dis-identification is to move our attention back to the body (The Center) and to enter into the flow (or the immediate gush) of life. In other words, we focus on the field, not the imagery we have of it.

An Exercise in Identity

Begin by getting comfortable in a place where you are not likely to be interrupted.

Make a list of the things you identify with, including:
Race
Nationality
Gender
Sexual preference
Occupation
Education
Political/ideological beliefs
Religious beliefs
Financial status
Dog or cat lover?
Are you creative?
Are you responsible?
Are you good at loving people?
Who made/makes you feel most loved?

Do you believe in yourself?
Do you want something you don't have?
What is it?

As a kid:
What did you want to be when you grew up?
What were your favorite indoor games?
What were your favorite outdoor games?
Who did you play with?
What happened to them?
What were they like?

Now spend a few minutes just thinking about your life.

You may find that the first things that emerge are repeats of recent recollections. These will pop up like recently opened files on a computer. Feel what you need to feel about these, but gradually shift your attention toward deeper memories. Maybe you will think of the place you grew up or your childhood family. **Just allow the images to roll.**

See if you can remember how you attached to people, places, and ideas. You were probably exposed to many of them. Write down some of the ones you most identified with.

If you have experienced trauma, take care that you have help on this journey and that you have a well-established sense of being grounded in your identity as a Learner.

Don't approach this work with a drive to accomplish anything. Enlightenment comes to those who are free from the scripts that are driving them to accomplish, master, or subdue. This is a gentle journey of just noticing where you gathered the bits of imagery that have shaped what you perceive as you.

Here are some hints at where to look:
Favorite stories and songs
People who impressed you
Favorite hiding places
Experience of people being sexual
Early expressions of your own sexual interest
Experiences of work and money
Early experiences of race and nationality
Experiences of embarrassment
Favorite experiences that inspired or moved you

The questions offer just a few prompts to begin your exploration of the imagery and scripts that accumulated in your early years, setting you on a course toward defining your identity. Once you have spent some time exploring these, try this:

Sit quietly

Allow your attention to flow towards your body

Close our eyes and look into the darkness

Notice your breathing

Bring the sounds around you into awareness

Take a moment to reflect on what you have explored — the images of your identity — and then let them all go.

Be nothing

Be nothing more than your sensations.

Let this be enough. No need to be anything else.

Practice letting go of all identity other than sensations. *Be* your sensations.

Notice what happens every time your thoughts and imagery distract you from your focus on sensation. What emerges may be worth noting. What is the thought or image? What made it urgent enough to interrupt your meditation? Which Affect made it urgent? For now, simply write it down and move back to the sensation of your being.

After you allow this to happen for a while (you may repeat this many times) return your attention to your body and give all of your attention to sensation for a minute or two.

Now I encourage you to bring back all the images you have explored of who you are. Just observe them without owning them. Move Alongside them and see their gifts and their limitations. These images of self have been the limits between which your identity is strung in a particular way — at a particular tension. How have these images defined the music of your life? Even the sour notes and the minor chords are all a part of that music. All along the way you were learning to play your life.

Return to your sensations and listen.

There is no shame in how you evolved.

You did your best in becoming who you are with the images you had available.

You are more than these images to which you identify.

You are Learning. Give that identity another name if you like.

If some of the images of your identity cause suffering for you or for others in your life, you can choose new images if you'd like.

You will always have and need an identity. To learn is a constant journey of identifying and dis-identifying.

At the root of all this change is the Silent Level of Awarenesss of your sensations. Here there are no words, no categories, no good or bad. Just being.

Chapter 20

Identity, Identification, and the Images We Own

Some of us have had experiences in our lives that are so intense that we have disowned them. What happens when this kind of trauma occurs is that the shock of the trauma that cannot be accepted as a part of our self is split off and often made unavailable in our memory. It is as if the core identity (Owner) cannot continue to operate with these memories present, so it disowns them. These experiences can create in us a problem called *dissociation*.

Now, it's important to understand here that dissociation is not just for traumatic events. Dissociation is a normal daily occurrence for all of us. Even the infamous "big boys don't cry" script involves the dissociation of Distress. Guys who have been indoctrinated into such scripts will also likely have challenges when in the company of someone who is crying. If you watch closely, you may see the telltale sign of dissociation in their eyes — frozen like a deer in the headlights. Dissociation from Distress can cause major disconnects in intimate relationships, but in most societies it is preferable. Men who cry are sometimes still perceived as weak, and men who do not cry under pressure or stressors may seem more adaptive.

Dissociation created from trauma is adaptive, too, but it also tends to create some less desirable dynamics. It is one thing for a guy to go all "deer in the headlights" while watching a chick flick with his girlfriend sobbing beside him. It is quite another for him to have flashbacks of being raped when she puts her hand on his leg.

Though dissociation is a normal adaptive process of our scripted imagery/emotions, many people suffer from its effects. Whether the memory images emerge in dreams or in unexpected waking moments when their present experience has just enough similarities to the traumatic scene, it can be utterly de-stabilizing. It is no wonder that the psyche may develop multiple identities to deal with the problem.

The dissociation of one identity from another is also a normal process. I don't think about being in my performing musician identity when I am deep in my intellectual identity, though I have learned to merge them more and more as I have grown older. In fact, an earlier version of this book was written as poetry, and I have included bits of that throughout this current text.

While the intensity of the Affects involved in trauma may be the biggest player in this process of splitting off, dissociation also involves disowning and disavowing those same Affects in order for the split to become well formed. Many victims of rape struggle with a sense that their body betrayed them by experiencing pleasure in a moment of being manipulated or controlled by a person they knew was doing something bad. In other cases, pain, torture, or even intense fear may generate shock, which is the psyche's way of disowning *everything* in order to survive an ordeal.

I have heard plenty of stories about how perpetrators of child sexual abuse used techniques that would force any child to dissociate. I will not describe them here. I only point to these dynamics as a way to add to the understanding of the phenomenon with hopes that we might all come to a greater appreciation of the challenges some of our friends and neighbors have suffered.

You may have had moments in which you disowned or dissociated an act of gluttony in order to salvage your self-image, saying something like, "How weird was that! It is *so* not *me* to eat a whole birthday cake!" But those who have experienced intense terror and humiliation have an exponentially greater intensity of their negative Affect to disown.

For many people who have experienced trauma, it helps to know that they are not abnormal in their dissociation or multiplicity of identities. It also helps to have a metaphor to provide some sort of map through these confusing and overwhelming experiences. I believe this exploration of consciousness can offer just that.

In my experience, those who suffer from DID, PTSD, and other dissociative issues need special support. If you would be the Ariadne to hold the thread of connection for someone who is working through these layers, you must be, above all, consistent in your presence. You have to commit for the long haul.

I do not advise revisiting any traumatic experience until a stable positive relationship is established. This stability is the light he or she needs to pierce the darkness. Focusing on their immediate challenges and the management of dissociative moments may seem counter productive to working through these past traumatic experiences, but only with strong stability can we make the journey. Once we find this stability, we can begin to work with the inner Coach, helping to establish a capacity to Move Alongside the dissociative experience with curiosity.

It is important for intense Affect to be processed in the body instead of allowing a flood of imagery to escalate the Affective responses. There are plenty of techniques for somatic, or affecting the body as distinct from the mind, processing of trauma available for those who are supporting these folks. I recommend Bessel Van der Kolk and Peter Levine whose works are trusted resources on the somatic processing of trauma.

If you have suffered from these kinds of issues, don't go it alone. Reach out for help. With the right support, you will discover that there are gifts that will arise from your suffering, and your creativity and your sensitivity can guide you to a new freedom. Your life experience has placed you on the cutting edge of evolving consciousness.

The Owner and the Goal

The Coaches in our consciousness are all guided by the images stored from our past experiences. The most durable and instrumental of these are those images we see as "us" (the Owner). You could also say that the Owner is also a projected image of "future me," although it seems that when we personalize these images it may feel like a current aspect of our identity. When I watched Glen Campbell on television as a child, I felt a subtle sense of my musician identity, right then and there. I saw myself as Glen, long before I ever picked up a guitar and began fixating on the repetitive mechanics of learning how to play it.

The imagery of Glen Campbell that I so identified with and stored in my memory was core to my motivation. It helps to notice this as we work with others or deal with conflict. Imagine that you are a 10-year-old boy sitting in detention for being repetitively non-compliant with a teacher's requests. The principal may not have learned about the Restorative Paradigm and believes that punishment is going to change you. But deep down you don't identify with the teacher *or* the principal. You identify with an older kid who lives near your house. He dropped out of school and is making lots of money on the Internet. He seems cool, well-off, well-liked, and he treats you like a grown-up. You don't follow the teacher's directions because they don't match up with your identity, and no amount of punishment is going to change that. We are all guided by the images to which we have identified — heroes as well as victims.

That older boy's rhetoric is basically an Attack-Other script, always criticizing authorities and education in general. But you, as this younger boy, don't see that. All you see is that this guy has already beat the system at which you are failing. You see him as heroic, and you identify with that. So when you are resisting the teacher or provoking outrage in the office, you don't perceive anything other than your own heroic resistance to the system. How might a school change its disciplinary practices with this kind of awareness?

Sometimes the issues with a student involve a Player (Affect) that is over (or under) functioning. Unregulated excitement has sent many a kindergartner to the principal's office. Hyperactivity can be a symptom of Fear or Shame avoidance. ADHD can be a name we give to kids who have habituated a way of avoiding negative Affects through active body movement to keep the interest/excitement Affect stimulated. Think about it. Could that be how their parents helped them modulate negative Affect all their lives – rocking them, jingling keys, and offering interesting or exciting distractions?

In these cases we can help by providing support instead of punishment. There is growing evidence that providing kids with Yoga and Mindfulness learning opportunities rather than suspension is highly effective at transforming behavioral issues in classrooms. I will repeat what I have shared previously. Most behavioral issues are actually emotional regulation issues. Add to that the individual dynamics of identification (The Owner) and the limited catalogue of plays to reflect on (The Coach), and we have pretty much addressed most of the common disciplinary issues of today's classrooms.

In some cases we need to address the Players involved in the problem and see what's happening there. At other times we need to help the Coach learn how to reflect in a different way. Yoga, meditation, and mindfulness help us do just that. The biggest problem with our self-reflection is that we assume that it is unaffected by the emotional dynamics at play within us. We can, however, learn not to believe everything we think.

We can help the Coach learn to move into observation mode and Move Alongside the emerging images and emotions without judging them. All of the information in this book may be helpful in developing skills to do this, and learning to empower and equip the Coach is at the very heart of Choosing to Evolve.

Sometimes the issues center on the Owner — and what that student has come to take on as an identity. It takes a little time to explore this, and we must be careful not to judge and trigger too much Shame and the scripted defenses that are sure to follow. Done carefully, however, these explorations often yield great opportunities for change and growth. That with which we identify most is right on the edge of our learning how to extend our consciousness.

Going to The Draft

One of the ways some of my clients have learned to transform dysfunctional scripts is to use a practice I like to call "The Draft." The Draft relies on the fundamental truth that it is easier to develop a new script than it is to unlearn an old one. So in The Draft we proactively seek out new imagery that will balance the team.

When the Coach and the Owner don't seem to have the inner resources to deal with the game, I suggest that they need a new player. (In the NFL, they call this "the player to be named later.") A new player can make all the difference to a team. In the middle of the season, when things are looking hopeless, a team can bring on board the precise skills they need to succeed.

This imaginary journey of "going to The Draft" involves researching movies, books, friends, and acquaintances in search of either an image for tolerating the intensity of the Affect involved, or an image that transforms a toxic traumatic scene into one that is less threatening.

Here's an example: My client is angry, but has no models for the healthy expression of that anger. We think together of movies where healthy anger is expressed. We find a character and name that character as a specialty player for intense anger. Then we practice acting that out as if it was a part in the movie. Gradually the new Player becomes a part of the team. There is, however, one very important caveat. We must fully *identify* with this new player and see our selves in them — and them in us.

Imagine that my client is embarrassed, but lacks any experience in managing this embarrassment in a healthy way. Shame in this case is so disabling it must be utterly avoided. First, we might explore the Compass of Shame scripts and recognize how everyone seems to use these at times. We then explore the ones this client has employed over the years. Then we explore the immediate "scene" of embarrassment and find ways to make it into a learning experience. Then we listen to a comedy sketch by someone like Jim Gaffigan and we make up a joke about this embarrassing moment. (Can you add a comedian to your team?) Then we revisit any more learning that might be needed from the scene.

In another case, we may revisit a trauma, but imagine bringing a new Player into the scene. This Player will need to be one we have discussed and determined to have all the necessary traits to deal with the situation. There are exercises like this to be found in practices like EMDR (Eye Movement Desensitization and Reprocessing, a type of psychotherapy used for treating trauma including post-traumatic stress disorder (PTSD).

Affect at the Heart of Dissociation

I once had a chance to hear Andreas Aamodt, present work he developed with Dr. Jon Monson at the University of Oslo. In their studies, which were based in a version of Affect Theory, schizophrenic patients were having complete remissions of symptoms as a result of a therapeutic intervention they called Affect Script Analysis.

The patients were first interviewed for how they tolerated the experience of the Affects. Each Affect was given a score. Then therapeutic interventions were aimed at aiding their capacity to tolerate higher levels of those Affects than they had been able to tolerate earlier. This work seemed to confirm for me that the primary locus of dissociative experience is at the Affect level. The upshot was that these studies further validated the understanding that the better we learn to tolerate *all* Affects, the less we need to dissociate.

I have worked with plenty of adults in their late 20s to early 40s who first began to struggle emotionally when they finally arrived at a place in their life that felt safe. They got married, succeeded in their careers, arrived at a financial goal, or something else that told their deepest consciousness that they were safe and could relax a bit. For them, however, to relax a bit meant that the game wasn't on the line anymore, and the dominant scripts that had helped them ignore certain Affects and images were not so dominant any more.

In some cases, these folks needed to go to The Draft and find some players that knew how to have fun. Some needed to draft a player that could find joy in adventure again — the Indiana Jones of their team. For others, it was important to finally face some of the traumatic events that had suddenly decided to bubble up into their awareness. The important thing to note is that human consciousness is an imagery system, and you can choose to add or delete images. All it takes is awareness (recognize where the need is), creativity (actively invent or innovate by finding a new image with which you can resonate), and commitment (rehearse that image until it is habituated).

The Draft provides an accessible metaphor for developing the capacity to adapt in these moments. If you find yourself overwhelmed, it is helpful to think of others you have known or witnessed who handled well the challenges you face. Everything we perceive is imagery, so why not identify with new images of ourselves that work better?

Layers of Neurosis

Long before I began to conceive this football team metaphor for imagining the workings of human consciousness, I had come to believe that emotional scripts are layered. By that I mean that one script tends to lead to the development of another, and another, and another — like layers of sediment. The insights I have shared around this idea often involve the ubiquitous experience of Shame-Humiliation. The scripts we engage to defend against Shame typically co-occur with most of the symptoms listed in a psychiatric diagnostic manual.

The first-layer script is originally developed as a way to cope. For example, imagine the experience of losing your family in a fire at age five. How might you cope with that? Perhaps you develop a script to avoid fires, or maybe you cope with the loss of your family with fearful attachment to anyone on whom you depend.

This anxiousness may work fine for many years. Your caregivers may feel compassion enough to humor your unusual needs for their attentiveness and constancy. But one day you find yourself with a teacher or a companion who doesn't.

At this point there will likely be Shame-Humiliation as your script of hyper-vigilance runs into a dead end. What you do then will determine the next layer. In almost every case I have experienced, Shame ends up being a co-occurring issue, adding a second layer to the complex. Then, as we have explored previously, you will likely manage or defend against this Shame with one or more of the scripts Nathanson described as part of the Compass of Shame.

This second layer to the Shame-Humiliation complex is something that has been overlooked and misunderstood by most psychotherapeutic theories and practices. I cannot stress how much the awareness of this layer has opened insight in both individual and couples' therapy work. And, as important as the second layer is, it is not the final layer that usually develops.

Over time, we may develop habituation to our Shame defenses that equals or surpasses our initial coping script. Shame scripts tend to spiral into more Shame, giving birth to more layers until eventually there comes a layer of scripting that simply grows out of the stuck cycles of the others. This script is marked by a sense of helplessness and negative self-imagery. This layer may be experienced as anxiety/panic (a feeling of loss of control of thoughts and emotions) or as depression (a withdrawal from continuing any efforts to change things). The inner dialogue (The Coach) is overwhelmed with doubt, "What's wrong with me?" Fears of being fatally flawed or defective are typical of this layer of scripting.

Though well meaning, those who seek to treat the presenting symptoms of a patient or client will likely miss the underlying dynamics. Treating the anxiety or depression after a 10-minute interview may offer symptomatic relief, but this does nothing to impact the underlying dynamics that have adhered themselves to someone's consciousness over time.

I have worked with many people who, despite their prescribed anti-depressants, continued to find their life to be a mess due to the layers of scripts such as those we have described. They just didn't feel as depressed about it anymore.

A more effective process of psychotherapy from this perspective is one of unraveling the layers. Even analyzing these layers can give someone the capacity to feel less crazy and more capable of moving forward. Soon the hopelessness/helplessness begins to shift, and we can turn our energy toward the Shame scripts that are defending the core issues.

Once we begin to deal with a core issue, we may need a variety of approaches, depending on the focus of the issue (Center, Player, Coach, Owner). Although the variety of these approaches and their relative effectiveness is beyond the scope of this book, in my work I have drawn from many of these including: Cognitive Behavioral Therapy, Existential, Positive Psychology, Gestalt, and various somatic approaches. In some cases I have worked in tandem with a psychiatrist who was also prescribing medication.

In many cases my work has been more educational, helping provide information that a client could use to transform their imagery. I have found in these cases that applied knowledge of Affects, imagery, and habituation make all the difference. Applying this knowledge, however, is only possible when the caregiver is capable of holding whatever the client presents with what Carl Rogers called "unconditional positive regard." It seems evident from our understanding of the Shame Affect that without this kind of relationship we are unlikely to reveal or face the aspects of our lives that are in the greatest need of healing.

Summary

In this chapter I have sought to share some of the insights I have found to be helpful in supporting growth and healing. We have raised several areas of focus for inquiry for uncovering the sources of suffering. In determining the source of a disturbance we can ask the following questions:

> Does the disturbance seem to involve a Center, a Player, a Coach or an Owner?
>
> Is there a dominant Player?
>
> How does this person reflect on his or her experience?
>
> What emotional dynamics seem to be present in "the Coach?"
>
> Are there conflicting identities (Owners)?
>
> What are the guiding images with which we are identifying?

During the course of this exploration we have made numerous suggestions on how to apply these insights, but before we leave this section, it seems worthwhile to lay out a clear process for Choosing to Evolve. Here are the basic components we have presented so far:

- Build awareness of the sources and limitations of your images.
- Recognizing these limits, hold an image of yourself as a Learner and cultivate the qualities of meekness.
- Build an awareness of the ways in which you tolerate or ignore each of your nine Affects and explore your own scripts.
- Practice Moving Alongside these scripted responses as you learn to recognize your own scripts.
- Participate in your consciousness as these images and scripts run into conflicts — and learn to give curious attention to them.
- Practice the arts of de-habituation and dis-identification in order to experience the true beauty around you and transform cycles of conflict into opportunities for growth and intimacy.

If you experience some disturbance or conflict, recognize that it is presenting you with an opportunity to consider the material we have explored, and use these insights to grow your awareness of your personal scripts and images. Calling again upon our football analogy, you may recognize that the issue at hand involves one or more of the players, coaches, or owners of Team You. Feel free to use the suggestions sprinkled throughout this book to address those dynamics in a new way.

SECTION V

Putting Concepts Into Play

Chapter 21

Our Scripts at Work

How we support ourselves economically and the work we choose to do is one of the most important aspects of life. And then there's money. How we get it, how we keep it, and how we use it — these things are so important to us that we speak of it in terms of "making a living."

As with all of our human experiences, the images we have around personal finances are those we picked up from what has happened in our past. To Choose to Evolve in the area of work and money, we will first need to become more aware of the images we carry — as well as our emotional attachments to those images.

In this chapter we will explore the work and money images that seem particularly important to our individual experience, the operation of a business, and the cultural dynamics created when we experience conflicts between these images.

This is not an exhaustive exploration, but it *is* meant to provide you with an example of how we can develop a deeper awareness of our images in this area. And, with that awareness we can then choose to keep those images — or trade them for some that will serve us better. We can also learn to practice how we talk about these guiding images when we find ourselves in times of conflict. Some of these images — and the emotions that accompany them — lie at the very heart of our cultural divisions.

To begin with, let's look at a few basic images we all have of work and money that play a big part in how we approach this important aspect of life. In addition to these general work and money issues, we also carry within our self-imagery some very important images of being both Providers and Consumers. As these defining images become clearer, we will begin to see how our perceptions have been shaped, and then we can make new choices that will offer us greater success and freedom. When we speak of freedom in this aspect of life, it is once again important to remember my guitar string analogy. Freedom, you'll remember, is not about being free from limits. Freedom is all about what we can create *within the limits we have.*

Images of Wealth and Money

We all have images of what money is — how to get it, what to do with it, how to feel about having it, and how to cope with not having it. Are you more of a "diamonds are a girls best friend" or a "can't buy me love" kind of person? Are physical comforts a big thing to you — or would you be content to live in the woods and fish for food? Do you feel insecure with only $100,000 in savings or are you content to have no money and no bills? Are you continually worried about not having enough money? Or do you tend to squander money when you have it? Do you admire rich people and want to be one? Or do you despise rich people and think they are selfish? How do you feel about people with no money at all? And finally, how are your boundaries with money? Do you tend to be a "what's mine is mine" kind of person — or a "what's mine is yours?"

All of these questions point to the images we carry about wealth and money, and these images play a big role in our experience of money and what we do with it. Money is important to all of us because it is our *currency* — the exchanges we make to meet our basic needs and to care for the needs of others. Money is also connected to our sense of adventure. We imagine that more money will give us more opportunities to follow our dreams and explore the world — and that less money will limit these opportunities and experiences. So money in this context represents a practical part of our ability to both reduce our negative Affects and increase our positive ones. What's interesting to note here is that some people have found ways to do both of these things with very little money.

Some of us carry deep wounds and Shame around money issues. It may sound crazy, but for some of us, having no money creates feelings of shame — and for others, having too *much* money brings on very similar feelings of shame. If you grew up around someone who had more wealth than you did and you experienced Shame because that person was always doing things you and your family could not, you may have feelings of shame around money whether you have it or not.

'Tis the Season

In American culture there is a practice of gift giving around special holidays, and Christmas in particular. Families and friends gather to exchange gifts in party-like settings where they also feast on their favorite foods. The amount of money that goes into these celebrations is astonishing — and this season of giving keeps many stores in business. Let's take a deeper look at the images and associations that are involved here, along with some of the intricate emotional dynamics around money and giving that we carry within us all year long.

As you will quickly see, this topic is expansive. It is also a good place to start when we're looking to uncover the scripts and images we carry about money because there is so much available in our memories to explore. Take a moment to recall the scenes you can remember that involve money. As you do, be sure to notice how your emotions get involved in motivating and directing your attention to those scenes. Keep in mind that it can be really hard to challenge these perceptions because of the cultural prohibitions around those who question cultural norms. Understanding what we now know about the concept of Moving Alongside, see if you can Move Alongside all of that, giving attention to what emerges spontaneously on its own without allowing cultural expectations to join in.

The After-Christmas Blues

Now, going back to our Season of Giving exploration, what some people discover is that beneath the façade of the beauty of the season there is always some degree of internal struggle over the *expense* of gift giving. In some cases, this can be a trigger for Shame so intense that we form scripts that deny our financial limitations. Some of us learned as children that to love someone means you must give them more than you can really afford. As adults, we load up our credit cards to meet our own gift giving expectations — and suffer later — but avoiding the Shame of not giving or giving only small things can be greater than the Shame of debt.

It's when our scripts around generosity and relational values come into play that the availability of credit can be particularly problematic. We find this same dynamic at play in how people drain their savings and even take on debt to hold more elaborate weddings and funerals than they can afford. Our social status, relational dynamics, and sense of identity all play a part in how we view spending in these recurring — or "once in a lifetime" situations. These events also create an opportunity to examine problematic spending and how and why it happens.

We all realize the complexities of disappointing a child or a spouse when they want something we may or may not be able to afford. The images with which we identify are challenged. And of course, what we want most is to see positive Affect on the faces of our loved ones — and what we *least* desire is to see their disappointment. For these most basic of reasons, it is often our "generosity" and not our greed that leads to insurmountable debt.

Wealth and Generosity — The Identity of Success

If the images you carry of wealth are negative ones (to hold onto money is selfish and greedy), you may find that you are not motivated to develop even a modicum of savings. You may also develop an Attack-Other script to justify your financial failures: "Those wealthy people don't deserve their money. They are all cheats and liars who use people."

And on the flip side, if the image you hold of wealth is such that you feel terribly insecure without a lot of it, there may be no amount of financial security that can ever resolve your fear. We all know that greed is a problem, both in an individual and in our world. Greed may develop in someone who has some insecurity scripts around money that are quite intense. Greed may also involve some sort of identification with images of self-reliance and self-importance. These scripted dynamics operate through emotional lenses that direct our attention in a way that makes the suffering of others less visible.

One way to develop more awareness of your own dynamics around money is to do a little journaling. Give it a try by using these questions as prompts:

How do you feel about having or not having money?

How many times a day do you think about money?

How do you feel about other people in your life who have less?

Where did you get your images about money and wealth?

What other images might you want to consider in order to live in a healthy and balanced way?

Sometimes just a little reflection can reveal images that undermine our capacity to manage money wisely or compassionately.

Images of Work

Where did you get your images of work? How old were you when you started doing chores or having a "job" of some sort? Do you see work as a burden, or do you never think twice about it? We will explore some of these memories further as we look at images of being a Provider or Consumer, but for now it is important just to note that we all have a general image in our minds of what work is.

Now, close your eyes and breathe for a moment and then tell me what you *see* when I say the word, "work." How does that word *feel*? What emotion does it trigger? Where did you get your images of work, and what are the feelings associated with these images? How much of your sense of overall identity comes from what you *do* at work? How has that changed over the years?

Work may feel like something we are privileged to do — or it may feel more like an expectation to which we give very little thought. Work may be something we feel should be rewarded and appreciated by others. Or it may even feel unfair to us that we should have to work at all.

Depending on what kind of experience of work, chores, and responsibility we've been taught to expect, our images of work can take on a wide spectrum of habituated patterns. I can think of more than a few clients I've worked with over the years who struggled with their jobs, always feeling underappreciated or overwhelmed. When we explored their expectations more deeply, we often discovered that they held a certain sense of resentment over having to do any work at all. Images of work become expectations, and sometimes they cause us a great deal of suffering. These images can also be a big source of conflict in intimate relationships.

Images of The Provider

Take a moment to reflect on how you see yourself as The Provider by considering the following questions. If you are not currently working to provide for yourself or your family, consider your image of what kind of The Provider you imagine yourself becoming.

- Do you approach work more as an entrepreneur or an employee?
- Where and when did you take on that image, and who modeled it to help you shape it?
- Do you feel that being The Provider is a burden — or just something everyone should expect?
- Do you ever complain about having to work so hard?
- How do you feel about others depending on you to provide?
- Do you ever feel frustrated and unappreciated for your work?
- As The Provider, do you expect to be inspired?
- Do you expect your work to be fulfilling?
- Where did you get these images and expectations?
- When was the last time your experience of being The Provider and that of your partner didn't match up with your images/expectations?

Even though women joined the American workforce en mass during and after World War II — and even after the push for women's equality in the 60s and 70s — the truth is we are still in the midst of a shift in the identities of men and women in the workplace. All across America today — and in some areas more than others — the images we carry about who we are when it comes to work have not yet completely shifted. In fact, for some, traditional work images have not shifted at all.

In the traditional American script, men left the home to work while women stayed at home and worked to take care of children, tend to all matters related to food and clothing, and generally run the household. This cultural arrangement was more than just an issue of economics. There is a lot of timeless mythology around men going out to conquer dragons or hunt to bring home the spoils, even though our hunter/gatherer days are well behind us in our patriarchal past.

These heroic mythological elements are worth examining here. The Providers in this imagery are the knights on white horses — protecting, rescuing, and providing heroically for their wives and family. It's also important to note that within this system of images where we see men risking and sometimes sacrificing their lives to provide for the family there are all sorts of ways these heroes are rewarded for this bold and brave behavior.

Within this system, a man knows who he is and when he has done his work as The Provider well. He has a clear image of both his role and the rewards he can expect for performing it. Naturally, this means that when he returns home after battling the dragons threatening the castle he will be celebrated and made to feel great satisfaction and pleasure.

Beyond Knights and Damsels

While it may seem hard to imagine, many men still carry these kinds of images, even in modern times. Whether the dragons they now slay come in the form of business deals or heartless bosses, these mythological images may still be present in the abstract imagery guiding our sense of identity, despite any newer images of equality we may have adopted. And, because these new images are in such conflict with the old, "knightly" ones, valuing the advancement of women, working to relieve their oppression and supporting their empowerment does not necessarily mean that we have also relinquished the old guiding images. In addition to managing those old images, today's man has the complex challenge of figuring out how to identify with newer images of what it means to be male.

Sexual equality and the rise of women in government and industry are still in process, despite persisting legal and judicial policies. While changing a law requires only that we convince enough people that a cause is just, the prospect of changing the images we carry in our minds is far more challenging than we might want to believe. What does it mean to you to be a good man or woman? If you are gender neutral, what does it mean to be a good non-binary person? What are *your* guiding images?

It's important to realize that the transformation of the images in our consciousness doesn't happen on its own. Though many individual men have struggled to shift their own image of The Provider, many men still carry those old images, and some become very frustrated when the conquering knight scenario fails to transpire in real life.

We are all approaching this shift in awareness in different ways. Some men have grown up with new scripts that retain their identities as heroes. They have become warriors for equality, fighting for the rights of the women in their lives. It is the same guiding myth, but with energies redirected to a new awareness.

For some men and women, the old myth must be totally destroyed. For them, true equality requires that women must also be heroes and the myth itself must be rewritten to include them. This kind of shift impacts the dynamics of power in the relationship on a much deeper level. If a man's wife becomes the hero of the story, does that make *him* the damsel in distress? Will her accomplishments make him proud? Or insecure?

We all operate from some guiding mythology, whether we realize it or not. Many of our cultural issues involve these guiding issues and our unconscious adherence to their unquestioned guidance. They are the glasses we wear without even knowing we own them. So where are the stories of heroes we need today? What new mythology (and high-order abstract imagery) will emerge as the story of humans in a world of equality?

There is an opportunity here for a type of partnership in intimacy that is new to the planet — joining in heroic actions *together*. To live in this deeply connected way, however, we will need to develop much greater skills at conflict and much more awareness of our own imagery and scripts than most people currently posses. Can you be a hero and still be meek? Or must your heroic endeavors reflect some other image you have of glory?

I realize — and apologize for — the myopic heterosexual focus of this section. We have all inherited some of the same mythological images, and many homosexual couples experience some of these same dynamics or variations on the same theme.

Affects, Mythology, and Provider Imagery

When the images of The Provider to which we have been programmed don't match our reality, the abstract anticipatory images trigger Affect in us just as readily as sensation triggers Affect in an infant. The mythological Provider images carried by many men have rewards far beyond receiving the love of their dependents. The role of the hero comes with a certain amount of freedom from criticism. In the extreme, this places all dependents including wives in a virtual state of slavery. This dynamic is not a relic of the past but quite common in the world today.

Nowadays, when women are also Providers, how is that supposed to work? Does she still offer him adoration for his hard work — or will she just shrug her shoulders and then match step with complaints about her own? And how are men supposed to provide the same rewards for *their* Provider mates?

These are questions that may help us make more conscious choices in the area of work. Without making conscious choices about our images of work, we simply run headfirst into more conflict and crisis. As I write this, there is a backlash in America against progressive movements for equality. I suggest that this resistance involves how our traditional, more mythological images are in crisis — and our lack of imagery to replace them. The shifting images also involve intricate dynamics of power and rewards that will require even greater skill for navigating conflict and creating awareness.

Given our new understanding of how human consciousness operates, we can begin to see how the images with which we identify around work set us up for strong feelings, depending on our degree of emotional investment and how much our experiences diverge from our images. When strong feelings emerge, men will most often respond with Anger; however, it's more likely that the initiating trigger will be Shame.

At this point, a man may want to focus the blame for his frustration outwardly — on women who have evolved into their own images of being Providers equal to them. Now these women no longer "play their part" in the old mythology that has unconsciously guided these men to understand their place in the world.

As more women take on more and more power and authority, men will deal with even more frustration to their old images of themselves as Provider. Right now, however, I am much more concerned about some of the young men I often work with who seem to have *no* meaningful image of being The Provider at all. I have a sense that they have been born into an age of male identity crisis.

As these twenty-somethings were growing up, they were exposed to the full force of women's equality. At the same time, women were being given images of themselves as powerful and independent, and the "dominant male" image was on its way out. Today it seems that some, perhaps *many* young men have found no alternative image. These young men often carry a need to live out heroic deeds as a way to prove their worth. Unfortunately, this need makes them particularly vulnerable to propaganda from fringe organizations and movements that provide both a community and an ideology through which they can focus those heroic images. The formula for a terrorist or an ideological killer is often just this kind of process — with some Shame scripts to motivate action.

While we could easily spend another entire book delving into and discussing these dynamics, I raise these questions for consideration here briefly for those who may feel inspired to do just that. If the old mythological male images of Provider/Protector are undergoing change due to the continued emergence of sexual equality, how can today's man deal with the "loss of status" — particularly the loss of a lover's adoration for their "sacrifices?" We are still learning new images for what intimate relationships can be when they happen between true equals.

The identity crisis many men are now experiencing to some degree lives in their imagery — and can be solved by *evolving* that imagery. I believe that for men to begin this journey of change they will have to hear from the women in their lives about their joy in gaining Provider equality — or of their suffering of not having it. In the long run, both sexes will need to continue reimagining their roles and rewards.

I am also suggesting here that just as shifts made long ago toward racial equality are still in the process, we are still working to re-imagine the imagery associated with the women's rights movement. While public policies may be slow to shift, the images we carry in our consciousness and our renegotiation of personal power and reward can be even slower. As we develop the capacity to be conscious of the images we carry — and become more capable of managing the emotional dynamics that occur when our images become obsolete — we will join the course of all human progress in a way that creates less disorder in our lives.

So what motivates that progress? We share a communal desire to increase positive Affect and decrease negative Affect. The most destructive dynamic to integration of new images will surface when Shame/Humiliation dominates our experience. This is what happens every time a new, progressive movement points our awareness toward new issues of justice and equality.

How can we help those around us to manage the collision of this new awareness of the need for equality with the images they carry that are at odds with it? For starters, we can now recognize that this collision will likely be experienced as Shame/Humiliation. With this knowledge we may have more success in our conversations. The traps we tend to get caught in when Shame/Humiliation is triggered are the same defensive scripts we have already explored. Now that we can recognize these defensive scripts, we can notice how the dynamics in our conversations are being guided not just by the collision of images and emotions, but also the defenses we have developed to deny, avoid, or manage those emotions.

Images of The Consumer

Advertisements feed us images of people smiling and ecstatic as they consume the products being sold. We are then emotionally motivated to feel the same ecstasy when we buy and consume them. Affects are the key to advertising because they are *also* the key to human motivation. For this reason we are constantly inundated with images that either seek to show how a product or service will increase our positive Affects or decrease our negative ones.

The agencies behind the advertisements may not have ever read Tomkins' work, but with enough study groups anyone can probably begin to predict human behavior. With the right emotional pitch, any product can seem important. This is not news — and even though we're all aware of this strategy created on Madison Avenue, we probably still think we enjoy the products we purchased only because they taste or look better. We forget that, at least in part, we bought them because we were programmed by a commercial to feel that way.

This classical conditioning has been made all the more effective by the advancements in digital media and the explosion of platforms used to transmit these messages. Here's an experiment to illustrate what I mean. Watch an hour of broadcast television with a pad and pen in hand, writing down the expressions/ dynamics of all the commercials. Now scroll through each of your social media feeds for 5-10 minutes each (Facebook, Twitter, Instagram, Pinterest, Buzzfeed, etc.) and do the same thing. I think you will quickly see how we are consistently manipulated — and from all possible angles — by people who know this game much better than we do.

To the advertisers of the world, we are The Consumer. That is not to say that all those creative people working in advertising are bad people. It is just to say that salesmanship is often about manipulating the very components of human consciousness we are exploring together and of which you are becoming more aware. By gaining and practicing this awareness, we develop greater freedom to choose *how* we consume.

How we respond to advertising is just a tiny part of the concepts involved in how we consume. We are also guided by a number of images that are a part of our identity. What is your image of being a

Consumer? Where did you get that image? What reinforces it? How does it meet your needs? Do you sometimes go shopping just to feel better?

We all carry some image of ourselves as The Consumer, and though these may not seem as significant as the images we have of being The Provider (with all its heroic dynamics), our role as The Consumer may well be even more important. As populations continue to rise along with the temperature of the atmosphere, the ways in which human beings consume resources is now becoming a much bigger deal. In fact, there is now at least as much heroism to be found in re-imaging how to be The Consumer as there was in our past images of being The Provider.

The term "conspicuous consumption" refers to a societal image of wealth and prosperity. Buying a car as a plaything is like a badge that says, "I am doing Really Well." In the past, this was all a part of the imagery of success. Now those images are shifting. Conspicuous consumption is now widely considered *unethical* in a world where most of the wealth is in the hands of a few and current consumption of the Earth's resources is unsustainable.

So now the tables have turned for the Consumer. Those who flaunt their consumption, living in mansions with big carbon footprints and polluting the skies with their private jets, are now subject to greater Shame. And now that you're aware of this shifting dynamic, watch for how this new brand of Shame is defended on all poles of the Compass of Shame (Avoidance, Withdrawal, Attack-Other, and Attack-Self). As all of humanity faces our looming resource crisis, we'll likely see more and more examples of wealthy individuals developing defensive scripts to manage the Shame involved in this new reality.

However, it is not just the wealthy and powerful whose image of The Consumer will have to shift as resources dwindle. We are *all* faced with the crisis of an unsustainable lifestyle, and if we deny it, it will be at the peril of our children and their children. Many voices have been trying to call our collective attention to our overuse and abuse of finite natural resources for decades. Why has there been so little progress — and so much resistance — to implementing change on a personal level?

Perhaps we believe that if we stop consuming at the level we are, the economy will crash, people will lose their jobs, and we will all be worse off and therefore less able to deal with the issues at hand. Even after 9/11 when America suffered the terrorist attack on New York and Washington DC, one of the first messages from the President was to keep shopping.

So here we are, caught in a conundrum of competing images for which we as The Consumer carry our own feelings of frustration and shame. While we can now rationalize our conspicuous consumption through a sort of patriotic sense that we are shopping for the greater good, this comes with an uneasy suspicious feeling that we are also screwing the future.

The Consumer image is also deeply connected to the pleasure center of the brain. We consume products and services that often offer us immediate gratification, and that is addictive. So not only is this image of The Consumer we carry one that can bring about Shame, it is also an image that can help us avoid/deny the very Shame it triggers.

Just as someone turns to alcohol for quick relief from social anxiety or to soothe a humiliation, some of us turn to spending money. When we spend money to buy things we experience a sense of power and control in a moment where we otherwise might feel empty or embarrassed. This is a quick fix that of course is much like putting a Band-Aid on a broken arm. At best, the deeper problem is only momentarily pacified.

I raise this issue now to point out how complicated the image of The Consumer can be — as well as the role it may play in other scripts we use to manage our emotional states. The reality is that both *having* money and *spending* money are intricately connected to the scripts we've developed to either enhance our positive or decrease our negative Affects.

Conscious Consumers

On the positive side, there is a great deal of power in being a Consumer, and if we are conscious of our images and emotions, we can claim that power in ways that are indeed heroic. In one of the poems I have shared, I wrote, "The power of the meek is in their non-participation." Let's revisit that idea as we begin to make more conscious choices as Consumers.

To this end, I want to raise the notion of Compassionate Boycotting as a way to effect change through the role of Consumer. By compassionate I am suggesting that there be a sense of empathy for those who are trying to create value in the world. These providers are trying to make a living just like we are, trying to support families like ours. Sometimes, however, they do business in ways that are absolutely ignorant in terms of sustainability or human rights issues.

A Compassionate Boycott is one in which a message is sent to a company, a store, power provider etc., pointing out the issue and offering a time frame under which the issue may be resolved before there will be a general boycott of their services. While this may seem unfeasible or unlikely to produce any real change, I would suggest to you that most companies respond to even a small percentage of loss in profits as they make decisions for how their market will behave in years to come. Even the consumption of staples like gas and electricity can be impacted when masses of people choose to deliberately lessen their consumption by a specific amount.

To be a conscious consumer in today's world is a powerful thing, and it is a power shared by all people everywhere. If there is a hope for the world, it is that masses of people will claim that power by transforming their indoctrinated images to their new image that asserts the power of their convictions. To do this well, merely critiquing the old images is never enough. We must replace these with positive images to which we can easily identify — new images that reflect our values and hopes for a safe, peaceful, and sustainable world. And, as we begin to wield this power, the key to keeping it is to remember to wield it compassionately.

There are plenty of naysayers who proclaim that the Earth party is over, the house has been trashed, and we are better off just living as we are and hope that NASA finds a way to continue human life elsewhere in the galaxy. I fear this to be a pipe dream that only serves us by providing an easy way to avoid the issue, or worse, propaganda to help stave off panic.

Choosing to Evolve in the here and now means claiming the power of The Consumer and discovering how the way of meekness can transform our addiction to things. Reimagine the world as a place where people live more simply, where conspicuous consumption is understood for the disease it is, and where true freedom and happiness are not found in the possession of things but in sharing the natural wonders of life, the Earth, and the amazing creatures that inhabit it.

An Equal Opportunity Shift

Going back now to our earlier exploration of how societal image shifting is affecting today's man, we can't leave this section without also addressing how these shifts in imagery affect women as well. No one gets off easy here. I think the shift for women is likely to be just as difficult as the crisis men face. However, the challenges faced by women are somewhat different.

For some women, this identity crisis is more about managing competing images. Though higher levels of financial success may mitigate some of these complexities, many women continue to struggle with the competing demands of work and family, and they often express resentment and frustration over not being able to find time for their own personal needs and dreams.

With these fundamental challenges already in place for women, it's easy to see that if there also happen to be any economic or marital instability issues in the mix, that underlying resentment can easily accelerate. Just as it is for men, when the image a woman carries doesn't match up with her external reality, emotions are triggered with intensity to match how deeply identified she is with these images.

Many of the women I've worked with whose images of being a Provider were at odds with their identity as a mother and spouse also feel a certain pressure toward perfectionism. The so-called "empowerment" images presented to women in the media during the past few decades may have inadvertently included some images that are simply unattainable to all but the very wealthy.

If a woman carries within her the image that hard work and perfectionistic devotion will lead to the perfect life, how will she experience failure of a business or a marriage? You guessed it. The traps of defensive reactions Nathanson described in his Compass of Shame model are frequently at play as women are set up to never "measure up."

Many who read this book will find it very easy to imagine what it would be like to be in a marriage or long-term relationship in which both partners are experiencing the kind of identity crisis and related Shame/Humiliation we're describing here. It is the most toxic of relationships when *both* people are engaging in defensive scripts to protect against their own Shame that is constantly being triggered. Money and work often play a part in marital issues, and this difficulty can be made even worse when one or both are in the midst of a shifting paradigm.

Summing Up

The images we have explored of the Provider and the Consumer do not exist in us beyond this discussion. What actually exists in your mind are a million remembered moments and associations that automatically tell you who you are, what you are supposed to do, how to do it, and what the rewards will be. Taken as a whole, these images define how we relate to not only earning and spending money, but also to the interdependent web of life around us. These remembered moments and associations define what you value and what you take for granted. They provide stability from the moment you wake up — and a trance to keep you partially asleep throughout your day.

We are not all the same, nor do we want to be. This work we are doing isn't about telling you how you should be or giving you 7 Steps to a Better Life. Choosing to Evolve is about gaining the freedom of choice. You are already brainwashed. Your life is "a dream you learned to have from a script you did not write." This book is simply your call to Wake Up. It is an opportunity to learn just enough about the way your consciousness works that you can participate in choosing the images you habituate and transforming the emotional scripts that drive your attention.

When it comes to providing and consuming, that journey toward freedom of choice has already begun. Now that you have read this chapter and considered your images from a new perspective, the choice is yours whether this is the right time to do some inner archaeology.

What kind of Provider and Consumer are you? What are the emotional scripts and core imagery that drive these economic activities for you? Where did you get those emotionally charged images — and can you get more curious about them? Do these images add to your sense of wholeness and wellbeing — or reduce it? Are there other images you would find more helpful that feel foreign to you?

Play with these questions and see what you can learn. Change in this arena doesn't have to feel difficult. Relax and learn. If you find that you have a major problem in this area, consider whether it is a Player (Affect), a Coach (Reflection) or an Owner (Identity and Imagery) that seems to be keeping you stuck. Maybe it's time to go to the draft and work intentionally to build a better team!

Chapter 22

Evolving Images of Intimacy

In the first sections of this book we explored the basics of how consciousness operates. The premise of Choosing to Evolve is that, although we cannot change the operating system of our consciousness (the habituation and scripting of emotions and images), we *can* Evolve our approach to it.

We have explored some of the reasons why working and participating with the elements of consciousness can be so tricky. The inner dialogue or Coach that would guide us toward the changes we seek is actually a part of the system and directed by the same scripts. We have recognized also that giving attention to the Silent level of our experience and the sensations of the body can provide a gateway for transforming the stuck revolutions of our patterns into an evolution of consciousness.

Our scripted emotional dynamics and defenses are evident in all arenas of life, but recognizing them is only the first step toward this personal and cultural evolution. In the last section we have toured a few of the arenas where we often find ourselves and others stuck in repetitive cycles of conflict or suffering. For those of us stuck in these scenes it can feel like life has become a warped record on a turntable where the song plays, the needle skips, and we get sick and tired of hearing the same bit of the same song, over and over again. Choosing to Evolve is about changing the record.

In order to do this we need awareness — and then we need creativity. The more we develop an awareness of our processes, including awareness of our particular images and our scripts, the more we can learn to step back from engaging in the stuck patterns of our lives. Instead, we turn our attention to the Silent Level of our experience. In this magical, mindful experience of now, we can practice de-habituating and dis-identifying with the images of our memory and imagination, and it is through this doorway that we can shift our inner dialogue toward curiosity.

For this reason, informed meditation and mindfulness are primary practices for Choosing to Evolve. Particular types of yoga, walking meditations, and many embodied movement experiences also serve as important practices for entering the Silent Level of awareness. Why do we need them? Because, as Einstein said, "You can't solve a problem at the same level of consciousness that created it."

Perhaps in the not-so-distant future we will see more yoga studios offering classes informed by these particular insights. And in addition to yoga studios, we will see more people attending dance studios where embodied movement can teach us how to give attention to the body — and more faith groups teaching and practicing meditation and contemplation. All of these can and should become our mental health centers of the future.

Learning to manage the constant flow of imagery in your head is likely to require a good deal of practice. As you develop this daily practice, however, you will begin to see a difference it can make. You gain the capacity to Move Alongside those moments in life where the record is skipping and repeating the same old patterns that have kept you stuck. So how do you change that record? Moving Alongside that feeling with creativity and love.

The love we need here is the compassionate curiosity for our own images/scripts and those of others. This is actually possible when we learn to dis-identify with these images by moving our awareness to the Silent Level *in the moment*. From there we can begin to tune into curiosity about what we *want* to create, seek new visions, and open ourselves to the tiny voices of our dreams that have been drowned out by the dominant scripts of our consciousness. It is through this vision quest that we can discover some beautiful new music to play!

In all the arenas of our lives, we can practice this process to transform our most intractable conflicts and issues. And, the more we practice, the more the habituation system of our consciousness begins to work for us. In other words, you can habituate your capacity for de-habituation!

We have briefly explored some of those arenas including work, economics, faith, education, parenting, and justice. To fully explore each of these is important but beyond the scope of this book. Before we finish this exploration, however, we have to take a look at how all this works within relationships. Rather than explore every type of relationship, including those between groups and countries, let's focus on our intimate relationships.

If you're looking for suggestions on how to apply this new understanding about human consciousness to your own intimate relationship, you'll find plenty of suggestions scattered throughout this book. As we have explored the habituation of our imagery, the scripting of emotions, and the patterns of our conflicts, I have tried to touch on some of the ways these play out in our experience of intimacy. Now as we near the end of this journey it will be easier to explore intimacy more completely.

Starting with the Ending

Most couples I meet have tried a few approaches to improving their relationships and have seen very little change over the long haul. Sometimes this is due to the lack of capacity for one or both people to become more conscious of their own images and scripts. Sometimes the therapeutic approach itself fails because it doesn't take into account the aspects of consciousness we have explored here. Sometimes, when the images and scripts two people carry are simply incompatible, no amount of evolving consciousness will keep them out of a state of continued crisis.

When we do not choose to walk away from an utterly toxic situation in which we do not have the tools or the influence needed for change, then we must ask why? Is this a pattern in our lives? Do we have a need to suffer? Do we know how to have intimacy that feels good? Remembering the four ways we explored for responding to conflict, this is a case to illustrate that Moving Away is sometimes the best option, even if it is temporary.

I have certainly been witness to many people having to make these kinds of difficult decisions. I have seen people choose to leave 30-year marriages, parents choose to Move Away from a child rather than to enable scripts that have become destructive, and adult children choose to distance themselves from parents who abuse or manipulate them. These are the kinds of painful decisions that also call into question the images we carry about loving families — and if these experiences and their associated imagery is not well-processed, they can leave permanent scars.

The evolution of consciousness we're discussing here can help us with all of these experiences, even when we do choose to Move Away, because greater awareness of the images we are holding always allows us to see everything and everyone more clearly. The images we carry of marriage and divorce will define the way we experience these moments, and sometimes we will need to acquire new images in order to heal.

The meekness that comes from recognizing the limitations of *everyone's* images — and the way we all tend to defend the narrow images we do have — can lead to greater compassion, even as we choose to part ways. Gaining awareness of our defensive scripts can also help us recognize the deeper dynamics involved in a break-up. Just knowing about the Compass of Shame can help us avoid some of the worst things that can happen in the process of a divorce.

Keep in mind, however, that evolving the way we Move Away from a committed relationship will never erase the negative feelings that will inevitably get triggered. However, we *can* use the insights we have explored here to turn that pain and suffering into learning, growth, and healing.

It is quite possible to say "no more" to a relationship and still hold onto our compassion — and even affection — for the other person. Now that we can recognize that the images by which we each have come to define our lives and our world are as much a matter of chance as of choice, it is much easier to forgive as we move on.

Evolving Together

Choosing to Evolve as a couple is simply the practice of putting our imagery/emotional awareness to work in the context of our most intimate relationship. Imagine what it would be like to join with someone who is committed to holding the thread of mindful connection with you, no matter what you feel or what screwy images you have habituated. Perhaps we are drawn to this kind of acceptance because we know that only in such a non-judging environment will we have the courage to enter the labyrinth of our defenses and expose the core issues that tend to drive us.

We feel that kind of safety the most when we see that our partner is attracted to us — and even more when we feel their adoring touch.

Sexual contact can be as much about safety as ardor. When you sense that your partner really wants to be with you, there is something that shifts in your defenses. The outer doors to the labyrinth seem to disappear.

These doors will return, however, at the slightest hint of rejection or revulsion from your partner. They will also return if there is even the slightest loss of the safety afforded by this mutual attraction and adoration. As the relationship moves from its early novelty of mutual discovery to the stage of taking each other's presence for granted, it is easy for us to slip back into our usual defenses.

At this point we set up a kind of norm for the level at which we will relate. How honest will we be? How freely will we express our feelings? How will we manage the unavoidable collisions of our differences? Will we allow these collisions to help us learn more and deepen our intimate connection — or will we find our differences to be too much of a threat to our images of self and demand that the other change to be like us?

Applying what we are learning as a couple begins with accepting the limitations of your individual experiences and entering into an honest effort to learn about each other's perspectives. In this kind of relationship all feelings are welcome, but all feelings are understood as temporary. We learn to treat even the strongest negative emotions as *information* about our attachments to images and *invitations* to deeper connection.

We re-imagine our intimate relationships from static to emergent, realizing that the imagery with which we identify is not something that is *ever* finished. In fact, a relationship itself is a part of what and how we identify, and that, too, changes over time. Imagine an intimate relationship that remains curious about what is emerging for both people and how identifying as Learners can transform conflict.

While most couples share information about their past experiences when they are dating, few couples have the awareness to explore the images likely to cause challenges to the relationship down the road. We know that a good deal of conflict in long-term relationships comes from a few things: money, sex, and power. To that typical list I would add: security and adventure. If you want to get to the heart of things, try having an open dialogue about your images of each of these, and notice where things get hairy or defensive.

It would be great if we had these conversations early-on in a relationship, but even after years of being together, this kind of dialogue can still deepen our connection to each other. For instance, you might find that simply exploring each of your histories of work and responsibility may offer up some insights about the images you each carry — and the payoffs you believe are promised for your efforts. With patience and practice you can search out the imagery that will inspire each of you and allow you both to minimize the experiences of Shame, Anger, and Distress that so many people struggle with in relationships.

Reading this book with your partner or spouse is a good place to begin the evolution of your relationship. Imagine how it would feel to share a relationship that has Evolved into a new capacity to de-habituate stuck patterns and transform its most destructive patterns of conflict into opportunities for deeper intimacy.

We are living in a time where the images for marriage are changing. With sexual/gender equality comes a whole new challenge to intimacy. When greater honesty and happiness are expected of intimacy, we also encounter more conflict. When power is shared rather than one dominating the other, we need new tools for managing this conflict. The thread of awareness we are spinning in Choosing to Evolve offers just such a set of tools.

Meet Stephen and Sally

Stephen was a 46-year-old sales rep married to a 35-year-old woman named Sally who worked in the upper management of an oil company. When they met there was an incredible chemistry between them, and they began moving toward a life together. However, even before they were married issues were beginning to emerge.

Sally would often criticize and correct Stephen. She seemed to always be focused on his flaws. Stephen, you see, did not always reflect the images Sally carried of how a spouse should be. There are many ways that this dynamic could be explored. Stephen and Sally had certainly developed different emotional scripts through the years. For one thing, Stephen was probably born with a lower threshold of sensitivity to stimuli — and was therefore less easily triggered emotionally. Sally, on the other hand, was very easily triggered and sometimes had difficulty regulating her Fear response, even when she was only slightly startled.

So Stephen and Sally were most likely experiencing differently what was going on in every moment of every day. What soon became most problematic in their relationship was the difference in the habituated ways each of them had learned to manage Shame. Stephen's pattern of managing the Shame triggered when Sally critiqued him was Withdrawal and Avoidance. (Remember these two opposite poles on the Compass of Shame?) Sally's habituated pattern of managing the Shame triggered for her when Stephen didn't measure up was to Attack-Other — and when that didn't work, to Attack-Self.

So with these Shame dynamics in mind, let's return to a common scenario for Stephen and Sally. Whenever Stephen's appearance or behavior didn't match up with Sally's imagery, she would critique him, sometimes in the presence of others. For Sally, pointing out Stephen's shortcomings was important for her to retain a positive image of her life — and how the man in her life should be. In response to this critique, Stephen would then Withdraw and begin to act out in ways that were both addictive and destructive.

Over time, this cycle became a toxic environment for both Stephen *and* Sally. Simply being in each other's presence seemed to trigger Shame in each of them, and this Shame was compounded by their frustration of being unable to change this dynamic of their relationship.

When someone we have chosen to be our most intimate partner doesn't live up to the images we carry of how our ideal partner should be, we not only experience Shame ourselves, but we also feel ashamed *of them*. Our self-imagery at some level may start to relate to how even being with them reflects badly on us — or our judgment. This is the part of the dynamic that explains the deep need in some men and women to have the most physically attractive partner available to them. We've all probably seen at least one instance (maybe even on TV) of how a "trophy wife" — or "trophy husband" — served to prop up someone's fragile self-image, right?

In Stephen, Sally did not possess a trophy husband, but she needed one to help her align with the image of success she had carried since she was a child. This was an image modeled for her in a thousand experiences (movies, television, and the performance of her peers) and to which she had been well indoctrinated. In fact, this was the image by which she had *always* judged herself with the harshest, most exacting, and consuming critique.

For Stephen, just being in Sally's presence was to be subjected to the same fierce judgment Sally had for herself. Stephen was therefore stuck in his hopeless desire to receive love and adoration from someone who seemed much more interested in making him feel embarrassed. This was the exact opposite of the image Stephen carried of a spouse and a marriage.

You see, the imagery of a wife and a marriage that were programmed into Stephen's heart and mind — and that motivated his generous nature — comprised a whole internal mythology for Stephen that was now completely obliterated. And, as he retreated into his defensive scripts it only made matters worse. In response, Stephen was now acting out with behaviors that brought on even more Shame for both of them.

Through years of this continuing dynamic, both Stephen and Sally went on with their lives. They went to work and continued to be responsible adults. They continued to interact with family and friends, although not quite as intimately as they once had. They tried to cover up the terrible pain that each of them felt as they continued their life together.

What would it take for a couple like Stephen and Sally to recover? Well, it's complicated, and not at all a one-size-fits-all remedy. Given the unimaginable diversity of life experiences, habituated images, and emotional scripting possible for any couple, the issues faced by every individual and every couple are unique. It is possible, however, to see how our individual images can give rise to these kinds of dynamics in our lives and relationships. We then become deeply confused and this feeling is intensified by our different defenses against the Shame that is triggered on both sides.

When Sally or Stephen spoke to their friends about their feelings, it didn't really help either of them to grow a deeper understanding of what was happening. In fact, most of the time their friends would simply resonate with the feelings and reinforce the defenses. Sally's anger was her truth of the moment, but that "truth" was actually a defense against a deeper, less conscious experience of Shame. Sally needed help learning to manage this experience of Shame more consciously.

Stephen's anger was almost non-existent and he avoided all of his Shame and frustration by seeking stimulation that would help him retain a positive self-image. His friends were more than happy to join him in seeking that stimulation, playing right into his Avoidance. He needed help in learning to own his anger, set limits, and manage Shame in a more productive way.

As these dynamics became clear to each of them, they chose to give each other the grace to work through them. They committed to a time of exploration and experimentation that brought curiosity and interest back to their relationship. It was not that they were ever going to be able to change some of their issues, but knowing them, naming them and learning to dance with them made all the difference.

If We Had a Magic Wand

Driven by the images we have received and the emotional scripts we have developed, every relationship we have is, by definition, a collision of individual scripts and images. The impact of these collisions will either open us to growth and learning or it will close us up in defensiveness.

As any parent knows, we can usually measure the quality of our adult children's relationships by observing the characteristics brought out in them. Is the child happier, more confident, and freer to be who he or she is? Or does the relationship leave his or her windows and doors locked and shuttered, isolated from support and consumed by jealousies, competitions, or distrust?

Sometimes we wish we could wave a magic wand and restore a sense of wholeness to our lives and to the lives of our children. We wish we could undo their defensive battles and erase the scars each skirmish has produced, but habituated scripts do not change easily.

The good news is that the commitment required to Evolve is born of this suffering, and there will come a time when we will look back on these struggles and see them as prerequisites to our evolutionary leap. And now, thanks to those who have explored this territory before us, we can see that beyond these defensive struggles there is a path ready to lead us out of our habituated experiences and into a new dawn of our own awakening.

Chapter 23

All My Relations

declaration
i've been listening to the news
'til i don't know what is true
and i don't know how to move
or what the hell to say to you
they give the count of casualties
like the stock market report
and there's no time for eulogies
of the lives that got cut short
but somebody's crying
over your sacrifice
your life was shattered
you paid such a price
will you be forgotten
so there's no downside to war
so the nation doesn't have

to be grieving anymore
seventeen-seventy-six
a declaration signed
with a list of grievances
to stand the test of time
a pledge to stand together
against all enemies
but we still haven't finished
setting ourselves free
now somebody's changing
and they see that its a shame

all the killing and the dying
in a god or nation's name
somebody's wondering
why we love these battle scenes
even though they massacre
so many people's dreams
is this some fatal attraction
are we just addicted to the action
could we wage the peace with equal passion
maybe then we'd see
what it feels to be
truly free

What I've offered here is a starting point for each of us to develop an awareness of the images we carry, and against which we are constantly evaluating our experiences. It's also very important to remember that we need to do more than just *critique* our old images. We Choose to Evolve by consciously selecting and living into new images that will serve us and others better.

When a critical mass of people becomes more conscious of the concepts we have explored here, it will make a dramatic difference in how we are able to transform the polarization of our culture, the conflicts within our relationships and marriages, and even across the public debate of policies. It is my hope that with this knowledge we will find better ways to connect with others and more sustainable ways to live in our interdependent world.

To Be Or Not To Be

Contrary to popular belief, it was not the invention of the wheel or the axe that brought us to where we are as a species. It was the evolution of human consciousness. And, even though this evolution was without a doubt our ancestor's greatest gift to us, that same gift is now one of the greatest threats to our personal freedom — and ultimately, our existence.

Within the pages of this book we have explored some of the ways in which the very structures of our human consciousness can cause

problems in our lives. In this exploration we have considered a path of
further evolution of our current consciousness for our own good and
for the good of our species. I believe we are now approaching a point
in our human existence at which these problems will either overwhelm
us or motivate us to new expressions of our humanity.

These new expressions of humanity must not erase all the good that
now exists. Losing the beauty that can be created through the fixation
of attention and the habituation of imagery would be tragic. Choosing
to Evolve is not about over-analyzing or controlling ourselves. It is
about gaining the insights and skills to know when to freely flow with
our emotions and imagery — and when to Move Alongside instead.

To gain this capacity to participate differently with the components of our consciousness requires learning about some of our unique
imagery and scripts. With this new awareness and the insights we have
explored, we can find the thread that leads us out of our programmed
life. And, as we all Wake Up, the world becomes a much cooler
place to be.

As we have just seen, the work of evolving our consciousness is
both an individual and a collective journey. Each individual person
on the planet is living in a bubble of his or her own personal reality.
Created through the habituation of his or her emotionally-charged
imagery, this individual reality is continuously being projected onto
their moment-to-moment experience. In fact, every single interaction
between two people is mostly an interaction between their personal
reality bubbles.

In these chapters we have explored tools and techniques for
building awareness of our individual imagery, recognizing the layers
of our emotional scripts, and managing the conflict that happens
as our own scripts collide with those of others. Without these tools
and techniques we will have little capacity for change; however, by
increasing our capability for personal awareness and developing new
skills for managing our interactions with others, we do more than just
change – we Choose to Evolve.

Facing the reality of this moment in our journey, our current state
of frustration and dysfunction signals the end. No, I'm not talking
about the end of the world. What I'm suggesting here is that if we
look hard enough we can see that our current way of being in and with
the world is entering its final days. Gone will be the way of being that

values knowledge for the sake of the power it can bring — and power for the purpose of dominating others. So what will happen when this ending arrives? Will our adolescence as a species find itself in a crash or in an evolution to adulthood?

Waiting for the World to Change

Maybe you have been waiting most of your life for just this sort of evolutionary leap. Perhaps you, like so many I have met, have come to sense more or less intuitively that it is time for you to become more than you have been. Maybe you have felt powerless to make a difference in the world around you — and each attempt has been more frustrating than the last. You were, in the lyrics of John Mayer, "waiting on the world to change." But here's the reality we all must face. The world is changing, whether we like those changes or not. As Harry Chapin wrote in his autobiographical song *There Only Was One Choice*, "If you just dream while you're asleep, there is no way for them to come alive!"

Before we start addressing the problems we see around us, it helps to develop a new understanding of how our consciousness operates. And then, in learning how to *apply* that knowledge to the issues that face us, we'll find our best hope of transcending them.

What do *you* see as the greatest threat to freedom and peace in the world today? Reflecting back on the information we have explored here, do you now see any different ways to think about that threat? Perhaps like me, you may begin to suspect that it is not the threats (nuclear war, inequities, global warming, etc.) that leave us most vulnerable as a species. It is our inability to de-habituate and dis-identify from the tribal and myopic images into which we have been indoctrinated.

The dynamics at the heart of our anxiety and depression, our brokenness, and our relationship failure are the same underlying forces that create the greatest threat to humanity. It is our lack of awareness about our emotional scripting that undermines our capacity to understand one another. The greatest threat to our species now is actually . . . our species because of the consciousness that has evolved within us. We cannot undo or change this part of who we are as humans. But we *can* Evolve in how we participate in it!

Instead of seeing our human experience as immutable, are you now beginning to understand why the habituated images and emotional scripts that guide us are the real threat? As you begin to work with and apply this information in your own life, you may notice for the first time that there are patterns to your own conflicts that are habituated dynamics, just like those we have explored here. You may even begin to recognize how the most powerful of your habituated images have formed identities that tend to fuel your most intense disagreements with others.

Now that you can see these things differently, do you see *yourself* differently? Do you see the limitations of your own images — and are you maybe a little less certain about your own indoctrination and identity? Admittedly, it can be a little scary to enter this labyrinth, but always remember this: You are *more* than those things that have become indoctrinated into your identity. You are, above all, a Learner — and Learners see, own, and *embrace* their limits. They become free from their attachments and defenses around the images they have picked up along the way. They are the meek who inherit the Earth.

This prophetic saying, "The meek shall inherit the Earth," in fact foretold the evolution of human consciousness we are now exploring. In fact, growing meek has always been the only hope of humanity. Meekness, you'll remember — is not about being shy or reserved. It is about becoming free from our defensive scripts.

Meekness in this framework is something of a spiritual practice. It is the mindfulness that comes from developing a new relationship with our *own* images and scripts. This new relationship requires the ability to Move Alongside the components of our consciousness that often lead to our repetitive cycles of stuck perceptions and emotional dynamics.

No Time Like The Present

We have been born into a unique time in history. Human beings have now evolved into their capacity to perceive life in ways that would leave our ancestors in shock and awe. And yet, with all of this evolved capacity we still struggle with how to live together as a productive and diverse species. We even struggle at times with how to live with *ourselves*.

I hope something in this work has stirred new perceptions for you that will lead to your own healing and the healing of your relationships. I sincerely believe it can, because we can now see how we are shaped by our biology and personal experiences to have emotional scripts and particular sets of images over which we had little or no choice. With this awareness how can we not become more capable of empathy and forgiveness?

Now, perhaps more than ever before, humans have the capacity to Choose to Evolve. Making that choice, however, requires a dramatic shift in how we approach what we "know." Choosing to Evolve entails paradigmatic shifts in how we talk about and think about nearly everything. It involves contemplation and mindfulness on an individual level, paired with communal actions directed toward transforming outdated systems that don't operate from the nuanced understanding of our human consciousness.

If we sincerely want to address the big issues now facing humanity, it will take a movement of the masses — an evolution not so much of our ideas, but how we *approach* our ideas in general.

At this point you may be asking yourself, "How can I Choose to Evolve? What is the process? Where do I start?" My briefest answer to that question would be to go back to page one of this book and read it again. If you do, I promise it will open up new insights you probably could not have fully grasped the first time through. When you read this book again from the very beginning, knowing what you know now, you'll likely find even more of your own answers spread throughout these pages. Next, find a group or a partner with whom to explore these insights and start to apply them to your life.

We Choose to Evolve when we meekly hold our own images and honor the limitations of our perspectives. We have only been exposed to a small slice of the great experience that is life, and when we Choose to Evolve we acknowledge how we have been socialized into a limited set of images. Within that recognition we gain the capacity for new choices.

We Choose to Evolve when we stop repeating some of the same patterns that have lost the capacity to inspire or heal us. The thread of Evolution is in our capacity to choose whether to *flow freely* with our more or less automatic images and emotions — or to practice Moving Alongside those responses with mindfulness and curiosity.

This new evolution of human consciousness is about *choices* made possible through our *new knowledge* of how our human consciousness actually works. These choices in turn offer us new opportunities for following that thread to create wellbeing in our own lives, in our relationships, and around the wider world.

This evolution will not come from the "top down" in our various cultures. This evolution will begin in individuals and small groups. In other words, if we want to see the *world* change we must start with ourselves and work outward.

To begin your practice of doing this work, you will first need to explore what you have read here from your own personal perspective. As we discussed in the previous section, it is likely that learning to Move Alongside the images we identify as "us" will offer the greatest freedom.

Developing the capacity to question what feels like our own identity is just part of the hard work of Choosing to Evolve. You may remember my sharing Karl Jaspers' observation: "The problem with enlightenment is that at first it's all bad news. I've been brainwashed." I remind you of this remark now, because after finishing a first read of this book I imagine that some people may find it to be a bit of a downer. This consciousness stuff is hard work!

I can only promise that if you Choose to Evolve in this way you will find that life has much to offer, much to share, and much freedom to be found — far beyond anything you can likely imagine right now. If you were looking for a quick fix to make you feel good, this is probably not it. This is a journey that begins with insight, evolves through practice, and creates a new way of being through how we learn to participate with consciousness.

I have tried to also describe why this work may well be the only sustainable evolutionary path for humankind. There is truth in all of us, wisdom in all of us, and inspiration to be found in all faiths. May we turn away from clinging to our narrow windows on the world and find common dialogue on those things that make us whole, renounce those images that only cause suffering, and acknowledge that we are more than that with which we have come to identify.

Like many of the people I know, I sense that the time is growing ripe for our transformation. The roots of change have been growing since ancient times and now, as always, the rains of suffering in the world and in our lives have stirred new things to sprout above ground. These same roots of change can be found in many programs that are now emerging around the world. The work we are doing as we Choose to Evolve makes the goals of these programs all the more recognizable and valuable.

The Rise of the Meek

The meek will inherit the earth, not dominate it into servitude. They will open their hearts and minds to others with curiosity, humility, and wisdom born from their awakening to the defining dynamics we have explored. The "new meek" will form charters, transform institutions, and resolve bloody conflicts. They will not cooperate or participate in the forms of communication that demonize and dehumanize others who have simply been exposed to different images and carry different identities.

The meek will bring truth to power, and they will do so with a much greater awareness and compassion. The meek will regularly gather in groups to explore their own images and scripts, making conscious what was once taken for granted. They will practice attuning to the sensations of their bodies and gain even greater skills at Moving Alongside their own emotional attachments to images, and even to their own identities.

The meek will be the first to celebrate their freedom from their own scripts and images. They will not be seduced by addictive escapes that promise no limits. The meek will not have their emotions manipulated by others for the purpose of promoting an agenda or a product. They will be so attuned to the energy of emotion in their own bodies that they can immediately begin to Move Alongside their scripts and emotions to make more conscious choices in the midst of conflict or calamity.

The meek will have the capacity to choose when and whether to *flow* with their lovely habituated emotions — or not. They will practice de-habituation and dis-identification and Moving Alongside until they do so with such ease that it becomes second nature — the new normal. And that, my friends, is when the evolution of human consciousness will take place — and we will witness the rise of the meek.

If you read this book and don't feel like you have evolved at all, then rest easy — you are completely normal. The insights available to you in this book just mark the beginning of your own journey. Now it's time to take the next step. Take a look around you and begin to notice the images and scripts that define the consciousness of the world we live in. Discover your own dynamics in the exercises peppered throughout this book. You will likely need support to make your evolutionary leap. Start your own study group with trusted friends or family where you make it a priority to address these insights to your own life, or check out My Leap Year, the specially created program designed to do all of that and more.

Of all the tensions at which our string of consciousness is strung, the most significant is birth and death. What will you do with these limits? Will you waste it mostly in indecision or make this year *your* Leap Year. Join the evolution of consciousness happening in our times to become part of the solution. In Choosing to Evolve you will Wake Up and join the rising tide of the Meek who have already inherited the world.

As Sure as The Moon
So many stories still untold
So many words I want to say
Could you hold my hand?
Let's embrace while we can
And try to make the moment stay
We share a second of time
The precious moments of our days
We didn't choose what we became
It was nature nurtures game
But we found a thread to lead us through the maze
And as sure as the moon
Is coming around to meet the sun
I know that we'll be gone
Before we're even done
So may the story that we live
And the glory that we do
Be to offer some salvation
As we're passing through
Some people have all the answers
They make the world seem so small
Put blinders on their eyes
Rehearse the same old lines
Til they see nothing else at all

You just keep asking the questions
You keep on hearing the call
To speak the truth you own
Embracing the unknown
Dancing through the wonder of it all
And as sure as the moon
Is coming around to meet the sun
I know that we'll be gone
Before we're even done
So may the story that we live
And the glory that we do
Be freedom to the captives
As we're passing through
I've been lost now and then
I can't pretend to conceal it
Now all I have to give
Are the lyrics that I live
And a song to help remember how to feel it
I've seen the gypsy inside you
You come and go like the tide
It's so crazy to reveal
That I can feel the things you feel
As if I were somehow there inside
And as sure as the moon
Is coming around to meet the sun
I know that we'll be gone
Before we're even done
So may the story that we live
And the glory that we do
Be guided by compassion
As we're passing through
May the story that we live
And the glory that we do
Shine all the light and love we have
As we're passing through

Resources

The following major works that have been my inspiration and shaped what has been presented here. I have learned more from conversations than from books, so rather than cite specific quotations, I offer these as the bodies of work from which I have drawn:

The writings and recordings of Silvan Tomkins:
Affect Imagery Consciousness, Volumes 1-4

The writings and recordings of Donald Nathanson, MD
"Shame and Pride, Affect, Sex and the Birth of the Self"

The writings of J. Samuel Bois edited by Gary David, PhD
"The Art of Awareness"

I have also been deeply influenced in my own imagery and insights by my interactions with:

James Kavanaugh, whose classic poetry book, *There Are Men Too Gentle to Live Among Wolves,* was an awakening in my college years and whose friendship in the 1980s encouraged me to continue on a path of creative living.

Sam Keen, who offered insights into the psychology of violence in my interview with him and whose "Faces of the Enemy" continues to offer timeless insight.

Bert Scott, whose relational theology awakened me to a larger world of faith and spirituality as we traveled many roads together in the 1970s. Bert is just another name for meek and wise.

Matthew Fox and his exploration of the mystical path found in Christianity that he elucidates in his many works including *Original Blessing.*

Joseph Campbell, particularly his interviews with Bill Moyers, "The Power of Myth."

Additional Resources

Affect Theory

Shame and Pride: Affect, Sex and the Birth of the Self, Donald Nathanson, MD

The Upside of Shame, Vernon C. Kelly, Jr. and Mary C. Lamia

Exploring Affect: The Selected Readings of Silvan S. Tomkins, E. Virginia Demos

Relationships

The Art of Intimacy and the Hidden Challenge of Shame, Vernon C. Kelly, MD

Emotional Safety: Viewing Couples Through the Lens of Affect, Don R. Catherall, MD

Parenting

What Babies Say Before They Can Talk, Paul Hollinger, MD, M.P.H.

Restorative Practices

The Psychology of Emotion in Restorative Practices, Vernon C. Kelly, Jr. and Margaret Thorsborne

Trauma

All the writings of Bessel Van der Kolk and Peter Levine

Education

Children of the Code, David Boulton, PhD

The Journey from Here

Reading a book can open your eyes to whole new world, but if you only think of that image you will not likely walk its shores. Take the next step. Commit to your growth through one of the opportunities available at www.myleapyear.com! There you will find trainings, groups and practices to help you on the journey of Choosing to Evolve.

Acknowledgments

Much of the material explored in *Choosing to Evolve* has come from a combination of theories and research to which I was introduced through associates connected with the Tomkins Institute. I am sincerely grateful for the friends and mentors that have engaged with me in regular dialogue as we explored a wide range of ideas and their relevance to our lives.

My deepest thanks to Gary David, PhD and Vick Kelly, MD for holding the thread of connection through multiple personal journeys through my own labyrinth of scripts. Their precious insights are only outweighed by their capacity for genuine caring.

In addition there is my friend Jonathan Grindlinger, MD, who passed away during the course of my writing. Jonathan was the most passionate learner of us all. I am reminded of this loss regularly as my cell phone seems oddly silent and his joyous voice echoes in my memory. Oh, my old friend, you are sorely missed, but your legacy lives on in so many.

Donald Nathanson, MD and Roz invited me into their home and gave me breakfast. I have never enjoyed Cheerios more. Perhaps they knew I wasn't there for the food. I had already been fed and continued to find sustenance in the insights Don shared about his life's work. We owe him so much for helping to extend Tomkins' work and for that and his friendship. I am deeply grateful.

Don's most popular book, *Shame and Pride*, was my first introduction to Tomkins. Bill Thrash gave me that book and helped me to understand why it was important. I hope my effort here honors Bill's passion for creating new avenues for transforming our public discourse into more productive dialogue. I also hope that in my attempt to make these ideas accessible to more people, I have not oversimplified the genius of all those whose work I have built upon.

I need to thank all those who have traveled this journey with me; I am grateful to Jen who has been my intimate partner and mirror. We have exposed our most challenging imperfections and had the courage to not look away much. Chelsea, Tiffany, Ben, John, Ronan and Lucy, being a part of your lives has taught me so much. I love you.

I could not begin to list the family, friends, and clients who have impacted my life and work, but please know that I am deeply grateful for your love and your courage. In some moments you allowed me into your darkest moments and in others you walked with me through my own. You have made my journey richer than I could have ever dreamed, and I look forward to hearing your experience of

Choosing to Evolve. Though I have not revealed any of our individual journeys, I have drawn from my experience of all of them.

And finally, a word of deep appreciation to my editor, Melinda Folse, whose tireless effort and belief in this project helped make it possible.

About the Author

Charles Gaby has spent more than 25 years in private counseling practice in addition to providing workshops and consulting with organizations on topics from Compassion Fatigue and Enhancing Intimacy to Restorative Practices in Schools and Communities. He has served as president of the Tomkins Institute and Lead Trainer for the Institute for Restorative Communities. He is co-founder of Sync Yoga & Wellbeing, where he teaches. His radio show, Roots of Change, is available online through www.myleapyear.com.